simsoc
simulated society

FIFTH EDITION

PARTICIPANT'S MANUAL
with Selected Readings

WILLIAM A. GAMSON

D1470569

with the assistance of
LARRY G. PEPPERS

*f*P

THE FREE PRESS
New York   London   Toronto   Sydney   Singapore

To my newest set of game players, Gilad, Ari, and Maya

THE FREE PRESS
A Division of Simon & Schuster Inc.
1230 Avenue of the Americas
New York, NY 10020

THE FREE PRESS and colophon are trademarks
of Simon & Schuster Inc.

Manufactured in the United States of America

20   19   18

Library of Congress Cataloging-in-Publication Data

Gamson, William A.
    SIMSOC : simulated society : participant's manual with selected readings.
  —5th ed. / William A. Gamson with the assistance of Larry G. Peppers.
      p. cm.
    Includes bibliographical references and index.
    (pbk. : alk. paper)
    1. Social sciences—Simulation methods—Handbooks, manuals, etc.
  I. Peppers, Larry G.   II. Title.

H61 .G27 2000
300'.1'13—dc21

                                                      00-037167

ISBN 0-684-87140-8

Contents

Tables and Forms

The Forms section (tear-out sheets) starts on page 119.

Preface

SIMSOC has been developed to make social science more vivid to students at the college level and to adults in leadership training programs. It focuses on what is perhaps the most central problem for a student of society: the establishment and maintenance of social organization. When citizens riot, when governments use indiscriminate violence against their citizens, when generals seize power and liquidate political opponents, when armed gangs terrorize their neighbors, we begin to recognize that the existence of order and legitimacy is a mystery to be explained rather than part of the world's natural organization.

There would be less mystery if societies provided full social justice for all citizens. But many instead provide great social, political, and economic inequalities, with some groups excluded and deprived of benefits that are enjoyed by others. Demands for inclusion and social justice inevitably generate conflict. SIMSOC attempts to create a situation in which participants must actively question the nature of the social order and examine the processes of social conflict and social control. As an inevitable by-product, participants find themselves dealing with a host of issues, including interpersonal trust, leadership, "deviant" behavior, social protest, and power relations.

SIMSOC is intended to be used in conjunction with conventional classroom discussion and readings. A selection of such readings is included in this manual. The manual also includes suggestions for study questions based on participation in SIMSOC. The current edition represents a newly revised version of the game, prepared with the assistance of Larry Peppers.

The use of games as a teaching or training device has a long history in many fields. Social scientists have developed a variety of games focused on social processes for use in teaching students about the society in which they live. Like all of these games, SIMSOC does not attempt to imitate a real society in every respect, but includes characteristics that highlight certain issues and problems. One can participate in SIMSOC at many levels. As in real life, what one learns will depend on what one puts into it.

WILLIAM A. GAMSON
August 1999

In Order to Play
SIMSOC

Each participant should have a copy of this *Participant's Manual,* which includes the necessary materials. The coordinator should obtain a copy of *SIMSOC: Coordinator's Manual,* which contains all materials required by the coordinator, provides complete directions on how to set up and run SIMSOC, and suggests how to handle a variety of situations that might arise. One copy of the *Coordinator's Manual* will be needed by the coordinator for each SIMSOC of up to 90 participants. The *Coordinator's Manual* is available for a $5.00 fee, and may be obtained by instructors who write, using their letterhead, to:

The Free Press
A Division of Simon & Schuster
Faculty Service Desk
1230 Avenue of the Americas
New York, NY 10020

NOTE: SIMSOC is pronounced *"sim*-sock."

simsoc

simulated society

1 RULES

SIMSOC Introduction

You will shortly be participating as a citizen in a simulated society.° If the society is to be a valuable learning experience, we will need your cooperation. Cooperation in this context means taking your objectives in the society seriously. We have tried to create a situation in which each of you has goals that depend on other people in the society for their achievement. Some of your goals will be held in common with other people, and some will bring you into conflict with others. Inevitably, some of you will do better than others in achieving your goals but, unlike some games, SIMSOC has no clear winners or losers.

You represent only some of the citizens of your society. Other citizens are present only in imaginary form—that is, certain rules of the game are based on assumptions about the reactions of these imaginary citizens. Nevertheless, this is basically your society to do with as you like.

COORDINATOR'S ROLE

The coordinator's role is kept to an absolute minimum once the society is in process. He or she will maintain the bank, receive forms, and carry out other tasks specified in the manual to make the game operate. If questions about the rules arise, the coordinator will guide you to the appropriate section of the manual and help you locate appropriate forms, but *will not interpret ambiguous rules or advise you how to deal with situations arising in the game.* The coordinator will do everything possible to avoid becoming enmeshed as a participant in your society once it has begun.

NATURE OF THE RULES

The rules in the manual are intended to represent certain "natural" forces in the real world rather than human laws. To ignore them by cheating simply renders the game pointless and meaningless. The coordinator should not be put in the position of having to monitor your observance of the rules, but should be able to depend on your cooperation to achieve the larger purpose of learning. The rules of the manual, as you will see, allow great leeway for you to add your own agreements and rules. The agreements that you make among yourselves are your own responsibility—these represent human laws rather than "natural" forces. If a player ignores or refuses to comply with a rule your society makes, you must face the issue of how to deal with this behavior. All players have a responsibility to observe the rules in the manual to make the game operative, but it is a matter of individual choice whether one observes the rules that you may establish to govern yourselves.

In spite of efforts to anticipate various contingencies, ambiguous situations will inevitably arise. When more than one meaning of a rule is possible, the coordinator will re-

---

°If you are unfamiliar with game simulations, you may wish to read the articles by Abt (pp. 41–43) and Raser (pp. 43–47) in this manual before reading the rules of SIMSOC.

fer the question to a group within the society for interpretation. The coordinator will be concerned only with those aspects of the ambiguous situation that affect his or her specific tasks as coordinator.

SUMMARY OF THE RULES

The rules that follow are detailed, but not as complicated as they first appear; you will discover this once SIMSOC is in process. A short summary of the rules is included here to give you a general sense of the nature of the society and the options available to you. It also includes page references so that later you can easily look up exact details as necessary. A careful reading of this summary is a helpful way to begin, but you should read the complete rules rapidly. Once you begin to play and attempt to achieve your goals, you will need to read various specific sections of the complete rules more carefully.

Simbucks

Simbucks are the basic currency in SIMSOC. Initially, they are held in a bank run by the game coordinator (see p. 7).

Region

All members of the society live in one of four regions (see p. 7).

Moving

A player may move to another region by paying a moving fee to the bank (see p. 7).

Travel

A person cannot travel between regions without having either a travel ticket or a Private Transportation Certificate. Travel tickets may be obtained from a limited number of players who have travel agencies and receive a supply of tickets each session. A Private Transportation Certificate may be purchased from the bank (see p. 8).

Subsistence

Every member of the society must, for every session attended, provide for his or her subsistence, doing this by means of either a subsistence ticket or luxury living. Subsistence tickets can be obtained from a limited number of players who have subsistence agencies and receive a supply of tickets each session. Luxury living may be purchased from the bank.

Failure to provide subsistence for a session will mean loss of one's job. Failure to do so in two consecutive sessions means one is considered dead and cannot participate in the society in any way (see pp. 9–10).

Munchies (optional)

The coordinator will maintain a Munchie Bazaar where Simbucks may be converted to food or beverages. Or, instead of Munchies, the coordinator may make other desirable items available for purchase with Simbucks.

Enterprises

Participants can invest their Simbucks to buy risky enterprises from the coordinator. The success of these enterprises depends partly on luck and partly on the skill of the investors (see pp. 10–11).

Basic Groups

There are eight basic groups in SIMSOC for which you can work. Only the heads of these groups will be designated by the coordinator at the beginning. The rest of the players must find jobs. The head of each group receives the group's income to dispense.

The groups include two industries (BASIN and RETSIN), two political parties (POP and SOP), an employee interest group (EMPIN), a human services group (HUM-SERVE), a mass media group (MASMED), and a rule-interpreting group (JUDCO). You should read the description of these groups before beginning play because you will be asked to designate a preference. If you are not picked as head of a group, you will be faced with the need for employment (see p. 11). You will also have an opportunity to support or withhold support from some of these groups.

National Indicators

Numerical values for four National Indicators are calculated at the end of each session. The indicators are Food and Energy Supply (FES), Standard of Living (SL), Social Cohesion (SC), and Public Commitment (PC). These National Indicators may be raised by investing Simbucks in either of two broad public programs—Research and Conservation, or Welfare Services. The National Indicators decline by a certain percentage each session and can be lowered further by various actions and events in the society. If the National Indicators decline below certain points, the income available to the basic groups in the society declines. If the National Indicators rise above a certain point, the income available to the basic groups in the society increases. If any National Indicator goes below zero, the society collapses and the game is over (see pp. 22–24).

Absenteeism

Certain National Indicators (described above) are lowered when members are absent, regardless of the reason for the absence (see p. 25).

Unemployment

Certain National Indicators are lowered if there are members of the society without jobs (see p. 25).

Death

Certain National Indicators are lowered if members die (see p. 25).

Minority Group (optional)

The coordinator will announce whether this option is in effect. It provides for the designation of some members of the society as Minority Group Members. These people may be removed from their positions at any time by action of any two non-Minority Group Members (see p. 26), or may face other obstacles.

Individual Goals

You will be asked to select certain personal or individual goals to pursue during the course of the society. You will have an opportunity to change these goals and to declare at each session the extent to which you feel you are meeting them (see pp. 26–27).

Simforce

Actual physical force is prohibited in SIMSOC but the equivalent of such physical force is provided. Any individual or group may create a Simforce with the power to arrest others and to protect specified others from arrest. A person who is arrested is restricted to his region and may not travel, may not hold any job or official position in the society, may not engage in any official transactions with the coordinator, and will have all possessions confiscated. All confiscated materials will be turned over to the head of the Simforce. A person is dead if his arrest is renewed for two consecutive sessions.

More than one Simforce can be created, and it is also possible to remove an existing Simforce. Arrests lower certain National Indicators (see pp. 27–30).

Simriot

Members of the society may riot by signing a riot form (Form M). Riots may be prevented, however, by the placing of a guard post. Riots lower certain National Indicators (see pp. 30–31).

Government

There is no requirement that the society establish a government nor are there any formal rules regulating a government (see p. 31).

Special Events (optional)

The coordinator may announce the occurrence of certain "outside events" affecting the society, but you will not know in advance when the events will occur or what their nature will be (see p. 31).

The Object of the Game

To achieve the individual goals you have set for yourself, to help the basic group to which you belong to achieve its goals, and to see to it that the society as a whole is a "success"—however you may choose to define this. If you try to achieve these objectives, the larger objective of learning will be achieved (see Summary, pp. 31–32).

GENERAL CONSTRAINTS

The "laws of nature" prohibit all of the following:

1. Taking resources from the bank or from other participants without their consent.
2. The use of physical force. (The game provides for a simulated version of this.)
3. Counterfeiting Simbucks or other resources.
4. Forging another person's signature without his or her consent.

SIMSOC Personal Life

SIMBUCKS

Simbucks are the basic currency in SIMSOC. They are signified in these instructions by "$." You can use them to buy things you will need to achieve your goals in the society. For example, they will help you to travel or to buy subsistence, Munchies, or other items. You can also invest them in various ways, or you may save them in any given session for later use. As you read the following instructions, you will discover the many ways in which you can spend your Simbucks. All Simbucks not owned by individuals or groups are the property of the bank kept by the coordinator. The bank does not make loans or extend credit.

REGION

All members of the society live in one of four regions, designated Red, Yellow, Blue, and Green. At the beginning of each session, you must go to your home region.

Moving

Any player may move to another region by filing the Moving Sheet (Form C) and paying a moving fee of $10 to the bank. The move becomes effective at the beginning of the session following the filing of this form. However, players may go to the new region immediately, if they provide their transportation as described in the next section.

Moving to a new region is subject to the following restrictions: First, no more than one-third of the total participants (including absentees) may live in any one region. Second, a player may be refused admission to a region by the *unanimous* consent of the inhabitants who are present (that is, excluding visitors or absentees).

TRAVEL

You may travel between regions in two ways:

1. *Public transportation.* A person who possesses a travel ticket may use it to travel between regions. A travel ticket is good for one trip, defined as leaving and returning to the home region with no more than one stop in each other region. A trip is over when the traveler returns to the home region or repeats a visit to any region. It is your responsibility to give the coordinator or an assistant your travel ticket at the beginning of each trip. Travel tickets can be obtained from people who head travel agencies (see discussion below).

2. *Private transportation.* Any individual may purchase a Private Transportation Certificate (Form D) from the bank at a cost of $25. Those who possess such a certificate may make as many trips as they like. In other words, a Private Transportation Certificate allows you to travel freely for the rest of the session and for all future sessions of the society. Only the individual who has bought a Private Transportation Certificate may use it. He or she may, however, sell or transfer a certificate to another individual by filing Form F and paying a transfer fee of $3 to the bank. The bank cannot buy back a Private Transportation Certificate once it has been issued.

No one may travel without either a travel ticket or a Private Transportation Certificate. A certain number of players will be designated as owners of travel agencies at the beginning of the game. These agency heads will receive five travel tickets in each session which they can use, hoard, dispense, save, or sell in any fashion they see fit. Unused travel tickets may be carried over to future sessions. A travel agency with its regular supply of five travel tickets may be sold or transferred (Form F), but a transfer charge of $3 must be paid to the bank.

Restrictions on Travel

Travel is subject to the following restrictions. First, no more than half of the total participants present at a session may occupy any region at any one time. A traveling member may not enter a region in which there are already 50% of the members of the society present. This restriction also applies to any other areas even if they are not official regions (for example, an "uninhabited region" used as a meeting place). Second, any player, even with valid transportation, may be refused admission to a region by the unanimous consent of the inhabitants who are present (excluding visitors or absentees). He or she may *not* be refused admission if one or more of the inhabitants is willing to have the traveler enter.

Calling or shouting between regions is prohibited. Players should act as if sound-barriers make it impossible for them to speak to each other unless they are physically present in the same region.

Reassigning a Travel Agency

If owners of travel agencies are absent, arrested, or have a Minority Group Member Action (Form K) filed against them, they lose their agency. The coordinator will reassign the agency at random to another member of the same home region. If the old owner has not yet received the allotment of tickets for the current session, the new owner will receive the supply for that session.

Cell Phones/Laptop Use (optional)

Cell phones or Laptops may not be used to communicate between regions unless the coordinator announces that this option is in effect. Then, they may be used only by MASMED (see pp. 18–19).

Location of Bank

The coordinator's desk or bank is considered part of every region, and transactions with the coordinator do not require travel.

SUBSISTENCE

All members of the society must provide for their subsistence for every session at which they are present (even if present for only part of the session). You can do this by presenting the coordinator with a subsistence ticket at any time before the end of the session. You can also provide for subsistence plus luxury by purchasing one of the luxury-living options described below.

A certain number of players will be designated as owners of subsistence agencies at the beginning of the game. These agency heads will receive five subsistence tickets in each session, which they can use, hoard, dispense, save, or sell in any fashion they see fit. Unused subsistence tickets may be carried over to future sessions. A subsistence agency, with its allotment per session of five tickets, may be sold or transferred (Form F), but a transfer charge of $3 must be paid to the bank.

The two luxury-living options are:

1. *Luxury-Living Package.* You may provide for your subsistence by purchasing a Luxury Living Package from the coordinator at a price of $15 per session. A Luxury Living Package includes subsistence for the purchaser for the session of purchase and, at the discretion of the coordinator, may include other benefits as well.

2. *Endowment.* You may purchase from the coordinator a Luxury Living Endowment at a cost of $25 (Form E). This endowment provides you with subsistence for the session of purchase and for all future sessions and, at the discretion of the coordinator, may include other benefits as well. You may transfer your Luxury Living Endowment to another participant (Form F), but a transfer charge of $3 must be paid to the bank. The bank cannot buy back a Luxury Living Package or Endowment once it has been issued. A Luxury Living Endowment can be used to provide subsistence for only one individual per session.

Reassigning a Subsistence Agency

The same rules apply as for a travel agency.

Subsistence Failure

If you fail to provide subsistence for a session, you suffer the following consequences: as of the end of that session, you are unemployed; if you are head of a basic group, you will be removed from your position and a new head will be chosen in the manner specified in the rules. If you own a subsistence or travel agency, you forfeit it, and it will be reassigned as specified in the rules.

These restrictions remain in effect until you provide a subsistence ticket or buy luxury living. During the period in which you are without subsistence, you are free to talk to others and to travel if you have the means of transportation. Even though you are officially unemployed, you may participate in ongoing activities and may continue to hold any Simbucks or tickets which you have saved from previous sessions. You may turn in Support Cards for basic groups and participate in other activities. Once you obtain subsistence, it is up to you to find a new job or regain your old one; you do not automatically assume your old position.

Repeated Subsistence Failure. If you fail to obtain subsistence in two consecutive sessions, you are considered dead and henceforth cannot participate in the society in any way. You will then be asked by the coordinator to observe the society and assist the coordinator.

MUNCHIES

(Option One) Munchies represent imported luxuries. Under this option, the coordinator will maintain a Munchie bazaar at which Simbucks can be used to buy food or beverages at rates posted by the coordinator. The bringing of any food or beverage to sessions of SIMSOC is prohibited if this option is in effect. Participants should act as if the Munchie bazaar is the only place where it is possible to get Munchies while the society is in session.

(Option Two) Instead of (or in addition to) a Munchie Bazaar, the coordinator may make other desirable items available for purchase with Simbucks. The coordinator will announce whether this option is in effect at the beginning of the simulation. If this option is used, prices of the various items will be furnished to MASMED in a catalogue.

ENTERPRISES

At any time during the life of the society, any individual participant or group of participants may invest in a maximum of one high-risk Enterprise per session. This Enterprise will consist of three puzzles to be solved before the end of the session in which the investment occurs. If all three are not solved, you will lose your entire investment. But even if all three are solved correctly, there is a 50-50 chance of losing your entire investment. (The Coordinator will role a die, with even numbers indicating a successful outcome and odd numbers indicating failure.)

However, if the enterprise is successful, the investors will receive two and a half times the amount invested. For example, if you invested 40 Simbucks, solved all three puzzles, and receive an even number on the role of a die, you will receive 100 Simbucks in return. All payoffs will be made at the beginning of the next session. A maximum of four Enterprises are available for the society as a whole in any given session.

The Table below indicates the minimum investment by Size Level and the return on investment for a successful Enterprise.

Table 1: Minimum Investments and Payoffs for Enterprises

Size Level	Minimum Investment	Payoff for Success
One	$20	$50
Two	$40	$100
Three	$60	$150
Four	$80	$200
Five	$100	$250

Probability of success: All three puzzles solved = .5
Less than three puzzles solved = 0

 Basic Groups

As noted, there are eight basic groups: two industries (BASIN and RETSIN), two political parties (POP and SOP), an employee organization (EMPIN), a human services group (HUMSERVE), a mass media group (MASMED), and a judicial council (JUDCO). The objectives of these groups and the resources and options available to them are described in detail below.

Before the society begins, you will be asked to express your first, second, and third preferences among the types of groups described below. These choices will be used only in selecting the head of each group, not the other group members.

Those persons not assigned as head of a group may then seek employment in one or more of the groups. In seeking employment:

1. You do not have to join the group you originally chose on Form A but can join any group that will hire you.

2. You can work for more than one group. This also applies to the heads, who may hold positions in other groups.

3. Ownership of a subsistence or travel agency is considered employment, but you may accept positions in basic groups as well.

Five different figures are given in the following sections for the basic income of the groups: Size Levels One, Two, Three, Four, and Five. The appropriate figure is determined by the total number of participants in your society. It will be announced by the coordinator prior to beginning the game and will not change. You may find it helpful to cross out the figures that do not apply to your society. Note that after the first session, a group may receive either more or less than its basic income, depending on changes in the National Indicators (see p. 24, "Consequences of Changes in the National Indicators").

BASIN (BASIC INDUSTRY)

Overall Objective: To Expand Its Assets and Income as Much as Possible.
BASIN represents a basic extractive industry such as mining. Its raw material is words, from which it extracts the vowels *a, e, i, o* and *u*. In each session, BASIN may purchase from the coordinator any number of verbal passages up to five. These passages need not all be purchased at the same time; they may be purchased any time during the session. BASIN's work on the passage consists of making a list of the correct number for each type of vowel that appears in the passage. All words should be included in the count—author names in references as well as text.

All purchases of passages must be authorized by the head of BASIN, using Form H. The passages purchased will vary in length, and hence in the labor involved in determining the correct number of vowels. The exact cost of a passage and the payment for a completed one vary depending on the size level of the society; they are summarized in Table 2. This table shows that BASIN receives a 25% profit on its investment for extracting the vowels correctly.

The return which BASIN receives for a completed passage is reduced if there are errors in the solution. Each number that BASIN is off from the correct solution counts as an error. Thus, if a solution has the correct number of *a*'s, *e*'s, and *i*'s, but has two fewer *o*'s than the correct answer and one more *u* than the correct answer, this constitutes three errors. Each error reduces the payment or credit to BASIN for a completed passage by 10% of the purchase price. For example, in a Size Level Two society, BASIN would pay $60 for a passage. If the solution had four errors, instead of receiving the full payment of $75 it would receive $75 − (4 × $6) = $51. BASIN receives zero payment for solutions in which there are six or more errors.

To receive credit for a passage, the solution must be turned in to the coordinator (using Form H) *during the same session in which the passage was purchased.* Passages purchased in one session cannot be held over to be completed in later sessions. Payment or credit for a completed passage is not received until the session is over. In other words, if BASIN completes a passage early in the session, it cannot use the payment for this product immediately, since it does not receive it until the session is over. The coordinator will keep track of BASIN's assets, and the head of BASIN will receive 10% interest on its assets at the beginning of each new session, including the value of work completed by the end of the previous session. *Note that the actual amount received is affected by the National Indicators. For example, if BASIN's assets were $200 and the National Indicators were down by 20%, instead of receiving $20 income, this would be reduced to $16 (80% of $20).* The head of BASIN can withdraw part or all of its assets from the bank at any time by filling out Form I and giving it to the coordinator.

BASIN can purchase passages by using its assets in the bank and its income from these assets. In the beginning of the society, however, BASIN assets and income are not high enough to purchase five passages. Therefore, if BASIN wishes to buy the greatest possible number of passages, it will need to raise Simbucks from other individuals and groups in the society. It may do this by promising others some return on their money, by persuading them that this will help the society, or by offering other inducements, arguments or even threats to get people to lend their money to BASIN.

Effects on National Indicators

The buying of passages and their successful completion by BASIN affect two of the National Indicators (these are described more fully later). The Standard of Living is raised for each acceptable solution (that is, each solution with fewer than six errors). The Food and Energy Supply is lowered for each passage purchased, on the assumption that this investment depletes existing resources in the society. In other words, buying passages entails short-term costs for the society but at the same time produces long-term growth in the economy.

Table 2. Summary of BASIN Assets, Income, Investment Costs, and Returns

	Starting Assets in Bank	Income in First Session	Cost per Passage	Payment for Completed Passage	Error Deduction[a]
Size Level One	$100	$10	$40	$50	$4
Size Level Two	150	15	60	75	6
Size Level Three	200	20	80	100	8
Size Level Four	250	25	100	125	10
Size Level Five	300	30	120	150	12

[a] BASIN receives no payment if there are six or more errors.

RETSIN (RETAIL SALES INDUSTRY)

Overall Objective: Like BASIN, to Expand Its Assets and Income as Much as Possible. RETSIN represents an industry that manufactures retail goods for sale abroad. The market for its product is less certain than BASIN's market. Its raw material consists of anagrams from which it can form smaller *marketable* words. For each anagram, there are only five marketable words, but RETSIN won't know which ones are of value. It knows only that all marketable words have exactly five letters, are common English words, and are not proper nouns or plurals.

In each session, RETSIN may purchase from the coordinator any number of anagrams up to five. These anagrams need not be purchased all at the same time; they may be purchased any time during the session. A completed anagram consists of a list of five-letter words, including as many marketable words as possible. Once a completed anagram has been turned in to the coordinator it cannot be reclaimed for further work in the event that some marketable words have been missed. Most marketable words, however, will be fairly obvious and shouldn't take more than five to ten minutes to discover.

All purchases of anagrams must be authorized by the head of RETSIN, using Form H. The exact cost of an anagram and the payment for each marketable word derived from it vary depending on the size level of the society; they are summarized in Table 3. This table shows that RETSIN receives a 50% return on its investment if it produces all five marketable words from an anagram, 20% if it produces four, minus 10% if it produces three, minus 40% if it produces two, and minus 70% if it produces only one marketable word. For example, in a Size Level Two society, RETSIN would pay $60 for an anagram. If its solution has four marketable words, it would receive $18 for each, or a total of $72.

To receive credit for marketable words, the solution must be turned in to the coordinator (using Form H) during the same session in which the anagram was purchased. Anagrams purchased in one session cannot be held over to be completed in later sessions. Payment on credit for marketable words is not received until the beginning of the following session. In other words, if RETSIN completes an anagram early in a session, it cannot use the payment for this product immediately, since it does not receive it until the session is over. The coordinator will keep track of RETSIN's assets, and the head of RETSIN will receive 10% interest on its assets at the beginning of each new session. *Note that the actual amount received is affected by the National Indicators. For example, if RETSIN's assets were $200 and the National Indicators were down by 20%, instead of receiving $20 income, this would be reduced to $16 (80% of $20).* The head of RETSIN can withdraw part or all of its assets from the bank at any time by filling out Form I and giving it to the coordinator.

RETSIN can purchase anagrams by using its assets in the bank and its interest from these assets. In the beginning of the society, however, RETSIN assets and income are not high enough to purchase five anagrams. Therefore, if RETSIN wishes to buy the greatest possible number of anagrams, it will need to raise Simbucks from other individuals and groups in the society. It may do this by promising others some return on their money, by persuading them that this will help the society, or by offering other inducements, arguments, or even threats to get people to lend their money to RETSIN.

Effects on National Indicators

The manufacture of marketable words from anagrams by RETSIN affects two of the National Indicators (as described more fully later). The Standard of Living is raised for each anagram that is converted into one or more marketable words. However, Public Commitment is lowered for completed anagrams on the assumption that RETSIN's product is for private consumption of goods that pollute the environment or are otherwise objectionable. Hence, the production of marketable words represents the privatizing effects of a consumer culture, reflected in a lowering of Public Commitment. In other words, buying anagrams entails short-term costs for the society but at the same time produces long-term growth in the economy.

Table 3. Summary of RETSIN Assets, Income, Investment Costs, and Returns

Size Level	Starting Assets in Bank	Income in First Session	Cost per Anagram	Payment for Each Marketable Word	Maximum Payment for Fully Completed Anagram
One	$100	$10	$40	$12	$60
Two	150	15	60	18	90
Three	200	20	80	24	120
Four	250	25	100	30	150
Five	300	30	120	36	180

POP (PARTY OF THE PEOPLE)

Overall Objective: To Determine the Major Public Policies Followed by the Society and to Develop Programs and Mobilize Supporters for This Purpose; to Be More Influential Than Its Rival. When the society begins, POP is a political party that has neither a program, a philosophy, nor an ideology. It is up to the members of POP to develop these things as they see fit. The content may vary greatly, depending on the circumstances in a given society and the beliefs of the citizens.

Income for POP

At the beginning of the first session, POP receives a starting income as follows:

Size Level One: $40

Size Level Two: $60

Size Level Three: $80

Size Level Four: $100

Size Level Five: $120

After the first session, POP receives an income according to the following:

$$\text{Income (after 1st session)} = \frac{\text{Number of Support Cards turned in during session}}{\text{40\% of members of the society}} \times \text{starting income}$$

To illustrate, in a Size Level Two society, POP would receive $60 for the first session. If POP received the support cards of 50% of the members in the first session, it would receive an income of $75 at the beginning of the next session (50% / 40% × $60 = 1.25 × $60 = $75). *Note that the actual amount received is affected by the National Indicators. For example, if the National Indicators were down by 20%, instead of receiving $75 income, POP would receive $60 (80% of $75).*

Turning in Support Cards

Each individual in the society *may* turn in one Party Support Card per session for either POP or SOP, but you are not obliged to turn one in if you choose not to.

Support Cards may be turned in at any time during a session, either directly by an individual or through an intermediary. To be valid, a Support Card must be signed by the individual expressing support. If the coordinator receives more than one Support Card signed by the same individual for a given session, all of that individual's Support Cards will be considered invalid for that session, and the person will be treated as having abstained. Support Cards from absentees or people under arrest are invalid and will not be counted.

The political parties may work together if they choose, and new parties may be created, but these actions do not affect the rules for receiving income which the coordinator follows. Members of the society are free to handle the distribution of this income once it is received in any manner consistent with the rules.

SOP (SOCIETY PARTY)

Overall Objective: Same as for POP.   Starting income for first session:

Size Level One:	$40
Size Level Two:	$60
Size Level Three:	$80
Size Level Four:	$100
Size Level Five:	$120

Income level after the first session is calculated the same way as for POP.

EMPIN (EMPLOYEE INTERESTS)

Overall Objective: To See to It That Members of SIMSOC Who Are Not Heads of Basic Groups Have Adequate Subsistence and a Fair Share of the Society's Wealth.   EMPIN may wish to organize the members of society working for the various basic groups in some manner. It may wish to propose programs for the society as a whole that would meet EMPIN's objectives. In doing so it may want to work closely with one or more other groups.

Income

EMPIN receives a starting income for the first session as follows:

Size Level One:	$30
Size Level Two:	$45
Size Level Three:	$60
Size Level Four:	$75
Size Level Five:	$90

In each subsequent session, it receives an amount of Simbucks equal to twice the number of valid EMPIN cards turned in to the coordinator. For example, if 25 members turned in valid EMPIN Membership Cards during a session, EMPIN will receive an income of $50 for the next session. *Note that the actual amount received is affected by the National Indicators. For example, if the National Indicators were down by 20%, instead of receiving $50 income, EMPIN would receive $40 (80% of $50).* EMPIN may solicit additional money from members of the society if it wishes.

Turning in EMPIN Membership Cards

As with the Party Support Card, each individual may turn in one EMPIN Membership Card per session or, if you choose, you may decline to turn in a card. EMPIN

Membership Cards may be turned in at any time during a session either directly by an individual or through an intermediary. To be valid, an EMPIN membership card must be signed by the individual member. If the coordinator receives more than one EMPIN Membership Card for the same individual during a session, it will count as only one membership. Membership cards from absentees and persons under arrest are invalid and will not be counted.

HUMSERVE (HUMAN SERVICES)

Overall Objective: To Make Sure That the Human Needs of Individuals in SIM-SOC Are Being Met as Well as Possible. HUMSERVE may wish to provide services for the physical, social, or emotional needs of participants. It may want to promote programs for the society as a whole to better meet human needs. In doing so, it may want to work closely with one or more other groups.

Income

HUMSERVE receives a starting income for the first session as follows:

Size Level One:	$30
Size Level Two:	$45
Size Level Three:	$60
Size Level Four:	$75
Size Level Five:	$90

In each subsequent session, it receives an amount of Simbucks equal to twice the number of valid HUMSERVE support cards turned in to the coordinator. For example, if 25 members turned in valid HUMSERVE cards during a session, HUMSERVE would receive an income of $50 for the next session. *Note that the actual amount received is affected by the National Indicators. For example, if the National Indicators were down by 20%, instead of receiving $50 income, HUMSERVE would receive $40 (80% of $50).* HUMSERVE may solicit additional money from members of the society if it wishes.

Turning in HUMSERVE Cards

As with Party and EMPIN cards, each individual may turn in one HUMSERVE card per session or, if you choose, you may decline to turn in a card. HUMSERVE cards may be turned in at any time during a session, either directly by an individual or through an intermediary. To be valid, the HUMSERVE card must be signed by the individual member. If the coordinator receives more than one HUMSERVE card for the same individual during a session, it will count as only one. Support cards from absentees and persons under arrest are invalid and will not be counted.

MASMED (MASS MEDIA)

Overall Objective: To Insure Good Communication Across Regions About What Is Happening in the Society.   MASMED does not have a monopoly over communication in SIMSOC, but it has certain advantages and information that make it easier for it to play a special role. The most commonly used form of communication in SIMSOC is face-to-face oral communication as participants travel from one region to another. To facilitate the role of MASMED in such communication, the head of MASMED receives a Private Transportation Certificate and a one-time supply of five travel tickets. This is initially issued in the name of the head of MASMED but it can be transferred by the usual procedures described above under "Travel" (p. 8).

The media of communication available to MASMED will be specified by the coordinator and will vary with the technical facilities available. Possibilities include the following:

1. Closed circuit television with broadcast originating only from MASMED but reception in all regions.

2. Videotape transmission with recording available only through MASMED but viewing available in all regions. The coordinator or an assistant will act as distribution agent for up to two taped broadcasts per session.

3. One-way intercom transmission with broadcast originating only from MASMED but received in all regions.

4. One-way computer transmission with sending capability available only through MASMED but terminals to receive messages in all regions.

5. Hard copy from a word processor or typewriter with transmission available only through MASMED. The coordinator or an assistant will act as distribution agent for up to two transmissions of hard copy per session.

6. Cell phones for the head of MASMED and for up to three reporters who may use them to communicate with their home bases while traveling to other regions.

After each session is completed and the coordinators have had an opportunity to calculate changes in the National Indicators, they will inform the head of MASMED of the current value of these indicators as well as the rates of absenteeism, unemployment, arrests, rioters, and death, and the *total* number of POP and SOP cards, EMPIN memberships, HUMSERVE cards, MASMED subscriptions, and Individual Goal Declarations turned in during the previous session. This information can be used by the head of MASMED in any way desired. However, all official forms filed by any individual with the coordinator will be treated as confidential and will be revealed only with the permission of the person filing the form.

Income

At the beginning of the first session, MASMED receives a starting income as follows:

Size Level One: $30

Size Level Two: $45

Size Level Three: $60

Size Level Four: $75

Size Level Five: $90

After the first session, MASMED receives income equal to twice the number of valid MASMED subscriptions turned in to the coordinator. For example, if 25 members turn in valid MASMED subscriptions during a given session, MASMED will receive an income of $50 for the next session. *Note that the actual amount received is affected by the National Indicators. For example, if the National Indicators were down by 20%, instead of receiving $50 income, MASMED would receive $40 (80% of $50).* MASMED may solicit additional money from members of the society or may charge for its services if it wishes.

Turning in MASMED Subscriptions

As with Party Support, EMPIN and HUMSERVE cards, each individual may turn in one MASMED Subscription per session or may choose not to subscribe. MASMED Subscriptions may be turned in at any time during a session either directly by an individual or through an intermediary. To be valid, a MASMED subscription must be signed by the individual subscriber. If the coordinator receives more than one MASMED subscription for the same individual during a session, it will be counted as only one subscription. Subscriptions from absentees, persons under arrest, or those without subsistence are invalid and will not be counted.

Summary of MASMED Resources

—One permanent Transportation Certificate.

—Five Travel Tickets (opening session only).

—Special access to information on National Indicators, other rates, Support Cards turned in for basic groups, and totals on Individual Goal Declarations.

—(If Available) Unlimited television, intercom, or computer transmissions per session.

—Two distributions of videotape or hard copy per session.

—(If Available) Use of up to four cell phones for communication between headquarters and traveling reporters.

—Starting income plus income based on number of subscriptions after first session.

JUDCO (JUDICIAL COUNCIL)

Overall Objective: To Clarify and Interpret the Rules as Honestly and Conscientiously as Possible. JUDCO members may be called on to decide issues such as the following:

1. whether the action or prospective action of some member or group of members violates the basic rules of the game;

2. whether an agreement among members of the society violates any basic rule of the game.

JUDCO may act when some action or agreement is challenged. JUDCO is the final arbiter on the meaning and interpretation of all rules, and the coordinator may refer questions to JUDCO for clarification.

JUDCO members should try to interpret ambiguous situations in good faith rather than use their ingenuity to evade the basic rules. The coordinators will accept JUDCO's judgment even though it might differ from their own interpretation, but arbitrary and capricious interpretations can render SIMSOC meaningless. If JUDCO, by its interpretations, removes the "natural constraints" which the rules are intended to simulate, the dilemmas the game poses will disappear—and the challenge of the game and its value as a learning device will disappear at the same time.

These rules govern the functioning of JUDCO:

1. To be valid, JUDCO decisions must be signed by a simple majority of its members. These decisions must be filed on Form J and signed by a majority.

2. JUDCO must have at least two other members besides its head, but it may have more than this as long as the total membership is an odd number.

Basic Income Per Session

Size Level One:	$30
Size Level Two:	$45
Size Level Three:	$60
Size Level Four:	$75
Size Level Five:	$90

Note that the actual amount received is affected by the National Indicators. For example, if the National Indicators were down by 20% in a Size Level Three society, instead of receiving $60 income, JUDCO would receive $48 (80% of $60).

THE GROUP HEAD

Powers of the Group Head

People are not considered officially employed by a group until the head of the group has filed a Job Schedule (Form G) listing them. Employment is assumed to carry over between sessions unless something happens to change a person's employment status. It is not necessary for group heads to file a Job Schedule after the first session unless they wish to make some change in employment, in which case they must file another copy of the Job Schedule indicating the nature of the changes.

No individual will be considered employed without his or her consent; an individual may quit any job by filling out the notice of resignation on the Job Schedule. Agreements on salary and working conditions are internal matters between the group heads and their employees and need not be reported to the coordinator.

Replacing the Group Head

1. *Voluntary removal.* The head of a group may resign at any time and simply appoint a successor of his or her choice. You do this by filling out the appropriate part of the Job Schedule (Form G).

2. *Involuntary removal.* Heads of groups are automatically removed from office if they (*a*) fail to provide subsistence, (*b*) are arrested, or (*c*) are absent. They may also be removed from office by the unanimous consent of all employees of the group who are present at that session. There is one qualification to this rule: the head cannot be removed by unanimous consent unless there are at least two official employees present.

Designating a New Group Head

In the case of voluntary removal, the old head can simply designate a successor. In the case of involuntary removal, we must distinguish three cases:

1. There are no other employees or all are absent. In this case, the coordinator will pick a new head at random from the same region in which the old head resides.

2. There is only one other employee present at the session. This employee automatically becomes the new head.

3. There are two or more employees present. They can select a new head by a simple majority. In the event that no employee has a majority, the group will remain without a head for that session. At the end of the session, the coordinator will pick a new head for the following session at random from among the employees.

The Job Schedule (Form G) is the form to use for all transactions regarding the removal and replacement of the head of a group.

MERGERS

Groups may make various alliances and arrangements with each other, including mergers, federations, and the like. All such agreements are internal matters among members of the society and do not involve coordinator transactions. For example, if two group heads join together to create a new group, the coordinator will continue to provide any resources to which individuals are entitled under the rules. The individuals are then free to pool these resources or not as they choose.

NATIONAL INDICATORS

Numerical values for four National Indicators are calculated by the coordinator at the end of each session as one means of measuring the general effectiveness and "health" of the society as a whole. Each indicator pertains to a different aspect of the society, as follows:

1. *Food and Energy Supply (FES).* This represents how well the society is adapting to its physical environment. Is it developing its natural resources to meet the needs of its population? (The words "population" and "citizens" in this discussion of National Indicators refer not only to the actual participants but to an abstract group of others who are represented here through the National Indicators.) Is it replenishing the resources it consumes? A higher score means an abundant Food and Energy Supply.

2. *Standard of Living (SL).* This represents the consumption level of the society. How well are the citizens of the society living at the present time? A higher score means a higher Standard of Living.

3. *Social Cohesion (SC).* This represents how well different groups of citizens are integrated. Are some groups isolated and left out? Are there destructive conflicts between subgroups? The higher the score on Social Cohesion, the less the presence of destructive intergroup conflict.

4. *Public Commitment (PC).* This represents the degree of commitment by citizens of the society to its social structure and values. Are there large numbers of alienated citizens who feel estranged from the society and do not participate in it in a constructive way? The higher the score on Public Commitment, the less the degree of alienation among the citizens.

PUBLIC PROGRAMS

The National Indicators may be raised by investing money in either of two broad Public Programs. The money is invested by giving it to the bank with the instruction that it be used for a specific Public Program. This money is "used up" in the Public Program—that is, once invested it cannot later be withdrawn from the bank.

The programs are:

1. *Research and Conservation.* The purpose of this program is to promote scientific research and activity in such areas as (*a*) developing and conserving the natural environment so as to increase the Food and Energy Supply, and (*b*) utilizing available manpower resources more effectively so as to raise the overall Standard of Living.

2. *Welfare Services.* This program creates and expands a variety of Welfare Services for the citizens of the society and thus copes with poverty, discontent, social unrest,

and so forth. Investments in this program help to raise the Standard of Living as well as Social Cohesion and Public Commitment.

Any individual or group can invest any amount of money in either or both of these programs. The specific effects of these investments on the four National Indicators of Food and Energy Supply, Standard of Living, Social Cohesion, and Public Commitment are discussed below. The effects take place at the end of each session.

Any individual or group may decide to aid the society by advising its members on investment policies, work organization, or other matters which may indirectly affect any of the National Indicators, and thus contribute to the overall vitality and effectiveness of the society.

CHANGES IN THE NATIONAL INDICATORS

Each National Indicator begins at 100 for the first session. Many of the actions that influence different indicators will be discussed further below. The effects are summarized here and in Table 4.

1. *Spontaneous decline.* Each indicator automatically declines by 10% between sessions to represent a spontaneous decay factor.

2. *Public Programs.* Simbucks invested in the two programs described above raise the National Indicators; however, these programs have "administrative costs," so that a Simbuck invested in them does not bring an equivalent rise in the National Indicators.

   a.   *Research and Conservation.* This program raises the Food and Energy Supply (FES) by 40% of the value of all new money invested in it and the Standard of Living (SL) by 10% of the value of all new money invested in it.

   b.   *Welfare Services.* This program raises the Standard of Living (SL) by 10% of the value of all new money invested in it and Social Cohesion (SC) and Public Commitment (PC) by 20% of the value of all new money invested in it.

3. *Industrial Production.* Each passage purchased by BASIN lowers FES by two units, but each passage completed raises SL by 1 unit. Each anagram invested in by RETSIN raises SL by 1 unit but lowers PC by 1 unit.

4. *Absenteeism.* Each absentee lowers SL and PC both by 2 units.

5. *Unemployment.* Each unemployed person lowers SL and SC by 3 units and PC by 1 unit.

6. *Riots and Guard Posts.* Each rioter lowers PC by 2 units and SC by the amounts indicated in Table 5 (p. 31). Each guard post lowers Social Cohesion by 5 units.

7. *Arrests.* Each arrest lowers SC and PC by 3 units.

8. *Deaths.* Each death lowers SL, SC, and PC by 5 units.

9. *Individual Goal Declarations.* Every *four* positive individual goal declarations ("Yes, I'm satisfied") raise PC by 1 unit; each negative declaration ("No, I'm not satisfied") lowers PC by one unit. Any declaration of change in individual goals leaves PC unaffected.

Maximum Decline

No National Indicator will be lowered by more than 30 units in a single session for any *single* cause although there is no limit to the size of decline from a combination of causes. To illustrate, if seven members were to die in a single session, SL, SC, and PC would be lowered only by 30 units rather than by 35. However, these indicators might also be lowered additionally by absenteeism, arrests, etc.

Table 4 summarizes these effects:

Table 4. Effects of Investment and Other Actions on National Indicators

	FES	SL	SC	PC
Research and Conservation	+40%[a]	+10%	0	0
Welfare Services	0	+10%	+20%	+20%
BASIN	−2 units	+1 unit	0	0
RETSIN	0	+1	0	−1
Absentees	0	−2	0	−2
Unemployed	0	−3	−3	−1
Rioters	0	0	—[b]	−2
Guard Post	0	0	−5	0
Arrested	0	0	−3	−3
Dead	0	−5	−5	−5
Individual Goal Declaration	0	0	0	±1[c]

[a]This means that if, for example, $10 were invested in Research and Conservation, FES would rise by 40% of this or by four units. Similarly, SL would go up by 10% while SC and PC would not be affected.
[b]See Table 5 (p. 31) for exact effects. Note that guard posts each lower SC by −5.
[c]Plus 1 for every four positive declarations; minus 1 for each negative declaration.

CONSEQUENCES OF CHANGES IN THE NATIONAL INDICATORS

The basic income which group heads receive at the beginning of each session is affected by the state of the National Indicators. More specifically:

1. If all four of the National Indicators are at 120 or above at the beginning of a session, basic income will be increased by 20% for that session.

2. If any of the four National Indicators is below 90, basic income will be reduced by 10%; if any is below 80, income will be reduced by 20%; if any is below 70, income will be reduced by 30%; and so forth, down to 90% less for any session in which any of the national Indicators is below 10. Note that this affects in the same way the *income* which BASIN and RETSIN receive, although their assets in the bank are not affected by the National Indicators.

3. **The society ends if any National Indicator falls below zero.**

 General Considerations

ABSENTEEISM

For every member of the society who is absent from any session, regardless of reason, Standard of Living and Public Commitment are each reduced by two units. Absentees are not required to supply subsistence for sessions which they miss, and therefore do not suffer the consequences of subsistence failure for the following session.

If heads of basic groups or agencies are absent, they are automatically removed from office and a new head is designated in the manner provided in the rules. Employees of the group continue to hold their positions while absent unless they are removed by the head. Members are not considered absent if they are present for any part of a session.

For any session in which there are five or more absentees (but fewer than ten), one subsistence agency chosen at random will not receive its allotment of subsistence tickets. For any session in which there are ten or more absentees, two subsistence agencies chosen at random will not receive their allotment of subsistence tickets.

UNEMPLOYMENT

Unemployment can result from any of five sources:

1. *Employer action.* You may be fired, or no one may be willing to hire you.
2. *Employee action.* You may resign from all your positions.
3. *Subsistence failure.* Failure to obtain subsistence means automatic unemployment.
4. *Arrest.* Arrest means automatic unemployment (see discussion of Simforce below).
5. *Minority Group action.* If the Minority Group option is in effect, some Minority Group Members may become unemployed by having a Minority Group Action (Form K) filed against them (see discussion in section below).

For each unemployed person in a given session, Standard of Living and Social Cohesion will each be lowered by three units, and Public Commitment will be lowered by one unit. (This does not include unemployment due to arrest, the effects of which on the indicators are already included.)

DEATH

You may die from failure to obtain subsistence in two consecutive sessions or from having your arrest renewed for two consecutive sessions (the second renewal is equivalent to execution). Members who die cannot henceforth participate in the society in any way; you will be asked to observe and assist the coordinator. Each death, regardless of cause, lowers Standard of Living, Social Cohesion, and Public Commitment by five units.

MINORITY GROUP MEMBERS (OPTIONAL)

The coordinator may include the following optional feature: As many as 20% of the members of the society may be designated by the coordinator as Minority Group Members when the society begins. They will be asked to wear some insignia or armband so that everyone can clearly identify them as Minority Group Members.

Minority Group Members will operate under the following special restrictions: any two non-Minority Group Members of the society may at any time, and without cost, have any Minority Group Members fired from their jobs and/or removed as head of a basic group or owner of a subsistence or travel agency. This is done by filing Form K with the instructor.

If a Minority Group Member is removed as head of a basic group or agency, a new head will be designated in the manner indicated in the rules.

Minority Group Members who are the recipients of such action retain all resources in their possession, including Simbucks and travel and subsistence tickets. They also retain their Private Transportation Certificate and Luxury Living Endowment if they own one. If they control a Simforce, this is not affected by Form K. In sum, *a Form K deprives Minority Group Members only of their positions, not of their possessions.*

Minority Group Members may reacquire any former positions in the next session if they are able to do so. They may not hold any position with a basic group or head any agency during the remainder of the session in which a Form K has been filed against them. Furthermore, a new Form K may be filed against them in subsequent sessions. In addition to these actions, the coordinator may introduce other obstacles for Minority Group Members.

Alternative Minority Group Option

If this option is in effect, the coordinator will administer a test. Only those who pass this test will be eligible to serve as basic group heads or agency heads.

INDIVIDUAL GOALS

In addition to pursuing basic group goals and various goals for the society as a whole, individuals are asked to pursue personal or individual goals. An individual goal emphasizes something for you *qua individual* (for example, being powerful) rather than a goal for the society (for example, making SIMSOC a place where people trust each other).

A short list of possible personal goals in SIMSOC is given below. You should choose one or more which you intend to pursue. In addition to or in place of those listed, you may substitute other individual goals you may wish to pursue, but be sure that they refer to something for you *as an individual.*

During the course of the game you will have an opportunity to change the goals you choose.

1. *Power.* I will try to influence what happens in the society as much as possible.
2. *Center of attention.* I will try to be a central figure in the life of the society, salient to as many people as possible.

3. *Style of life.* I will try to enjoy the highest standard of living available, including as many Munchies as possible.

4. *Security.* I will try to lead a life in which I will not be threatened by lack of subsistence, by loss of job, by arrest, or by any other misfortune.

5. *Popularity.* I will try to be loved and admired as much as possible.

6. *Fun and adventure.* I will try to lead an exciting life, filled with adventure and challenge.

7. *Other.* (Please specify.)

Individual Goal Declaration

Each individual may turn in one Goal Declaration Card per session, choosing one of the following three answers to the question: "Are you satisfied with how well you are meeting your personal goals?"

1. Yes, I'm satisfied.

2. No, I'm not satisfied.

3. I've changed my individual goals as follows: (specify the nature of the change).

Note that you have the option of not turning in *any* Individual Goal Declaration, either because you are uncertain or for any other reason. Individual Goal Declarations may be turned in at any time during a session. Unlike Party Support Cards, EMPIN Memberships, or MASMED Subscriptions, Individual Goal Declarations may not be turned in by an intermediary but must be given by the individual directly to the coordinator. No more than one option may be checked, nor more than one turned in per session, or all for that individual will be considered invalid for that session. For example, if you indicate a change in your goals but also check that you are satisfied, such a declaration will have no effect. Individual Goal Declarations from absentees or from people under arrest are invalid and will not be counted.

Effects of Individual Goal Declarations on National Indicators

One of the National Indicators, Public Commitment, is raised by one unit for every four persons turning in a positive Goal Declaration, and is lowered by one unit for each negative declaration. Abstentions or changes in goals do not affect Public Commitment.

SIMFORCE

For better or worse, physical force, or the threat of physical force, plays a role in the life of real societies. It may take various forms—police arresting citizens, secret terrorist organizations threatening citizens, guerrilla forces attacking government officials, or even two armies fighting against each other as in a civil war. Actual physical force is prohibited in SIMSOC—no participant can physically restrain the movement of other participants or in any other way use physical force against them. The *equivalent of such physical force* is, however, provided in the game.

Initiating a Simforce

Any individual or group of individuals may create a Simforce by filling out Form L; the minimum cost is $25 (paid to the bank), but a larger amount of money will create a larger Simforce. Form L requires a stated authorization rule telling the coordinator what constitutes an order of the Simforce. This statement may take any form desired (for example, "An order must be signed by a two-thirds majority," "An order must be signed by any one of the following people," or "An order must be signed by all of the following people"). The only requirement is that the statement be unambiguous. Any persons authorized to give orders may issue orders changing the authorization rule itself (see Form L).

A Simforce must be renewed during each session following its creation or it will be considered defunct and its orders will not be carried out by the coordinator. The renewal cost is $10 (paid to the bank) for a force of any size; this payment is for maintenance and does not increase its size. The size of a Simforce may be increased by giving additional money to the bank for this purpose.

The Simforce must also designate a head, but the powers of this head are regulated by the authorization rule that is chosen. The head of the Simforce receives the confiscated possessions of those arrested (as described below) and is the communication link with the coordinator. The designated head of a Simforce may be replaced by any valid order that follows the stated authorization rule for the Simforce. If a Simforce head is absent during a session and no one present is authorized to give orders to replace the head, then this Simforce will be considered dormant and will lose all powers during this session. If the Simforce head returns in subsequent sessions, the Simforce may be renewed with its full powers restored.

Powers of a Simforce

A Simforce has three powers: (1) *to arrest persons,* (2) *to protect persons from arrest,* and (3) *to attack another Simforce.*

1. *Arrest.* An arrest is initiated by filling out Form L. (One must, of course, already have a Simforce to arrest someone.) There is a cost of $10 (paid to the bank) for each person placed under arrest. The actual arrest is made by the coordinator, who will carry out the orders of the Simforce. If the coordinator cannot carry out an ordered arrest because the target is under the protection of another Simforce, the head of the Simforce attempting the arrest will be informed that the order cannot be carried out, but the $10 will not be returned.

Arrests of unprotected persons will take place as soon as the coordinator is able to carry out the order and will last for the duration of the session. Arrested citizens will be informed by the coordinator of their status and all their personal possessions will be confiscated (see restriction #4 below). Note that if the head of BASIN or RETSIN is arrested, only their own Simbucks are affected, not those that are held by the coordinator in the bank accounts for these groups.

The coordinator will not reveal the identity of the arresting Simforce unless asked to do so by the head of the Simforce. All confiscated possessions will be turned over to the head of the Simforce.

An arrested person may be released at any time by order of the arresting Simforce.

The return of confiscated materials upon a person's release is an internal matter and is not specified by the rules. At the beginning of each session following an arrest, the Simforce head should inform the coordinator whether he or she wishes to renew existing arrests for the session or release those under arrest. Renewals require a payment to the bank of $10 for each arrested person per session. The coordinator will inform those under arrest of their status for the session.

All arrested individuals are automatically, immediately released if the arresting Simforce is removed (see discussion below on removing a Simforce.)

a. Restrictions on the arrested person. Members who are under arrest—

(1) are restricted to their own region and may not travel;

(2) may not hold any official position in the society (including any position in a basic group or agency);

(3) may not engage in any official transactions with the coordinator (i.e., turn in any forms, invest Simbucks, etc.);

(4) will be obliged to surrender all Simbucks and subsistence and travel tickets in their possession at the time of arrest;

(5) are provided with subsistence while under arrest, but if released during a session must provide subsistence for that session;

(6) maintain their Luxury Living Endowments and Private Transportation Certificates if they own them, but cannot use them while under arrest;

(7) will have their POP and SOP support cards, EMPIN and HUMSERVE cards, MASMED Subscriptions, and Individual Goal Declarations become invalid for the period of the arrest (they will not be counted by the coordinator);

(8) and whose arrests are renewed twice consecutively are dead and cannot henceforth participate in any way. They will be asked to observe and assist the coordinator.

b. Fines. A Simforce may wish to institute a schedule of fines for given actions. The coordinator, however, will *not* act as the agent of the Simforce in collecting such fines. If a fine is assessed against people and they refuse to pay, the matter may be dropped, or else some action such as arrest may be carried out against the refusers. In short, the collection of fines is the responsibility of the participants and will not be assumed by the coordinator.

2. *Protection from arrest.* Any person who is under the *protection* of a Simforce cannot be arrested until the protecting Simforce is removed (see below). All individuals authorized to sign orders of the Simforce (as indicated on Form L) are automatically assumed to be protected by it; in addition, the Simforce may place any other individuals under its protection by so indicating on Form L. In order to be effective, protection must be extended to persons prior to the time the coordinator informs them of their arrest.

3. *Attack and removal of another Simforce.* A Simforce may be destroyed by an attack from another, larger Simforce. An attack is launched by filing an attack order on the Simforce action form (Form L). An attack is successful in removing the target if, and only if—

a. the target is correctly identified by the name of the official head;

b.   the attacking Simforce is at least $25 larger than the target force.

If an attack is successful, the coordinator will inform the attacker of this fact and will inform the head of the now defunct Simforce that his or her force is no longer in effect. In this case the attacking Simforce will be reduced in overall size by an amount equal to 50% of the size of the Simforce that was destroyed.

The coordinator will not reveal the size of any Simforce or the name of the official head. If an attack is unsuccessful because of a failure to identify the head accurately, the head of the attacking Simforce will be informed of this and will be charged $10. If an attack is unsuccessful because the attacking Simforce is insufficient in size to overcome the target, the attacking Simforce will be reduced in size by 50%, and the head will be so informed. The head of the Simforce that was attacked will be informed of the unsuccessful attack on his force but will not be told the identity of the attacking Simforce.

To illustrate this rule, assume that a Simforce of size $70 attacks another Simforce of size $50 and correctly identifies the head. The attack is unsuccessful since the attacking force is not $25 larger than the target. The unsuccessful attack means that it is reduced in size by 50% to $35.

Once an attack order is filed with the coordinator, the attack is considered in progress. Neither the attacking Simforce nor the target Simforce may be enlarged in size while an attack is in progress.

Effects on National Indicators

There is no expectation that a Simforce will necessarily be created. It is only a possible option, and the society may end up with several, one, or no forces depending on the decisions of its members.

Arrests affect the National Indicators thus: For every individual who is arrested, Public Commitment and Social Cohesion are reduced by three units.

SIMRIOT

Members of the society may riot by signing the Simriot Form (Form M). An individual may sign only one riot form in any given session. If more than one is signed, his or her signatures on all such forms will be considered invalid. A riot does not occur until and unless the riot form is presented to the coordinator; thus, the existence of a signed riot form does not guarantee that a riot will in fact occur. Signatures on riot forms are valid only for the session in which they are signed. Individuals under arrest cannot riot.

Preventing a Riot

Any individual may, by payment of a fee of $20, place a guard post in any designated region. The posting of a guard will be indicated by the coordinator's placing of a Guard Post Form (Form N) in a visible place in the designated region. The guard post is valid only for the session in which it is posted, but the original poster has the option of renewing it at the beginning of each session for a fee of $20 per session. The presence of a guard post in a region makes it impossible for a riot to occur there, but it lowers Social

Cohesion by 5 units. Signatures on a riot form will be considered invalid if a guard post is in effect in the region at the time a riot form for that region is filed with the coordinator.

Effects of a Riot on National Indicators

1. Public Commitment: −2 for each rioter.
2. Social Cohesion: Calculate the percentage of the total population of the society represented by the rioters to the nearest 5% and apply Table 5 below:

Table 5. Effects of Riot Percentage and Guard Posts on Social Cohesion

Percentage of Rioters	Social Cohesion
5	0
10	−2
15	−6
20	−12
25	−20
30 or more	−30
Guard posts	−5 each

GOVERNMENT

There is no requirement that the society establish a government, and it may wish to operate without one. If members wish to form a government, they may do so at any time. If a government is created, its supporters may organize and conduct it in any manner they choose. There are no formal rules regulating such a government.

SPECIAL EVENTS (OPTIONAL)

Sometime during SIMSOC, the coordinator may announce the occurrence of certain outside events affecting the society. You will not know in advance when such an event will occur or what its nature is. These events are mentioned here so that you realize that they are part of the game and not an arbitrary intervention by the coordinator.

sımsoc Summary

The rules are less complicated than they first appear, as you will discover once SIMSOC is in process. All the details have been included here, but they will not all be needed by everybody. The basic question many people have at this initial stage is simply, "What is the object of the game?" For you as an individual participant, there are several objectives:

1. To achieve the individual goal or goals you have set for yourself;

2. To help the basic group or groups to which you belong achieve their goals;

3. To see to it that the society as a whole is a "success"—however you may wish to define this.

If you conscientiously try to achieve these objectives, the larger objective of learning will be achieved.

At this point, take out your Choice Sheet (Form A) and indicate on it your choice of basic group and individual goals. Put only your name on the Assignment Sheet (Form B) and hand this in also. This will be filled out by the coordinator and returned to you at the beginning of the first session.

SELF-TEST ON SIMSOC RULES

To make sure that you understand enough of the rules to begin play, a short, self-administered quiz on the rules is included in this manual (Form O). You should take it and check your answers before you begin play.

SOME COMMON QUESTIONS ABOUT PLAYING SIMSOC

Some of the most typical questions asked by participants before playing SIMSOC are included below, with answers indicated:

QUESTION: Does each person get a certain number of Simbucks?

ANSWER: No. Only the heads of the basic groups receive Simbucks, but they can give them to others.

QUESTION: Does a group gets its income only once, or does it get a fresh supply of Simbucks at each session?

ANSWER: The head of a group gets a fresh supply at each session. Similarly, the owner of a travel or subsistence agency gets a fresh supply of tickets at each session.

QUESTION: Can the members of the society decide to make travel free if no one objects?

ANSWER: No, because that violates the basic rules in the manual. The rules in the manual are like the laws of nature—the travel ticket represents the cost in time, manpower, and energy consumption of travel from one place to another. The rules you make among yourselves are like the laws of society—they can be changed or broken—but you should all try to observe the rules in the manual or else the game will not work properly.

QUESTION: Does one need a travel ticket to give something to the coordinator?

ANSWER: No. The coordinator and the bank should be regarded as part of every region. You are not considered to have left your region when you approach the coordinator for any transaction. You have traveled only when you go to some other region.

QUESTION: Suppose a majority of the members of society agree that some obnoxious individual should not be allowed to travel. Would the coordinator enforce this rule?

ANSWER: No. it would be up to you to enforce it, using the means provided in the game. The coordinator will carry out only those actions specified in the manual.

QUESTION: Are the four regions separate societies?

ANSWER: No. They are four parts of the same society. The National Indicators, for example, affect all of you the same way regardless of region. The region is just the place where you live.

QUESTION: Does it make sense for us to pool our travel tickets?

ANSWER: It's up to you to figure out what makes sense and what does not. There is no rule prohibiting you from doing it.

QUESTION: Will everyone be assigned to some basic group and region?

ANSWER: Everyone will be assigned to some region, but only eight people will be assigned to groups—the eight heads. The rest of you will need to find jobs.

QUESTION: Can you work for more than one group?

ANSWER: Yes.

QUESTION: Will we be told what caused the National Indicators to change as they did?

ANSWER: No. MASMED will be told the end result and all of the relevant rates that go into it. It can do whatever it wants with the information.

QUESTION: If BASIN finishes a passage during a session, can it use the money it gets for that to buy another passage?

ANSWER: Not during that session because it does not receive credit in its bank account for solved passages until the end of the session. It can use the money it makes to buy passages during the following session.

QUESTION: Can JUDCO make laws?

ANSWER: Any group can make laws. The question is, who will obey them? The coordinators will not enforce the laws which members of society choose to make, including JUDCO. They will carry out only those actions specified in the manual. If these are ambiguous, they will accept the judgment of JUDCO on how they should be interpreted. For example, suppose JUDCO made a ruling that only members of JUDCO were allowed to create a Simforce. If some group ignored this and filled out the proper forms to create a Simforce, following the procedures described in the manual, the coordinator would carry out their Simforce orders. JUDCO's ruling would have no effect unless members chose to observe it or unless JUDCO had worked out some way of making it effective.

QUESTION: Will there be enough subsistence tickets for everybody?

ANSWER: You will have to wait and see about that when the society begins.

QUESTION: Must the owners of a subsistence agency use one of their five tickets for their own subsistence, or do they not need one?

ANSWER: They need one the same as everybody else does unless they buy a Luxury Living Option.

QUESTION: Can people get subsistence even though they do not have a job?

ANSWER: Yes. Someone might give them a subsistence ticket.

QUESTION: Can a Simforce arrest someone without a reason?

ANSWER: Yes, if it follows the procedures described in the manual.

QUESTION: Doesn't SIMSOC create a capitalist society?

ANSWER: No. It is true that the income for the basic groups is given to individuals, but they do not necessarily have to operate as private citizens. You can set up a system of state ownership or ownership by groups and call the head a manager or secretary; or you can allow the individual group heads the freedom to decide for themselves how to use the group's income. It is up to you to create the kind of economic system you think is best. Whatever the system, however, some individual must still be officially designated as the head, and the rules do give this person important powers which you will have to come to terms with in some way in any system.

QUESTION: Is the object of the game to keep the National Indicators as high as possible?

ANSWER: That's one possible objective but not the only one. It's up to you how much you choose to emphasize the National Indicators compared to other objectives. This is not the kind of game where there is one clear goal of "winning." It's more like life, in that you usually want to achieve several different goals at the same time.

 Study Questions (Optional)

ASSIGNMENT ONE

Answer three or more of the following questions, using events in SIMSOC and the selected readings for illustration, but drawing on other material as well where applicable:

1. Under what conditions could a society manage to function without a formal agency to administer sanctions for deviance (i.e., a police force)?

2. What may prevent people in authority from using their authority for selfish ends?

3. Under what conditions are people most likely to keep agreements which they make, and under what conditions are they most likely to break them?

4. Imagine a situation in which people hold many different goals, some of which conflict with each other. Imagine that there are also certain things that help or hurt everybody equally. Describe several different ways in which a society can get its members to contribute to the general interest, even when this detracts from their pursuit of their private interests.

5. What factors keep a society from breaking down into a series of small communities that have no contact with each other or whose only contact is to make war on each other? To what extent are these factors present or absent among the different countries of the world?

6. Some studies of leadership have shown that the persons who work hardest to move a group toward its goals are not the most popular or best-liked members. Why do you think this is so, and what do you think the best-liked members are likely to contribute to the group?

7. Under what conditions will efforts to induce conformity produce non-conformity or deviance by the persons at whom these efforts are directed? Under what conditions are efforts at producing conformity most likely to meet with success?

8. What kinds of people are most likely to deviate from group norms?

9. What features would you build into or prohibit in a society if you wanted to keep yourself from being influenced or constrained by others as much as possible? What features would you build into a society or prohibit in a society if you wanted to make sure you could influence others as much as possible?

10. Some people argue that conflict is always bad for a society, whereas others see it as healthy and making positive contributions. For each of these viewpoints, discuss the conditions under which it is likely to be valid.

11. Under what conditions will groups within a society rebel, and under what conditions will their rebellion be successful?

12. When will a protest group decide to work within the system rather than try to overthrow the system?

13. What determines how effective a government is in putting resources to work to solve a society's problems?

14. What are some effective mechanisms for handling social conflict in a society?

15. How do feelings of powerlessness affect one's social interaction with those on whom one is dependent?

16. How are those with power able to deal with the potential or actual resentment of those who are affected by their power?

17. Under what conditions do members of a society begin to question basic values and goals that have heretofore been accepted by almost everybody?

18. What kinds of social institutions foster close interpersonal relations and a sense of community?

19. Under what conditions would a fully collectivized society emerge in SIMSOC?

ASSIGNMENT TWO

Imagine that you are back at the beginning of SIMSOC, except that you know what you now know. Other are in the state of relative innocence and confusion which prevailed then. Describe in detail what you would do to achieve any three of the following goals:

1. to get as many people as possible to participate in the running of the society;

2. to create conditions under which people could be trusted to keep agreements;

3. to make yourself the best-liked person in the society;

4. to create conditions under which you and others would be as free as possible from other people's influence, particularly the influence of societal leaders;

5. to create conditions under which you would have maximum influence over others;

6. to make sure the National Indicators of your society would be higher than those of any other SIMSOC that has been run.

Suppose you were trying to achieve all three of your selected objectives at the same time. To what extent do they conflict with each other, and to what extent do the same actions contribute to more than one objective simultaneously (either positively or negatively)?

Finally, suppose that the society were to start again at the point at which it ended. To achieve the same objectives discussed above, would you do anything different from what you described above? If so, what would have to be done differently and why?

ASSIGNMENT THREE

Imagine that you have been hired by the superintendent of a large metropolitan school system. Your job is to develop an educational game to teach social science material to high school seniors. Pick any body of material in this course as subject matter of your game, specify what it is you intend to teach in the game you develop, and then describe the educational game you would use to teach it.

You may wish to read one or both of the following books if you become especially interested in this: Samuel Livingston and Clarice Stoll, *Simulation Games* (New York: The Free Press, 1972), and Michael Inbar and Clarice Stoll, editors, *Simulation and Gaming in Social Science* (New York: The Free Press, 1972). The former is a brief paperback which includes a substantial section on how to develop games. The latter is a collection of descriptions by simulation game designers of how they developed their simulations.

SIMSOC
simulated society

2 SELECTED READINGS

The following selections deal with some of the issues that SIMSOC is designed to highlight. You should be able to relate your experiences and observations from SIMSOC to these readings and thus understand their points more thoroughly and personally.

SELECTED READINGS

What are simulation games? Why do people use them and what do they hope to achieve with them? The selections by Abt and Raser introduce the reader who is unfamiliar with this technique to its basic purpose. They try to make clear what it is about simulation games that gives them their potential as a teaching and a learning device. They also explain how and why any social simulation deliberately ignores certain aspects of reality in order to highlight others.

The Reunion of Action and Thought

Clark C. Abt

Physically inactive thought (mistrusted by Nietzsche) and mentally inactive action (mistrusted by all sensible men) are diseases of civilized man. He often wars without thinking and thinks without reward. Physical action in affluent civilization today is reserved for brutalities, chores, and play. Mental action is practiced chiefly by the physically inactive.

The classic Greek ideal embodied both thought and action, both individuation and participation, *in the same activities.* Today, intense participation in social decision-making is limited to a few individuals appointed, elected, or permitted to represent the larger society. Yet individuals can once again become involved, and thought and action can again be integrated, in games created to simulate these social processes. The zest for life felt at those exhilarating moments of history when men participated in effecting great changes on the models of great ideas can be recaptured by simulations of roles in the form of serious games.

"In dreams begin responsibilities," said the poet, and in games begin realities. Games offer expanded possibilities for action in a mode that, while chiefly mental, includes the felt freedom, intuitive speed, and reactive responses of physical movements.

The word "game" signifies one of those incredibly rich concepts of human activity that have many roots and implications. Even the barest dictionary definition suggests protean significance. "Amusement, diversion" "Fun, sport"—with sport suggesting a physical activity combined with an entertaining mental one. "A procedure for gaining an end," as in playing a waiting game. "A field of gainful activity," like the newspaper game. "A physical or mental competition conducted according to rules with the participants in direct opposition to each other," a general but misleading definition since the participants need not be in direct opposition. "A situation involving opposing interests given

specific information and allowed a choice of moves with the object of maximizing their wins and minimizing their losses," a useful, if incomplete, economic definition. As a verb, "to play for a stake." As an adjective, "having a resolute unyielding spirit," presumably in some serious or sporting conflict.

Consider the words appearing in these definitions: amusement, sport, procedure, gain, activity, competition, rules, participants, opposition, information, moves, object, maximizing, minimizing, win, lose, play, spirit. Some of these words describe the formal structure of games: procedure, rules, participants, information, moves, winning and losing. Others suggest the motivation of the participants: amusement, gain, competition, opposition, maximizing, minimizing, play, spirit. Yet all purposeful human activities involve participants, rules and procedures, success and failure. And indeed, the wide use of "game" as a metaphor for many social, economic, political, and military activities shows how much we assume about the formal similarity between games and real-life activities.

My own quite impressionistic view is that a game is a particular way of looking at something, anything. This "way of looking" has two main components, a rational, analytic one and an emotional, creative, dramatic one. The game's analytic component sees in certain aspects of life—family, love, friendship, education, profession, commerce, war, politics, partying—common formal or structural characteristics identical to those of games. These formal characteristics include some or all of the game elements of competing actors or roles or players, objectives or goals that are usu-

This reading is reprinted from Clark C. Abt, SERIOUS GAMES *(New York: The Viking Press, 1970), pp. 4–7 and 9–14. Copyright © 1970 by Abt Associates, Inc. All rights reserved. Reprinted by permission of The Viking Press, Inc.*

Clark Abt, a political scientist, heads Abt Associates, Inc., a private firm specializing in the use of simulation techniques.

ally unattainable by all actors at once, resources and powers that the actors use to try to gain their objectives, rules or laws or customs that limit or handicap the actions of the actors and tend to balance them so that the outcome tends to be uncertain, and definite conceptions of winning or losing that are important but mercifully impermanent.

The emotional, creative, dramatic component of the game is made up of a curious combination of optimistic beliefs in the luck of "another chance" and a pessimistic respect for the odds, the chanciness of it all. It is basically an existential view of man's acting, despite uncertainty, to achieve conflicting goals that end up mattering less than the action itself. "It's how you play the game. . . ." Ignorance need be no bar to action. It is, also, pessimistic (and romantic) in its view of life as conflict—with others, with nature, with self—but always unresolved oppositions, uncertainties, overcomings of obstacles. And it offers a kind of spiritual conquest of all evils by incorporating them into stimulating adversary roles that are as necessary to the good as the black is to the red—something the religion game developed long ago.

Games also include a no-nonsense operational ethic that allows no real excuse for losing. It has respect for "the money ball-player" who delivers despite obstacles and knows there is no justification—in game terms—for not doing so. This is an ethic of personal responsibility, in which there are no real excuses except "bad luck," which is a viable excuse only once in a while.

Reduced to its formal essence, a game is an *activity* among two or more independent *decision-makers* seeking to achieve their *objectives* in some *limiting context*. A more conventional definition would say that a game is a contest with rules among adversaries trying to win objectives. The trouble with this definition is that not all games are contests among adversaries—in some games the players cooperate to achieve a common goal against an obstructing force or natural situation that is itself not really a player since it does not have objectives.

Of course, most real-life activities involve independent decision-makers seeking to achieve objectives in some limiting context. The autonomy of human wills and the diversity of human motives result in gamelike forms in all human interactions, and in this sense all human history can be regarded as gamelike in nature.

o   o   o

Games may be played seriously or casually. We are concerned with *serious games* in the sense that these games have an explicit and carefully thought-out educational purpose and are not intended to be played primarily for amusement. This does not mean that serious games are not, or should not be, entertaining. We reject the somewhat Calvinistic notion that serious and virtuous activities cannot be "fun." If an activity having good educational results can offer, in addition, immediate emotional satisfaction to the participants, it is an ideal instructional method, motivating and rewarding learning as well as facilitating it.

The term "serious" is also used in the sense of study,

relating to matters of great interest and importance, raising questions not easily solved, and having important possible consequences. None of these aspects of serious games need be associated with their customarily heavy behavioral baggage of piousness and solemnity. Games may be significant without being solemn, interesting without being hilarious, earnest and purposeful without being humorless, and difficult without being frustrating. They may deal with important behavioral problems, and they may concern substantive problems in almost all academic and intellectual fields.

o   o   o

The need to experiment inexpensively and creatively is pervasive. Most people experiment with psycho-social situations throughout their lives in ways having most of the elements of games. What we are discussing here are the extended and novel applications of a very traditional developmental mode of human behavior. The oxymoron of *Serious Games* unites the seriousness of thought and problems that require it with the experimental and emotional freedom of active play. Serious games combine the analytic and questioning concentration of the scientific viewpoint with the intuitive freedom and rewards of imaginative, artistic acts.

The abstract representation of real life in game form does not render the game any less capable of teaching "true" knowledge. One does not have to be Shakespeare to understand his plays (which are, after all, monumental literary games), but acting in the plays can yield a more vivid and lasting view of Shakespeare than would a teacher's reading of the plays to a class.

Jean Piaget has said, "Knowledge is not a copy of reality. To know an object, to know an event, is not simply to look at it and make a mental copy, or image, of it. To know an object is to act on it. To know is to modify, to transform the object, and to understand the process of this transformation, and as a consequence to understand the way the object is constructed. An operation is thus the essence of knowledge, it is an internalized action which modifies the object of knowledge." He adds, "Intelligence is born of action," and "Anything is only understood to the extent that it is reinvented." People in daily life constantly invent and reinvent situations in order to learn from them. Yet too often people fail to recognize that reinventing a situation in which one has been an actor and perhaps reliving or revising decisions made is, in effect, to play a game. People tend to look for an abstract pattern within the situation or to compare situations in order to come to some new abstract conclusion. Yet they often fail to realize that it is an active situation which has led to their new abstract knowledge.

o   o   o

Games are effective teaching and training devices for students of all ages and in many situations because they are highly motivating, and because they communicate very efficiently the concepts and facts of many subjects. They create dramatic representations of the real problem being studied. The players assume realistic roles, face problems, formulate strategies, make decisions, and get fast feedback on the consequences of their action. Also, with games one can evaluate the students' performances without risking the costs of having errors made in "real-world" tryouts and without some of the distortions inherent in direct examination.

In short, serious games offer us a rich field for a risk-free, active exploration of serious intellectual and social problems. In games man can once again play the exciting and dynamic roles he always enjoyed before society became so compartmentalized. The role-playing that stu-

dents undertake in games that simulate life is excellent preparation for the real roles they will play in society in later life.

BIBLIOGRAPHY

Jennings, Frank G. "Jean Piaget: Notes on Learning." *Saturday Review* (May 20th, 1967).

What and Why Is a Simulation?

John R. Raser

Man uses verbal or logical analogies because they are esthetically pleasing or because they communicate vividly: "The vessel ploughed through the water." Analogy, or metaphor, is so deeply embedded in language that we are unaware of all but the most obvious. Verbal and logical analogies might almost be called the foundations of thought. By the use of analogy, what is abstract may be made concrete, and what is complex may be made simple. Thus, in the words of Socrates, Plato told his audience that the just man can be understood more clearly by examining the man "writ large," the just state. John of Salisbury reversed Plato by describing the state as a man, with the king as the head, the soldiers as the arms, and God as the soul. And Jesus told his followers that the man of true faith is like a lily of the field that takes no thought of the morrow.

Such analogies and similies are bridges that enable us to move from the simple, the concrete, and the specific, to the complexities and abstractions with which we wish to grapple. Analogies are tools for turning the *symbolic* into the *iconic*, thus giving form and substance to what is illusive and invisible. Think of the power of the Cross as a Christian symbol, an enormously economical abstraction; and of the even greater emotional and intellectual power of a painting (an "ikon") of the Crucifixion.

When the social scientists speak of "simulation," however, they are restricting the term to a much narrower sense than that used in the paragraphs above. Before it is possible to understand just how and why social scientists use simulation, it is necessary to grasp the exact sense in which they use the word.

A simulation is a model of a system. Other models . . . may attempt to represent a system through verbal means, mathematical means, or pictorial means. Like simulations, they involve the abstraction of certain aspects of the system one is studying

and an attempt to replicate these aspects by other means, such as words or mathematical symbols. But the simulation model differs in that it is an *operating* model. Once the variables that have been selected are given values within the simulation and the relations among the variables are specified, the model is allowed to operate. It may operate through the interaction of people who play roles within the model; or it may operate on a computer. The rules given to the human participants in the simulation or the computer program represent the premises of the model. Its operation produces the implications.[1]

As compared with a Tinker Toy model of a molecule, which can represent only static structure, not process, a simulation can be thought of as a *dynamic model*. Simulators, therefore, must try not only to build a model of system *structure*, but also to incorporate system *processes*. In doing so, they abstract, simplify, and aggregate, in order to introduce into the model more clarity than exists in the referent system.

ABSTRACTION AND SIMPLIFCATION

What is abstracted? That is, which components and relationships are included in the simulation and which are not? This will depend on the purposes of the simulator; it cannot be decided in a vacuum. Relevance or irrelevance

---

[1]Sidney Verba, "Stimulation, Reality, and Theory in International Relations," p. 491.

This reading is reprinted from John R. Raser, SIMULATION AND SOCIETY *(Boston, Allyn and Bacon, 1969), pp. 5, 10–12, 15–19, 29–30, 32, 35–37, and 43–44.*
John R. Raser is a political scientist.

can be determined only within the framework of a particular goal. Let us take, for example, the simulation of an aircraft in flight. If the aim is to study the "lift" provided by a particular type of airframe configuration, then a wooden form shaped like the aircraft in question placed in a wind tunnel will provide the data needed. We can eliminate all the internal workings of the plane, except, perhaps, those needed to provide for the aileron and tail settings that govern its flight. Details such as radio equipment, seats, wiring, fuel tanks, and stewardesses, which, from one point of view, would make the simulation a more complete and accurate representation of an aircraft in flight—and thus more "valid"—are, in fact, only expensive and distracting rubbish. The usefulness and, thus, the "validity" of the simulation are achieved through intelligent abstraction and simplification, not through detailed and accurate representation of the entire system in question.

If, on the other hand, the aim of the simulator is to study human fatigue on an aircraft in flight, then a fairly detailed simulation of the interior of the aircraft will be needed, with its space limitations, its physical layout, its vibrations and noises, and its human occupants. The external configuration and air speed can be ignored.

So the design of the simulation is determined by the specific problem to be studied, not by general considerations of "perfect replication." In fact, the entire idea of perfect replication is nonsense. No two things can be identical in *all* respects; they have differing positions in time and/or in space, if nothing else. When we say that a model is a *representation* of something, we imply that the two differ in some respects. It is important to bear in mind that all modeling begins with *abstraction* and *simplification;* they constitute "the name of the game" rather than being inconvenient limitations that simulators could overcome if they had more funds, better facilities, more computer memory-space, or a more comprehensive theory.

It is equally important to recognize that for some purposes a very simple model is preferable to a more complicated one, if only because it is cheaper and easier to manipulate. The difficult questions that model-builders face concern *which* elements, *which* relationships, *which* processes should be included, and which can be neglected. It is to answer these questions that modelers cry for better theory. The theory regarding airfoil lift, for example, is so well worked out that the problem could probably be solved in a few minutes on a computer rather than in a wind tunnel. But the theories regarding human fatigue and its relationship to noise, space limitations, the presence or absence of other people, or the activity being engaged in, are so primitive that the simulation builder would be hard put to know just what he should include in his simulation and what he may exclude in order to obtain useful and generalizable results.

In sum, then, simulations tap into different bodies of theory about referent systems, depending on the simulation purposes. It is not possible to judge the merits of a simulation on the basis of its simplicity or complexity except in terms of its purpose. It is certainly possible, however, to judge a simulation according to the validity of the theories or part-theories that it incorporates. A simulation, for example, that attempts to represent the movement of the heavenly bodies in space would be rejected if it were based on the theory that space is filled with ether. Simulation shares the problems of all other scientific endeavors in that the usefulness and generalizability of its results depend on the adequacy and validity of the theory on which it is based.

o   o   o

WHY SIMULATE?

Why do people build simulations? The primary answers can probably be subsumed under the headings of *economy, visibility, reproducibility,* and *safety,* although there are certainly other reasons as well.

Economy

It is frequently cheaper to study a given phenomenon in a model or in a simulation than in its natural setting. So whereas constructing and operating a simulation frequently is an extremely expensive proposition, it is usually less so than the alternative of attempting to gain the desired information from the referent world. For example, to build a scale model of an air frame and place it in a wind tunnel, operate the wind tunnel, and make observations of the flow of smoke over the foil under different configurations is time consuming and expensive, but far less so than to build a full size air frame, incorporate it into an aircraft, and to fly it under the same variety of conditions. Experiments can be performed on the model much more economically than on what it models.

Furthermore, experiments performed on a model can eliminate costly mistakes that might cause waste or disaster if not caught. Assume for a moment that our intrepid simulator has been able to overcome all the difficulties we discussed in connection with the harbor simulation, and that it functions properly. Now the construction of a breakwater is contemplated. By adding a model of the proposed breakwater to his simulation of the harbor, he can determine whether its presence will set into motion any new currents or other unforeseen developments which might have undesirable consequences for the harbor as a whole. Lacking this kind of predictive device, the real breakwater might indeed reduce the chop and swell—but at the unanticipated cost of depositing a sand bar requiring monthly dredging of the navigational channel!

So there are two senses in which the use of simulation may be economical. First, because it is usually cheaper to experiment with a model than with the real thing; and, second, because costly mistakes can be avoided by "running it through in advance."

Visibility

Using a simulation frequently increases the visibility of the phenomenon under study in two ways. First, the phenomenon may be physically more accessible, and hence more readily observed. Sitting behind a glass and watching smoke flow past an air foil in a wind tunnel is much easier than trying to measure the airflow past the wing of a plane in flight. Watching a silt deposit build up in a table top replica of a harbor is much easier than trying to measure what is occurring under 80 feet of muddy sea water. In fact, the "accessibility gap" may be so wide in some instances that observation of the phenomenon under study may be virtually impossible in nature, but extremely easy in a simulation. A working model of the solar system is one example; another example is the computer simulation of nuclear warfare that enables strategists to study the amount of destruction resulting from differences in weather conditions, weapons yield and reliability, time of warning, and extent of preparation.

A second way that simulation may increase the visibility of the phenomenon under study is by bringing it to the foreground, highlighting it, *clarifying* it. It is difficult to study the circulation of blood in a living organism, for the system of which it is a part is so complex that interference with it may radically affect the entire system. But in a *simulation* of blood circulation, it is possible to block the flow of blood at various points and observe the results.

Frequently, the phenomenon under study is so confused and chaotic that it is hard to make any sense of it. Consider the student who wishes to test the basic principles of international relations, who wants to look at world affairs in order to understand them. What does he need to look at? How shall he decide what is relevant? Where shall he start, what should he observe? The United Nations? The daily newspapers? The International Court of Justice? The flows of international trade? The national military postures? The thousands of intergovernmental and private agencies? If he tries to become *au courant* with all the elements of international politics, he will almost certainly end up confused and exhausted.

But if someone has built a simulation of international relations that incorporates most of the salient elements in simplified and explicit form, the student can study it and so gain a grasp of general outlines, an operating framework, upon which he can then elaborate the details in which he is particularly interested. For him, the simulation has functioned to *simplify* a system whose complexity obscures specific phenomena. Hydraulic models of the economic system or little plastic digital computers for children serve this same purpose of clarifying and simplifying the complex by eliminating all but the salient and relevant phenomena. So simulations aid visibility by making certain kinds of phenomena more accessible for observation and measurement, and by introducing clarity into what is otherwise complex, chaotic, or confused.

Reproducibility

Simulations allow scholars to reproduce chains of events that they could not otherwise observe repeatedly. There are at least two reasons for wanting to reproduce events. The first reason involves the element of *chance*. For example, suppose a researcher wants to find out how long passengers will have to wait for buses at the peak rush hour. He could station observers in the bus terminal for 360 days in a row, and through an hour by hour count, gain some understanding of those elements of chance which simply cannot be predicted, such as how many buses will be stopped at how many red lights, or how many passengers will not have the correct change at ticket windows. But a computer simulation of the operation of a bus terminal is not only far more economical, but also allows the researcher to build the element of chance into his simulation, run it repeatedly, and learn that the wait will be "X" minutes under given conditions with a probability of, say, .86 that it will be no more than "X plus 1" and no less than "X minus 1" minutes. These probabilities can be derived only by letting the simulation run often enough to allow all the possible outcomes to occur, and by observing the frequencies with which they do in fact occur.

Also, of course, simulations allow the student to reproduce many times a situation that might never occur again in real life: this aspect enables him to examine certain variables and relationships with respect to their influence on the outcome of the real life situation. It enables him, in effect, to play the fascinating historical game, "What might have happened if . . . ?"

In the terminology of research, simulation allows us to observe the effects of different kinds of manipulation of the input variables: it is possible to change assumptions, to alter the input parameter values, and to modify the relationships among elements of the system. For example, in the simulation of a nuclear exchange, we might want to ask, "What difference does 15 minutes' warning as opposed to 30 minutes' warning make in the amount of destruction? What difference does it make in the severity of the retaliation that will be suffered if the counterforce missiles are only 70% reliable instead of 90% reliable?" Changing input variables is closely related to the technique of allowing chance to operate in a random fashion, except that in this case we alter the variables in ways that interest us. We might ask, as another example, "What difference will it make in the international system if the chief of state of one of the major powers is highly paranoid as opposed to self-confident and trusting?"

So simulations are valuable because they allow phenomena to be reproduced, and thus (1) enable the experimenter to derive statistical probabilities when the outcome is uncertain, and/or (2) enable him to vary numerous aspects of the system in ways that yield profitable insights into how the system operates. In other words, simulations allow controlled experiments to be made that would otherwise be impossible.

Safety

Frequently, propositions may be tested in simulations more safely than in the real world. There are two senses in which this is true. The first is best illustrated by the "flight trainer" for prospective pilots, or by the "reflex test" equipment sometimes used to determine whether a given person is qualified to operate certain machines safely. These are essentially training or testing simulations—laboratories for measuring or increasing human skill. The safety features of such simulations are obvious. Pilot error in the flight trainer may result in a scowl from the instructor, but it won't produce a fiery death or the smashup of a multimillion-dollar aircraft. Discovering that one's reflexes are slow may be humiliating, but it is better to discover it in a laboratory than at 70 miles per hour on a super-highway.

Not only do simulations allow us to avoid putting human beings in dangerous situations, but they also allow us to study dangerous situations themselves without actually creating them. The simulation of a thermo-nuclear exchange is one example. The computer simulation of a controlled nuclear reaction is another example; it produces information about tolerances of stability without risking the hazards of a real reactor's going "critical." So simulations are used for safety purposes, both to protect human beings while they are being trained or studied, and to produce laboratory analogues of dangerous phenomena that we need to study.

The decision to use a simulation may be governed by one or another of these features of economy, visibility, reproducibility, and safety, depending on the research situation. Still other reasons for using simulations are that participation in a simulation deepens the involvement of the subjects, and that simulations offer an opportunity to stage "future events" so that they may be analyzed and "played through." These other reasons for simulating will be elaborated more fully in the context in which they occur.

So far, we have discussed simulations without drawing a distinction between those used in the physical sciences and those used by social scientists. In many cases, the distinction is not clear cut—the computer simulation of a bus terminal is an example—for both physical and human behavioral factors must be built into the model. However, most of the examples given so far have been drawn from the physical sciences and from engineering, because in many ways the problems are more straight-forward and the examples clearer. In a sense. I have attempted to use a principle of simulation in this chapter, by using the more simple to provide a model for understanding the more abstract and complex. The following section deals with the special problems and promises of simulation and games in the social sciences.

° ° °

THE GAMING APPROACH TO SIMULATION

In a simulation, the rules for translating external variables into simulation variables are highly formal; in more colloquial language, the rules are tight and tough. All substitutions and analogies must be defended; the relations between variables must be carefully specified; the operation of the simulation must be governed by mathematical rules. Clearly, then, the translation of variables must be based on adequate theory and data.

In a "game," according to my definition, there is more leeway with respect to analogical consistency and strictness. The rules for translating "real life" variables into simulation variables are less demanding, so it is possible to "play around" a bit and "make do."

° ° °

Thus, *the game can serve as a "pre-simulation," to be used both as a laboratory for studying basic principles of human behavior and as an admittedly inadequate framework for conducting research leading to improvement of the framework itself.*

This "gaming" approach to simulation building is one that a colleague refers to as "messing around" in science. This is not a disparaging phrase; "messing around" is a legitimate way to increase knowledge. In fact, some philosophers of science have argued that this approach to building a body of knowledge about human social behavior is sounder and more productive than the more traditional methods.

° ° °

The "gaming" approach to simulation-construction is similar to lifting oneself up by one's bootstraps or, perhaps more accurately, to rebuilding an airplane while it is in flight. Although this may at first seem like an exercise in absurdity, there are sound reasons for advocating it as a research strategy. But whether we turn to games as "pre-simulations"—as a means of elaborating and refining theory that can then be embodied in a simulation devoid of human participants—or whether we use games as a laboratory for studying the behavior of human subjects, we confront certain basic epistemological questions.

° ° °

The kind of "knowing," which comes from the recognition of patterns and thus of the subunits of those patterns, is called *distal* knowledge. We confront a collection of fragments—bits of punctiform data, each of which is uninterpretable—and suddenly we see the entire pattern or context. Common expressions used to describe this experience include "insight," "revelation," "seeing how it all fits together," and "having it suddenly all make sense." They all express the recognition that when an entire context or pattern is grasped, *each part of the pattern* is also more clearly apprehended. In a sense, we may say that the whole is greater than the sum of its parts.

° ° °

Now we can use pattern-recognition not only in understanding concrete physical phenomena, but also in handling abstractions—in testing concepts and in building theory. An idea acquires new meaning when it is set in the context of other ideas; then, both idea and context enrich and illuminate each other. Scientists increasingly recognize that the inclusion of theories and part-theories in a larger construct is a powerful technique for enhancing data-gathering and theory-testing, *even though the scientists may lack confidence in the absolute validity of many of the theories included in the construct.* As Donald T. Campbell observes, the certainty of identifying any single part is facilitated by a prior identification of the whole, even if the prior identification is uncertain and partially erroneous.

We are now back to our starting point; this is the process in science we referred to earlier as "messing around." It is the process involved in constructing a "game" that you hope eventually to develop into a simulation. Instead of waiting to build a construct (simulation) until you are certain of the nature of all its elements, you build a game that requires tentatively postulating the entire model. By watching the behavior of the operating subparts of the tentative model and by noting how they "fit" with its other parts, you can check and refine both the subparts and the model as a whole.

°   °   °

These arguments point directly to "games" as ideal laboratory environments, if we are interested in the interaction between a human being and the system of which he is a part. Games provide a powerful research tool for generating information. As knowledge about basic human behavior increases, the game evolves towards its end point—simulation.

BIBLIOGRAPHY

Campbell, Donald T. "Pattern Matching as an Essential in Distal-Knowing." In *The Psychology of Egon Brunswick,* ed. K. R. Hammond. New York: Holt, Rinehart & Winston, 1966.

Verba, Sidney. "Simulation, Reality, and Theory in International Relations." *World Politics,* 16 (1964).

PART 2 / INTERPERSONAL INFLUENCE AND LEADERSHIP

SIMSOC is intended to be a simulation of a society, but at the same time it is a relatively small group of individuals engaged in what is frequently a highly intense interaction. Rich and dramatic interpersonal dynamics are produced in the course of most SIMSOCs, and some game coordinators choose to make this a major focus of the postgame discussion. This section of readings focuses on one aspect of this interaction—interpersonal influence and the emergence and exercise of leadership.

The selections by Senge and the summary of his work emphasize leadership as a collective and shared phenomena and the importance of what he calls "Fifth Discipline" thinking.

The selection by Blau analyzes the emergence of leadership and power differentiation within a group as an outgrowth of a process of social exchange. It has the merit of linking interpersonal processes to the emergence of more permanent social institutions. Verba examines a special problem of leadership—trying to meet the emotional and human needs of the members of a group while, at the same time, having to push people toward the accomplishment of some task. It is a problem which many groups solve by using different leaders for the social-emotional and instrumental areas; these leaders, however, must cooperate if the group is to be effective. The tension between the two leadership tasks is greatly reduced, Verba points out, if leaders have high legitimacy. Under such conditions, efforts to move the group toward its goal are not regarded by group members as exercises of personal power, which cause resentment. Burns examines various aspects of leadership, especially the kind of *transforming* leadership that engages with others in such a way that both leaders and followers raise one another to higher levels of motivation and morality.

Communities of Leaders and Learners

Peter M. Senge

Almost everyone agrees that the command-and-control corporate model will not carry us into the twenty-first century. In a world of increasing interdependence and rapid change, it is no longer possible to figure it out from the top. Nor, as today's CEOs keep discovering, is it possible to command people to make the profound systemic changes needed to transform industrial-age institutions for the next business era. Increasingly, successful organizations are building competitive advantage through less controlling and more learning—that is, through continually creating and sharing new knowledge. The implications this change will have for the theory and practice of management are impossible for us to overestimate. But, we can start by rethinking our most basic concepts of leadership and learning.

Leadership first. In the knowledge era, we will finally have to surrender the myth of leaders as isolated heroes commanding their organizations from on high. Top-down directives, even when they are implemented, reinforce an environment of fear, distrust, and internal competitiveness that reduces collaboration and cooperation. They foster

This first selection by Peter M. Senge is reprinted with permission from the HARVARD BUSINESS REVIEW 75 *(Sept.–Oct., 1997)*.

Peter M. Senge teaches organizational learning in the Sloan School of Management at MIT and is the author of *The Fifth Discipline* (Currency Doubleday: New York, 1990).

compliance instead of commitment, yet only genuine commitment can bring about the courage, imagination, patience, and perseverance necessary in a knowledge-creating organization. For those reasons, leadership in the future will be distributed among diverse individuals and teams who share responsibility for creating the organization's future.

Building a community of leaders within an organization requires recognizing and developing:

- local line leaders, managers with significant bottom-line responsibility, such as business unit managers, who introduce and implement new ideas;
- executive leaders, top-level managers who mentor local line leaders and become their "thinking partners," who steward cultural change through shifts in their own behavior and that of top-level teams, and who use their authority to invest in new knowledge infrastructures, such as learning laboratories; and
- internal networkers, people, often with no formal authority, such as internal consultants or human resources professionals and frontline workers, who move about the organization spreading and fostering commitment to new ideas and practices.

In knowledge-creating organizations, these three types of leaders absolutely rely on one another. None alone can create an environment that ensures continual innovation and diffusion of knowledge.

As for learning, after six years of collaborative experimentation as part of the MIT Organizational Learning Center (OLC), companies such as Ford, Shell Oil, Harley-Davidson, Hewlett-Packard, Chrysler, EDS, FedEx, and Intel are finding that enduring institutional learning arises only from three interrelated activities:

research, the disciplined pursuit of discovery and understanding that leads to generalizable theory and method;

capacity building, the enhancement of people's capabilities and knowledge to achieve results in line with their deepest personal and professional aspirations; and

practice, the stuff that happens in organizations every day—people working together to achieve practical outcomes and building practical know-how in the process.

Today the knowledge-creating process has become deeply fragmented. The three core activities are typically carried out by specialized, disconnected, often antagonistic institutions: universities, consulting firms, and businesses. Too often, the results are ivory-tower research that is rarely applied, consulting projects that offer recommendations for solving problems but rarely build people's ability to stop creating the problems in the first place, and nonstop fire fighting as managers carom from crisis to crisis.

The deep systemic problems that afflict our institutions and society are not likely to be remedied until we rediscover what has been lost in this age of specialization: the ability to honor and integrate theory, personal development, and practical results. In fact, the former corporate members of the OLC, along with MIT, have re-formed as the Society for Organizational Learning to do just that.

In a sense, such a change involves returning to an older model of community: traditional societies that gave equal respect to elders for their wisdom; teachers for their ability to help people grow; and warriors, weavers, and growers for their life skills.

Poised at the millennium, we confront two critical challenges: how to address deep problems for which hierarchical leadership alone is insufficient and how to harness the intelligence and spirit of people at all levels of an organization to continually build and share knowledge. Our responses may lead us, ironically, to a future based on more ancient—and more natural—ways of organizing: communities of diverse and effective leaders who empower their organizations to learn with head, heart, and hand.

*Inter*dependency Rules and "Wins the Day"

Peter M. Senge

Ours is a highly individualistic culture. In our minds and myths the ideal of the solitary hero facing every challenge and virtually single handedly conquering every frontier dominates our self-perceptions as a people. In reality, we are the product of one great mass movement after another. We are, in fact, almost totally *inter*dependent, not "independent." So are all of our social and economic systems.

Peter Senge teaches us about an MIT market-example simulation called *the beer game.* Like most human systems, that "system" was larger than what was local. The players in

These summaries and syntheses of Peter M. Senge's arguments in THE FIFTH DISCIPLINE *were prepared by Ronald Lee Logsdon, Executive Director, Audubon Area Community Services in Owensboro, Kentucky and are reprinted with permission of the compiler.*

that system created their own "crises"—which is typically what people do. They did not consider the "law of unintended consequences." Like most of us, when things seemed to go awry they thought only to do something that had worked for them in the past. When that strategy did not work as expected they only did the same thing again, but more aggressively. Things then got only worse. The reason: *They failed to understand the system in which they operate and then to act "sensibly."* Specifically, they failed to understand the interdependencies within their system and act considerately and patiently.

There weren't any villains, but they blamed each other for the *self-created instabilities* in their "system." Their emotional reactions created "panic" and worsened conditions.

Regardless of where we wish to consider our "place"— in an organization, a family, a community, a nation—we are part of a human system. Peter Senge points out that the nature of these systems is subtle *because we are part of the structure*—and as "the eye can't see the eye"—we're just too close to easily get a proper perspective.

Players in our systems—all of us—look for heroes and, when things go wrong, culprits—someone to blame. It's a "kneejerk" reaction—we look for some*one* to fault, and we get upset! Instead, we should look to understand the way the structure of human systems influences our behavior.

Peter Senge lists three lessons for us:

- *Structure influences behavior.* "Different people in the same structure tend to produce qualitatively similar results." ". . . More often than we realize, *systems cause their own crises,* not external forces or individuals' mistakes."
- *Structure in human systems is subtle.* ". . . Structure in complex living systems (as in the human body) means the basic interrelationships that control behavior." It includes *how* we make decisions, including how we "translate perceptions, goals, rules, norms into actions."
- *Leverage often comes from new ways of thinking.* Our tendency is to focus on our own actions and ignore how those affect others. They create extreme instability because they don't understand how they are creating the instability in the first place.

So "refine your scope of influence." How? Be deliberate. *Be a calming influence.*

We must work to see and understand the "systemic structure." That, Senge says, is the "underlying *patterns of interdependency.*"

As in the "beer game," if everyone in the system is experiencing virtually the same problem, they *must* have something else in common. And that is the nature of the system itself. The failure to recognize these *systems* in which we function is what tends to make us so often feel like "victims."

The interesting thing about the **patterns of interdependency** is that we tend to be relatively unaware of them. We like to tell ourselves the fables of our independence. It just isn't so. Senge demonstrates his point with the example of the automobile, which he describes as one of our "prototypical examples of independence." But contrary to the mythical image, we literally place our lives in the hands of strangers when we drive our automobiles. Our roads are "an extraordinarily *inter*dependent system" which we only realize, it seems, when there is an accident.

"We live our lives in webs of interdependence," says Peter Senge. We must "unlayer" our *mental models* about life, work and society. Eventually we must come to realize the "larger systemic set of forces" rather than blaming *someone* or *something* before we can benefit from systems thinking.

Correcting our problems have mostly to do with **understanding how the world works** and **how we work.** We must begin to think in terms of "how our actions might be creating our own reality."

The logic is so simple, but we just don't get it easily. The reason? We learned in infancy (playing with blocks) that a consequence immediately follows an action. When consequences are not immediately apparent, we don't get it (the connection). When longer term consequences are not at all what we wanted, we don't see their direct connection to our earlier actions.

People consistently take actions that today make apparent "good sense" based on the limited information and understanding they have, but they don't see the connection with longer term consequences. Indeed, many later problems surely do occur because of our "best efforts." **The problem is more in how we think rather than the situations to which we react.** As Pogo's wisdom says, *"We have met the enemy and they is us."* Senge asks the crucial question, **if we start to think systemically, how might we act different?** Will it make us more able to create what we really want?

"The discipline of systems thinking begins with a shift in awareness. You become aware of interdependencies," he says. Thus aware, realize that you must function at a pace the system can handle. *Acting precipitously, things typically get worse, not better.* The action becomes counterproductive. That's what happened in "the beer game." Senge also uses the example of a shower with a slow response time. Turn the handle too aggressively and you will freeze then scald alternatively. Haven't we all experienced that?

As expressed in the **"Take two aspirin and wait"** rule, *"the key leverage point is* **patience**," Senge says. He continues:

> The promise of systems thinking is very simple. If we can begin to learn to shift our ways of looking at the world to begin to see the interdependency that actually exists, we will begin to think differently and therefore, we will begin to act differently. This con-

dition afflicts human civilization worldwide, the condition of working hard and producing outcomes which are *not* what we want to produce. It's having problems all around us and knowing that despite our best efforts these problems persist—and *not* realizing that it may be *because* of our "best efforts."

With systems thinking, we could actually move to be more able to create the type of world we truly would like to live in. After all, we are creating the world we have right now.

A Shift of Mind—Seeing the World Anew: *Whole!*

Peter M. Senge

Systems thinking is the most direly needed discipline in today's complex, often overwhelming, seemingly out-of-control world. Our fragmented, linear, cause-effect, culprit-focused approaches to dealing with contemporary life and its institutions are not working—at least not very well.

"Systems thinking is a discipline for seeing wholes. It's a framework for seeing interrelationships rather than things, for seeing patterns of change rather than static 'snapshots,'" says Peter Senge, author of *The Fifth Discipline.* This statement and the previous two segments of this paper simply help set a stage for changing our mind set and helping us, as Senge describes it, "seeing the world anew." He asserts that so much of "the unhealthiness in our world today is in direct proportion to our inability to see it as a whole."

To correct that—even in our little corner of the world—we must develop a sensibility for the "subtle interconnectedness that gives living systems their unique character," he says.

So why do we attempt to solve every problem by breaking it down into unconnected parts and attempt to rebuild each one independently then re-create a new whole? Senge says the roots of this approach lie in our culture—in "linear" Western language and the mind set of the Industrial Age.

But today, things are more "complex" than our ability to comprehend, much less solve. Why? Senge says there are two kinds of complexity, and Western man is good at one, but poor at the other.

The first kind of complexity is *detail complexity.* This is linear, sequential, cause-and-effect, "snapshot" kind of detail. It's like having all the parts and a clear understanding of how to assemble them into, say, a bicycle. It may be a challenge, but we're very good at this kind of detail complexity. The second kind of complexity is *dynamic complexity.* This is more about "process" than tangible product. Its "cause and effect" are subtle at best—and often obscure or totally hidden to us. Its "structures" are the patterns of interrelationships that recur—again and again, but the appropriate interventions are not obvious to us. We're usually not very good with **dynamic** complexity.

Instead of "linear" language in its written form, the *real/leverage* thinking, as in our dealing with dynamic complexity, says Senge, comes from looking for "circles of causality." This comes from understanding three crucial variables in every "system": 1) *Reinforcing* or **amplifying feedback,** 2) *balancing* or **stabilizing feedback,** and 3) **delay.**

Reinforcing feedback is both the "engine of growth" and the agent of decline—as in the "snowball effect." With reinforcing feedback, "momentum is everything," regardless of its forward/backward, up/down direction.

Balancing feedback is the force—whether pedal or brake—behind all goal-oriented behavior. Life as we know it is a "balancing process." These processes—except for obvious resistance—are difficult to see, so it often looks like nothing is happening when they are at work, whereas reinforcing processes are usually obvious.

The third factor in circles of causality is delay. "Systems seem to have a mind of their own," Senge says. We don't like impediments when we want something done, so as in the "beer game" we've already reviewed, we just do more of what we "know" to do and do it more aggressively. We then expect sure results, but they don't come. In fact, matters usually get worse the more we "proact."

We've already discussed in this series the importance and virtue of **patience!** It's a lesson we cannot learn too well. Senge says that we are in a dynamically complex environment "when the effect of one variable on another takes time." Failure to recognize systemic delays simply produce "overshoot," and thereby, instability and ultimate breakdown. Senge offers this advice: "Things do happen . . . *eventually.*" He concludes: The systems viewpoint is generally oriented toward the long-term view. That's why delays and feedback loops are so important. In the short term, you can often ignore them; they're inconsequential. They only come back to haunt you in the long term.

Reinforcing feedback, balancing feedback, and delays are all fairly simple. They come into their own as building blocks for the "systems archetypes"—more elaborate structures that recur in our personal and work lives again and again.

We are now preparing to move from the "introductory" to the meat of Senge's "Fifth Discipline" thinking. But before we do let's stop and cover what he terms *The Laws of the Fifth Discipline.*

1. **Today's problems come from yesterday's "solutions."** Like neighborhood drug arrests, we often merely shift the problem elsewhere.
2. **The harder you push, the harder the system pushes back.** It's called "compensating feedback."
3. **Behavior grows better before it grows worse.** Our "solutions" often make things *look* better only in the short run.
4. **The easy way out usually leads back in.** So why then do we so eagerly embrace nonsystemic but familiar "solutions"—even when they are so fundamentally wrong?
5. **The cure can be worse than the disease.** Shifting the burden—as we usually do—is both addictive and dangerous.
6. **Faster is slower.** Just remember the story of the tortoise and the hare. The corollary is, we'll either do our "favorite intentions" or do nothing at all.
7. **Cause and effect are not closely related in time.** "There is a fundamental mismatch between the nature of reality in complex systems and our predominate ways of thinking about that reality," says Senge.
8. **Small changes can produce big results—but the areas of highest leverage are often the least obvious.** It's the difference between our "snapshot" views and the deeper, better understanding achieved through "process" thinking.

9. **You can have your cake and eat it too—but not at once.** It's not "either-or": real leverage—through a better understanding of "circles of causality"—can improve both over time.
10. **Dividing an elephant in half does not produce two small elephants.** It produces a mess! "Living systems have their own integrity," says Senge. A key principle is: *The Principle of the System Boundary.* **It's OK to see the parts, but understand the integrity of the whole!**
11. **There is no blame.** Senge asserts: "You and the cause of your problem are part of a single system. The cure lies in your relationship with your 'enemy'." This is wrapped inside an overarching reality, according to Senge, and that is: **"There is no outside."**

As we discussed in an earlier segment, everything in our system—and all systems—is interdependent. As much as at any time before in man's history, this is **"the age of interdependence."** "Everybody shares responsibility for the problems generated by a system" and "the search for a scapegoat is a blind alley." Peter Senge says, "Nature loves a balance, but many times human decision makers act contrary to the balances and pay the price." The human body requires "homeostasis" to survive, so does any other system, be it an organization or a society.

And, says Senge, "That's one of the lessons of balancing loops, with delays. Aggressive action often produces exactly the opposite of what's intended. It produces instability and oscillation instead of moving you more quickly toward your goal."

Shared Visions: Powered by a Common Caring

Peter Senge

Shared visions, while held in common, are **not commonplace.** But Peter Senge says that shared visions are the required second discipline for organizations to be truly effective today. And its prerequisite is personal mastery, or *personal vision.*

According to Senge, when a vision is shared:

- *People have a* **similar picture** *of the vision—it reflects their own personal vision.*
- *People are* **"committed** *to one another" having that vision.*

- *People are* **"connected,** *bound together by a common aspiration,"* as well as to "an important undertaking."
- People are **excited.** Their vision is powered by a common deep **caring.**
- **It is growing**—providing the "focus and energy for *generative* learning" and "expanding your ability to create."
- It may be *extrinsic*, that is, focused on a competitor or "territory," or *intrinsic*, focused on inner standards of experience; or a combination of both. Both types can coexist.

A "shared vision" is—must be—**compelling,** or it's not likely to be either **shared** or possess any of the other characteristics Senge mentions. Beyond that, it's hard to specify exactly what such a vision might be. Kazuo Inamori of the Kyocera Company perhaps explains it best when he says, "It's not what the vision is, but what it does." Senge says, "A shared vision, especially one that is intrinsic, uplifts people's aspirations."

Senge says further that shared visions:

- Change people's relationship with the enterprise—it's no longer "theirs," but *ours.*
- Allow those previously mistrusting to begin to work together.
- Create a commonplace image, identity, purpose, and set of operating values.
- Compel courage—and new ways of thinking and acting.
- Establish overarching goals.
- Foster risk-taking and experimentation.
- Foster long-term commitment.

These factors may speak to the great power of "an idea whose time has come." But Abraham Maslow once observed that *shared purpose and vision* were the most striking common characteristics of high performing teams. A Senge colleague, Robert Fritz, said, "In the presence of greatness, pettiness disappears." Senge's corollary is: "In the absence of a great dream, pettiness prevails." But in truth, a shared vision is not just "an idea," but "a force in people's hearts."

But force needs direction. Peter Senge warns that in the highly complex real world, we must still see both "the forest" and "the trees." We must be able to resolve the problem of complexity, see through it, and organize it into a "coherent story that illuminates the causes of problems and how they can be remedied in enduring ways." He continues, "What we need most are ways to know what is important and what is not important, what variable to focus on and which to pay less 'attention' to—and we need ways to do this which can help groups and teams develop shared understanding."

Many enterprises resort to "strategic planning" to achieve these ends. But Senge also warns that this is no panacea. Why the cautionary note? Because those efforts tend to:

- Be reactive and short term in their focus.
- Reveal more about today's problems than tomorrow's opportunities.
- Emphasize extensive analyses of current *"W-O-T-S,"* competitors, niches, and resources.
- Lack "a goal worthy of commitment."
- Fail to "nurture genuine vision."
- Be top-down or outside-in.
- Function like "blinders" to continually new and emerging needs, dangers, and opportunities.

"The plan" will not energize us. From 1987-92, GE nearly lost out as a result of its Strategic Plan. Meanwhile, its foreign competition beat their socks off. Strategic Thinking Consultant Dr. William Corley says that strategic planning is "a skeleton unconnected by muscle, ligaments—worse, it has no heart. It lacks the ability to marshall energy for the 'last kick'." "There are two fundamental sources of energy that can motivate an organization," says Senge: **fear** and **aspiration.** Aspiration drives **positive** visions and is a "continuing source of learning and growth."

Shared visions are a powerful source for that energy. But how do we achieve it? It's more than mere can-do optimism, which Senge refers to as a "thin veneer over a fundamentally reactive view."

People are so used to top-down "marching orders." But Senge says leaders must give up that approach. *Leaders'* visions are just their *personal* visions, **not** "automatically" the organization's vision. It's fine—even important!—for leaders to share their visions, just don't impose them. Leaders should share their visions, and then ask, "Will you follow me?" **Build on people's personal visions,** says Senge. "Official visions" fail to foster energy, commitment, or passion.

Building shared vision results from "a course of action that transcends and unifies all our individual visions"—and even allows multiple visions to exist. Building shared vision is "a central element of the daily work of leaders." As one CEO said it, "My job, fundamentally, is **listening** to what the organization is trying to say and then making sure that it is forcefully articulated." Senge later refers to "the *art* of visionary leadership."

"Visions that are truly shared take time to emerge. They grow as a by-product of the interactions of varied individual visions. Experience suggests that visions that are genuinely shared require ongoing conversation, where individuals not only feel free to express their dreams but learn how to listen to each others' dreams. Out of this listening, new insights into what is possible gradually emerge," writes Senge.

There are no canned "formulas" for how to find or build shared visions, but Senge offers these principles and guidelines in what he calls . . .

The Discipline of Building Shared Vision

A. Encourage personal vision and respect individual freedom. "Shared vision is rooted in personal visions."

B. Move from "personal mastery" (personal visions) to shared visions.

C. Spread shared visions through the processes of "enrollment" and commitment, not compliance. Be flexible.

D. Create synergy. Combine shared vision *and* systems thinking. "Vision paints the picture of what we want to create. Systems thinking reveals how we have created what we currently have."

"The only vision that motivates you is *your* vision," says Hanover Insurance CEO Bill O'Brien. Caring is personal. It is rooted in one's own set of values, concerns, aspirations."

Senge likens the process of combining individual visions into shared visions to *a hologram,* which he terms "a three-dimensional image created by interacting light sources." In a hologram, each piece "represents the image from a different point of view" and "each individual's vision of the whole is unique." But Senge says that if you add the pieces, "the image of the whole does not change fundamentally," except that "the image becomes more intense, more lifelike." Each of the parties to the shared vision is *a partner,* co-creator, nurturer, co-supporter.

Senge also presents the variety of possible attitudes one can feel toward a vision. He charts the responses as follows:

- **Commitment.** "Wants it. Will make it happen." Within legal and ethical constraints, will give "whatever it takes."
- **Enrollment.** "Wants it," and will offer whatever it takes within **"the spirit** of the law."
- **Compliance** (three types):
  - **Genuine Compliance.** "Good soldiers." Sees benefits; does what's expected and more. Follows the "letter of the law."
  - **Format Compliance.** "Pretty good soldiers." Sees the benefits on the whole, but does only what's expected.
  - **Grudging Compliance.** Does enough of what's expected—because he "has to," but he's openly "not really on board." Does not see the benefits, but does not want to risk his job through noncompliance.
- **Noncompliance.** Does not see the benefits of the vision; will **not** do what's expected. Thinks: "I won't do it; you can't make me."
- **Apathy.** Neither for or against the vision. Has no interest, no energy. Thinks: "Is it five o'clock yet?"

Clearly, commitment to shared vision is what's most desirable, and apathy is perhaps the worst response of all. So how do we get commitment or at least enrollment? Senge offers this advice to management leadership:

1. Be enrolled yourself. Don't "sell." **Show** your support!
2. Be on the level. Be honest: don't "inflate" the benefits or "cover up" on the downside.
3. Let others choose. Assure "freedom of choice."

". . . There is nothing you can do to get another person to enroll or commit," Senge says. Words are not enough. To get others to share a vision, you must "paint pictures of the type of organization we want to be," says Hanover's Bill O'Brien. The vision is *the what,* says Senge—"the picture of the future we seek." That picture, that *vision* along with

the *purpose* (or Mission) and *core values* of the enterprise provide its three governing ideas—or "the company creed." They tell me the "what," the "why," and the "how" which moves a group along "the path toward achievement." Taken together, they answer the question, *"What do we believe in?"*

And again, the last principle in the discipline of building shared vision is to synergize your shared dreams with systems thinking:

1. Learn how existing policies and actions are creating the "current reality";
2. Understand those forces and where there is "leverage" for influencing them; and
3. Accept that "the reality we now have is only **one of several possible realities."**

Finally, Senge gives warnings against those threats which might cause the visioning process to wither. There are always "balancing processes" at work against any force that exerts itself. At least six such processes can affect the building of shared vision:

1. As more people get involved, there's an **increasing diversity** of views—which is **not** necessarily bad.
2. Spells of **"reduced clarity"** can impede the vision's spread. (Conversely, if increased clarity occurs, the spread continues.)
3. **Unmanageable conflicts**—even polarization—may occur. "Diversity of visions will grow until it exceeds the organization's capacity to 'harmonize' diversity," says Senge.
4. **Discouragement.** If unable to bring a vision into reality, people may be unable to "hold" the "creative tension," i.e., commitment to truth and what they really care about.
5. People get overwhelmed by the demands, they **lose focus** on the vision. The current reality is simply too much, they may feel, to overcome.
6. People **forget their connection** to one another. They stop asking, "What do we really want to create?" And they may begin "proselytizing" members toward their point of view rather than continuing the visioning process as a "joint inquiry."

It's daunting, but shared visions are realized somewhere, probably many times over each day—and it makes all the difference in some great endeavor(s). And it can happen with us too!

Shared visions come from people. Shared visions take lots of time. "The visioning is the work," says Senge. "It never stops." That's why he calls it **a discipline.**

But once again, **It's not what the vision *is,* it's what the vision *does.*** It's a "conversation that spawns the imagination, the creativity, all the daring things that people do."

It begins with personal visions. And always, people keep **their** visions—not as inflexible "advocates," but as receptive inquirers to others' visions. They "remain open to the possibility for **the** vision to evolve, to become 'larger' than (their) individual visions. **That** is the principle of the hologram."

Senge asserts:

"The underlying precondition for shared vision to exist is that **people must believe** that they can create the future." Systems thinking helps people "understand systemically the causes of their problems and how they are a part of those causes." When people accept that, they inevitably say, "Ah, now we understand how we're creating the mess we've got now. Well, what would we like to create in the future?"

"Systems thinking and shared visions," says Senge, "reinforce this underlying shift of mind towards **creating** rather than just reacting."

Social Exchange, Power, and Leadership

Peter M. Blau

Unilateral Dependence and Obligations

By supplying services in demand to others, a person establishes power over them. If he regularly renders needed services they cannot readily obtain elsewhere, others become dependent on and obligated to him for these services, and unless they can furnish other benefits to him that produce interdependence by making him equally dependent on them, their unilateral dependence obligates them to comply with his requests lest he cease to continue to meet their needs. Providing needed benefits others cannot easily do without is undoubtedly the most prevalent way of attaining power, though not the only one, since it can also be attained by threatening to deprive others of benefits they currently enjoy unless they submit. The threat of punishment, although it exerts the most severe restraints, creates the dependence that is the root of power indirectly, as it were, while recurrent essential rewards that can be withheld do so directly. The government that furnishes needed protection to its citizens, the employer who provides needed jobs to his employees, and the profession that supplies needed services to the community, all make the others dependent on them and potentially subject to their power.

Emerson has presented a schema for examining "power-dependence" relations and their consequences, which can be reformulated to specify the conditions that produce the imbalance of power itself.[1] Individuals who need a service another has to offer have the following alternatives: *First, they can supply him with a service* that he wants badly enough to induce him to offer his service in return, though only if they have the resources required for doing so; this will lead to reciprocal exchanges. *Second, they may obtain the needed service elsewhere,* assuming that there are alternative suppliers; this also will lead to reciprocal exchanges but in different partnerships. *Third, they can coerce him to furnish the service,* provided they are capable of doing so, in which case they would establish domination over him. *Fourth, they may learn to resign themselves to do without this service,* possibly finding some substitute for it, which would require that they change the values that determine their needs. Finally, if they are not able or willing to choose any of these alternatives, they have no other choice but to comply with his wishes, since he can make continued supply of the needed service contingent on their compliance. In the situation specified, the supply of services inevitably generates power. The absence of the first four alternatives defines the conditions of power in general.

This schema can be employed to indicate the conditions of social independence, the requirements of power, the issues in power conflicts, and their structural implications. The conditions of social independence are characterized by the availability of the first four alternatives, which enables people to evade the fifth one of dependence on services from a given source. First, strategic resources promote independence. Specifically, a person who has all the resources required as effective inducements for others to furnish him with the services and benefits be needs is protected against becoming dependent on anyone. The possession of generalized rewards, such as money, is evidently of major significance in this connection, although wealth is

---

[1] Richard M. Emerson, "Power-Dependence Relations," *American Sociological Review* 27 (1962), 31–41. Suggestive as the underlying conception is, the focus on balancing operations is unfortunate and somewhat confusing inasmuch as it diverts attention from the analysis of power imbalance, His schema deals with the balancing operations consequent to given differences in power-dependence, whereas the reformulation derives power imbalance from the conditions of exchange.

This reading is reprinted from Peter M. Blau, EXCHANGE AND POWER IN SOCIAL LIFE *(New York: John Wiley & Sons, 1964), pp. 118–125, and 199–205, by permission of the Publisher.*
Peter M. Blau is a sociologist.

not a perfect safeguard against dependence, since many benefits a person may want, such as fame or love, cannot be obtained for money but only with other resources.

The fact that there are alternative sources from which a needed service can be obtained is a second condition that fosters independence. If there is only one employer in a community, or only one expert consultant in a work group, others are likely to become dependent on him. The situation, however, does not have to be that extreme. As a matter of fact, any commitment to a social relationship entails a degree of dependence by excluding alternatives. An employee presumably remains in a job either because alternative employment opportunities are less attractive to him or because his investment in this job is so great that moving to another would be too costly for him. Whatever the reason, his lack of equally preferable alternatives makes him dependent on his employer.[2] The degree of dependence of individuals on a person who supplies valued services is a function of the difference between their value and that of the second-best alternative open to them. The more employees prefer their own job to any possible alternative, the more dependent are they on their employer and the more power does he have over them. The employer can cut the salary of employees who are very dependent on their job, assign them unpleasant duties, or force them to work harder, and they have no choice but to accept the decisions and to comply. Yet by doing so the employer makes the job less attractive to the employees and other employment opportunities relatively more attractive, decreasing the difference between the present job and alternatives, and thus reducing his employees' dependence on him and his power over them. Generally, the greater the difference between the benefits an individual supplies to others and those they can obtain elsewhere, the greater is his power over them likely to be. Hence, others can increase their independence of a person who has power over them simply by accepting fewer benefits from him—no more than they can get for their services elsewhere—except that this is often not so simple for them.[3]

A third condition of independence is the ability to use coercive force to compel others to dispense needed benefits or services. The inability to use force may be due to weakness or to normative restraints that effectively prohibit resort to coercion, or it may be due to the fact that the desired benefit loses its significance if given under duress, as is the case for love and for social approval. Superior coercive power makes people relatively independent of others inasmuch as power includes the ability to prevent others from interfering with one's conduct. Since there is strength in numbers, independence can be won through forming coalitions capable of enforcing demands.[4]

A lack of need for various services constitutes the fourth condition of independence. The fewer the wants and needs of an individual, the less dependent he is on others to meet them. Needs, however, do not remain constant. By providing individuals with goods and services that increase their satisfaction, their level of expectations tends to be raised, and while they were previously satisfied without these benefits, they are now desirous of continuing to obtain them. The development of new needs in this fashion underlies the increasing consumer demand that is an essential element in an expanding economy. But emergent needs serve this function by strengthening the dependence of people on those who can supply the resources required to meet these needs, notably employers. Religious and political ideals derive their driving force in large part from imbuing adherents with values that make the satisfaction of material wants comparatively unimportant and that, consequently, lessen men's dependence on those who can supply material benefits. By reducing material needs, revolutionary ideologies become a source of independent strength and resistance to power.

The fourfold schema can also help to delineate the strategies required to attain and sustain power, which are complementary to the conditions of independence just discussed. To achieve power over others with his resources, a person must prevent others from choosing any of the first four alternatives, thereby compelling them to comply with his directives as a condition for obtaining the needed benefits at his command. This requires, first, that he remain indifferent to the benefits they can offer him in exchange for his. The strategies of power designed to preserve this indifference include denying others access to resources that are vital for the welfare of a group or individual, for example, by fighting attempts of working-class parties to take over the government; securing needed benefits from outside sources rather than subordinates, as illustrated by the gang leader's disinclination to borrow money from his more affluent followers;[5] and encouraging competition among the suppliers of essential service, for instance, by opposing the formation of unions that would restrict competition for jobs among workers.

A second requirement of power is to assure the continued dependence of others on the services one has to supply by barring access to alternative suppliers of these services. Monopolization of needed rewards is the typical means of achieving this purpose. The only firm in town where jobs can be found, the only child on the block who

---

[2] The counterdependence of the small employer on the employee's services may create interdependence and neutralize the small employer's power, but the large employer is not so much dependent on single employees as on a labor force whose turnover can and must be taken into account in management, and his independence of any one employee sustains his power over all of them, unless it is reduced by their collective action.

[3] Accepting a job at a higher salary than one can command in the market, buying from an acquaintance at wholesale prices, gaining acceptance in a more eminent group than one's achievements warrant, and generally obtaining any recurrent benefit that is superior to what could be obtained elsewhere entails dependence and loss of power.

[4] Emerson, *op. cit.*, p. 37.

[5] William F. Whyte, *Street Corner Society*, 2nd ed. (Chicago: University of Chicago Press, 1955), pp. 257–258.

has a bicycle, the political society that is the sole source of national security and glory, the church that is the only avenue to salvation, and the police that alone can offer protection against violence—all these have power due to their monopoly over important benefits.

The ability to prevent others from resorting to coercive force to effect their demands is a third prerequisite of maintaining power. Discouraging coalitions among subordinates that would enable them to extract demands is a strategy that serves this end, as is blocking their access to political power. Such organizations as unions and working-class parties have two analytically distinct, though actually inseparable, functions in the fight against existing powers. Their success threatens those in positions of power, on the one hand, by making them dependent for essential services on these organizations (for example, for labor supply) and, on the other, by subjecting them to their coercive power (for instance, the union's sit-down strike or the executive power of the labor-party government). Obstructing such coalitions, therefore, protects power against being undermined either by withholding vital services or by employing coercive force. Probably the most important strategies for safeguarding the power that rests on the possession of important resources, however, are support for law and order and resistance against political control of exchange processes. These defenses protect the power potential that resides in superior vital resources not only from the threat of violence but also from being curbed by the legitimate power of the state.

Fourth, power depends on people's needs for the benefits those in power have to offer. Materialistic values, which make money and what it can buy of great significance, strengthen the power of employers. Patriotic ideals, which identify people with the success of their country in war and peace, fortify the power of the government. Religious convictions, which make the blessings of a church and the spiritual counsel of its representatives rewards of great saliency, reinforce the power of church dignitaries. Revolutionary ideologies, which define the progress of a radical movement as inherently valuable for its members, bestow power on the movement's leadership. Groups and individuals in power have a stake in helping to perpetuate and spread the relevant social values and in opposing counterideologies that depreciate these values. Dominant groups whose power rests on different social values have some conflicting interests, therefore, although their common interest in preserving the existing power structure may well override these differences.

The conflict between the powerful (who have an interest in fortifying their power) and the people over whom they have power (who have an interest in strengthening their independence) centers around four types of issues, which again correspond to the four alternatives outlined. First, there is the issue of the resources of subordinates. If their resources were sufficient to obtain the benefits they need in exchange for them, they would cease to be subject to the power of the others. Granted that every single subordinate's resources are inadequate for this purpose, the issue becomes that of pooling the resources of all subordinates who confront a superior or group of superiors to extract demands from him or them. The second issue is that of the alternative opportunities available to subordinates for obtaining needed benefits. Competition among superiors for the services of subordinates increases the subordinates' independence, whereas monopolistic practices increase the superiors' power. These two conflicts are complementary, since the question in both cases is the degree of collective organization permissible to restrain free competition, although it is the organization of the powerless that would husband their resources in one case, and the organization of the powerful that would monopolize needed benefits in the other.

The third conflict is political. At issue here is the use of coercive force in the fight against powers based on superior resources. The prototype is the conflict over the use of the legitimate coercive power of the state to regulate exchange transactions and restrict power that rests on economic strength. Fourth, there is the ideological conflict between social values that intensify the need for the services the powerful have to offer and counterideologies that mitigate this need. In the process of decreasing the need for some services, however, radical ideologies increase the need for others—namely, those that contribute to the reform movement—with the result that ideologies make adherents less dependent on the power of some but more dependent on the power of others.

Finally, tracing the implications of each of the four alternatives leads to the analysis of basic problems of social structure. First, the fact that benefits can be obtained by reciprocating for them with others directs attention to the study of exchange processes and the distribution of resources. Second, the exploration of alternative opportunities points to the investigation of the emerging exchange structures, the competitive processes in them, the going rates of exchange, and the normative standards that tend to develop. Third, the study of coercive power raises questions concerning the establishment of coalitions and organizations to mobilize power, the differentiation of power in social structures, and the processes that govern the struggle over political power in a society.[6] Fourth, the ability to get along without something originally needed calls attention to the modifications of social values that occur under various conditions, the formation of new ideologies, and conflicts between ideologies.

The main points of the entire discussion presented are summarized in the schema below.

Dependence on the benefits a person can supply does not make others subject to his power but gives him only potential power over them. Realization of this power requires

---

[6] These could also be considered to be implications of the fifth alternative. The third and fifth alternatives are complementary, as they are concerned with power from the perspectives of the two different parties.

Alternatives to Compliance	Conditions of Independence	Requirements of Power	Structural Implications
1. Supply inducements	Strategic resources	Indifference to what others offer	Exchange and distribution of resources
2. Obtain elsewhere	Available alternatives	Monopoly over what others need	Competition and exchange rates
3. Take by force	Coercive force	Law and order	Organization and differentiation
4. Do without	Ideals lessening needs	Materialistic and other relevant values	Ideology formation

that he actually supply the benefits or commit himself to do so. In a technical sense, we are dependent on all employers who are in a position to offer us better jobs than those we have, but these employers have no power over us, while our employer has the power to command our compliance with his directives, because the salary and other benefits he furnishes obligate us to comply lest we cease to continue to receive them. He alone can withdraw from us benefits to which we have become accustomed, whereas other employers can only tempt us with greater rewards.

The ability to provide superior benefits than are available elsewhere, in a situation where these benefits are needed and cannot be extracted by force, constitutes a very strong claim to power, although not a completely inescapable one. If the power demands are too severe, relinquishing these benefits may be preferable to yielding to the demands. Moreover, a person's or group's resources may not be adequate to obligate others to comply. For these reasons coercive force, which can hardly be resisted, is important as a last resort for exercising power over individuals who cannot otherwise be made to yield. Whereas physical force is a perfect protection against power—killing a man or incarcerating him disposes of his threat—it is an imperfect tool for exercising power, since people can choose even death over compliance. Hence, coercive force differs only in degree from the power that rests on the supply of needed benefits, albeit an important degree.

° ° °

LEGITIMATION AND ORGANIZATION

Organization involves the coordination of collective effort. Some form of social organization emerges implicitly in collectivities as the result of the processes of exchange and competition, in which the patterns of conduct of individuals and groups and the relations between them become adjusted. These processes have already been discussed. But other organizations are explicitly established for the purpose of achieving specified objectives, whether they are manufacturing goods that can be sold for a profit, participating in bowling tournaments, collective bargaining, or winning political victory. In these formal organizations, special mechanisms exist to effect the coordination of tasks of various members in the pursuit of given objectives. Such coordination of efforts, particularly on a large scale, requires some centralized direction. Power is the resource that makes it possible to direct and coordinate the activities of men.

Stable organizing power requires legitimation. To be sure, men can be made to work and to obey commands through coercion, but the coercive use of power engenders resistance and sometimes active opposition. Power conflicts in and between societies are characterized by resistance and opposition, and while the latter also occur within organizations, effective operations necessitate that they be kept at a minimum there and, especially, that members do not exhibit resistance in discharging their daily duties but perform them and comply with directives from superiors *willingly*. Only legitimate power commands willing compliance.

Legitimate power is authority, which Weber defines as "the probability that certain commands (or all commands) from a given source will be obeyed by a given group of persons." He adds that a basic criterion of authority "is a certain minimum of voluntary submission," although the specific motives for the obedience to commands may vary.[7]

[7] Max Weber, *The Theory of Social and Economic Organization* (New York: Oxford University Press, 1947), p. 324.

His analysis of three types of authority centers on the value orientations that cause people voluntarily to submit to orders from an authority they accept as legitimate.[8] What is left implicit in this analysis is the specific criterion in terms of which authority can be distinguished from other forms of influence to which individuals voluntarily submit. Indeed, the emphasis on voluntarism is misleading without further specification, since an authoritative command is one a subordinate cannot dismiss at will.

It may be suggested that the distinctive feature of authority is that social norms accepted and enforced by the collectivity of subordinates constrain its individual members to comply with directives of a superior. Compliance is voluntary for the collectivity, but social constraints make it compelling for the individual. In contrast to other forms of influence and power, the pressure to follow suggestions and orders does not come from the superior who gives them but from the collectivity of subordinates. These normative constraints may be institutionalized and pervade the entire society, or they may emerge in a group in social interaction. The latter emergent norms define leadership, which, therefore, is considered a type of authority. The authority in formal organizations entails a combination of institutionalized and leadership elements.

LEADERSHIP

Furnishing needed contributions in a group empowers a man to effect compliance with his demands. The exercise of power exerts restraints, which are, in effect, inescapable if the need for the contributions is great and no alternative sources for them are available. Compliance is a cost that is judged on the basis of social norms of fairness. Excessive demands in terms of these social standards, though those subject to the power may not be able to refuse them, engender disapproval. A person whose demands on others are fair and modest relative to the great contribution he makes to their welfare, however, earns their approval. For example, a laboratory study of small groups found that the emergent leader was more apt to be liked by the rest if the initiative he took in social interaction was accompanied by a high rate of response from others, that is, by their frequently agreeing with him and turning to him with comments and questions, than if the rate of such feedback was low.[9] This may be interpreted to imply that excessive demands by a leader, as indicated by a low rate of feedback, create disapproval that make him less liked.

Compliance can be enforced with sufficient power, but approval cannot be forced regardless of how great the power. Yet the effectiveness and stability of leadership depend on the social approval of subordinates, as several

studies have shown. Thus, the results of two experiments demonstrated that leaders who were accepted and approved by subordinates were more effective in exerting influence on them than superiors who were not.[10] A study of army leadership found that trainees who approved of their officers and noncommissioned officers were less likely to express various forms of aggression, such as going "AWOL" (absent without leave), "blowing their top," drunkenness, and gripe sessions, than those who described their superiors as arbitrary or weak.[11] The findings of another experiment indicated that group leaders whose suggestions and directives engendered a disproportionate amount of resistance and disagreement were relatively unstable, that is, they were more likely than others to be displaced as leaders in subsequent experimental periods.[12] The disapproval some leadership practices evoke among followers impede a leader's effectiveness because they create resistance, aggression, and possibly opposition that may lead to the downfall of an informal leader.

Collective approval, in contrast, legitimates leadership. The abilities that enable a person to make major contributions to the achievement of a group's goals command respect. The respect of others for him prompts them to follow his suggestion, since they expect to benefit from doing so more than from following the suggestion of someone whose abilities are less respected. The actual contributions to their welfare resulting from following his guidance not only validate the others' respect for such a person but also obligate them to comply with his directives regardless of whether doing so is in their personal self-interest. It is their obligation to comply with his directives, not simply their respect, that bestows leadership upon a person and empowers him to coordinate the activities of the members of a group, which involves directing individuals to do things that are not to their own immediate advantage. The effective coordination of effort produces rewards, and the leader's power enables him to exert a predominant influence on their distribution—how much of the honor and glory of the winning team will reflect on the rest rather than on himself, or how large a share of the material benefits goes to others and how much remains in his hands. It is this distribution of rewards that most directly effects the legitimation of leadership.

If the benefits followers derive from a leader's guidance exceed their expectations of a fair return for the costs they have incurred, both by performing services and by complying with directives, their collective approval of his leadership legitimates it. Their joint obligations for his contributions to their welfare and their common approval of

[8] *Ibid.*, pp. 329–363.
[9] Robert F. Bales, "Task Status and Likability as a Function of Talking and Listening in Decision-making Groups," in Leonard D. White, *The State of the Social Sciences* (Chicago: University of Chicago Press, 1956), pp. 148–161.

[10] John R. P. French, Jr., and Richard Snyder, "Leadership and Interpersonal Power," in Dorwin Cartwright, *Studies in Social Power* (Ann Arbor: Institute for Social Research, University of Michigan, 1959), pp. 118–149.
[11] Hannan C. Selvin, *The Effects of Leadership* (Glencoe: Free Press, 1960), chapter v.
[12] Elihu Katz, Peter M. Blau, Morton L. Brown, and Fred L. Strodtbeck, "Leadership Stability and Social Change," *Sociometry*, 20 (1957), pp. 36–50, esp. 44–46.

his fairness, reinforced by their consensus concerning the respect his abilities deserve, generate group pressures that enforce compliance with his directives. These social pressures constrain individual group members who for personal reasons are inclined to resist the leaders guidance to submit to it lest they draw on themselves the social disapproval of their peers. Legitimate leaders command willing compliance, which obviates the need for sanctions to compel or induce others to comply with directives, because the group of subordinates exerts pressures on its members to follow the leader's orders and suggestions.

The social approval of followers that legitimates leadership is distinct from the respect they may have for the leader's abilities. Although the two go often together, a person in power may have abilities that command the respect of subordinates yet make oppressive demands on them to which they react with disapproval. Respect probably does, however, act as a catalyst of legitimate leadership, since it seems to make compliance with a person's directives less burdensome. Indirect support for this statement is provided by some findings from a study of sixty caseworkers in a welfare agency.[13] Generally, the factors that distinguished workers who were often consulted from those who were rarely consulted also distinguished those who were highly respected from those who were not. But some kinds of Workers, such as oldtimers, were often consulted without being highly respected. The obligation incurred to consultants inhibited informal sociability with them if the consultants were not particularly respected, but it did not inhibit sociability if they were. This finding suggests that respect for a person legitimates the obligation to comply with his wishes and thus makes this obligation less of an impediment to informal intercourse with him.

Stable leadership rests on power over others and their legitimating approval of that power. The dilemma of leadership is that the attainment of power and the attainment of social approval make somewhat incompatible demands on a person. To achieve power over others requires not only furnishing services that make them dependent but also remaining independent of any services they might offer in return. To legitimate a position of power and leadership, however, requires that a leader be concerned with earning the social approval of his followers, which means that he does not maintain complete independence of them. An individual's refusal to accept offers of favors from others who are in his debt and his insistence on remaining entirely independent of them are usually experienced as rejections and evoke their disapproval. By asserting his dominance over the rest of the group in the process of becoming their leader and exercising his leadership, a person can hardly help antagonizing at least some of them, thereby endangering his chances of having his leadership legitimated by social approval. Conversely, preoccupation with the approval of followers interferes with a leader's ability to com-

mand their respect and compliance by making the greatest contribution to their welfare he can, because concern with being liked prevents him from basing his decisions consistently on criteria of effectiveness alone. Such preoccupation, in other words, induces a leader sometimes to refrain from making what is the best decision in his judgment for fear of antagonizing subordinates.

The dilemma of leadership can be epitomized by saying that its legitimation requires that a leader be magnanimous in the exercise of his power and in the distribution of the rewards that accrue from his leadership, but such magnanimity necessitates that he first mobilize his power and husband the group's resources, that is, act in ways that are the opposite of magnanimous. Once a man has attained much power, however, be can easily make demands that appear only moderate in view of his strength and capacity to supply benefits. In other words, extensive power facilitates obtaining legitimating approval for it.

Two different sets of expectations govern the process of legitimation, since the leader's general expectations define what is extensive or insufficient power, while those of the followers define what are moderate or unfair power demands. The less the leader expects to achieve with his power, the less power will be sufficient to meet his needs and the less demands be will make on those subject to his power. The reactions of the followers to the leader's demands, in turn, are contingent on their normative expectations of how much a leader can fairly demand in return for his contributions. Small needs for power as well as great power make it easy for a man to exercise his power in ways that elicit legitimating approval from subordinates. The line between exploitative oppression and legitimate leadership is defined by the interplay between the expectations of the man in power that define his needs and the expectations of those subject to his power that define their needs and his complementary rights.

Power must be mobilized before it can be legitimated, because the processes involved in mobilizing it are not compatible with those involved in legitimating it. The dilemma of leadership is resolved by devoting different time periods to coping with its two horns, so to speak. This parallels the conclusion of Bales and Strodtbeck that the dilemma of group problem solving posed by the need for a cognitive orientation to the task and the need for a supportive orientation that reduces tensions, which are incompatible, is resolved by devoting different time phases to meeting these two needs.[14] The potential leader of a gang uses his physical strength first against the other members to assert his dominance over them. Only then can he organize their activities and lead them in gang warfare, now

---

13 Blau, "Patterns of Choice in Interpersonal Relations," *American Sociological Review*, 27 (1962), pp. 41–55, esp. 50–51, 55.

14 Bales and Strodtbeck, "Phases in Group Problem Solving," *The Journal of Abnormal and Social Psychology*, 46 (1951), 485–495. Another method for resolving the leadership dilemma is a division of labor within the leadership group, that is, having those leaders who exercise power and restraints supported by other leaders who do not and who command the approval and loyalty of followers; see Philip E. Slater, "Role Differentiation in Small Groups," *American Sociological Review*, 20 (1955), 300–310.

using his strength and other resources in behalf of his followers against outsiders. If he is successful, his contributions to their welfare evoke legitimating approval of his leadership, which makes his continuing dominance independent of his use of physical sanctions against followers.

The situation of formal leaders in organizations is different from that of informal leaders who emerge in a group. Resources and institutionalized mechanisms place managers in organizations a priori in a dominant position over subordinates, thereby obviating the need for initially asserting their dominance and facilitating the development of legitimate authority.

Leadership: Affective and Instrumental

Sidney Verba

The purpose of this chapter is to explore one aspect of the leader-follower relationship as it is found in both small experimental groups and on-going social systems. This aspect is the dual function that the leadership structure of a group must perform if the group is successfully to reach the goal that brought it together. In attempting to achieve its goal, a group must . . . direct activities both toward the instrumental task it faces and toward the maintenance of the internal structure of the group. The group's internal maintenance function must be performed in such a way that the individual members find their participation in the group at least satisfactory enough to keep them from leaving the group. And . . . it is the function of the group leadership to operate in both these areas—the instrumental and the internal group maintenance.

The importance of the affective tone and emotional aspects of the leader-follower relationship in political and other social situations has long been recognized. Individuals do not give their allegiance to a state or their support to a political leader solely because of the material benefits they receive in return. The decision on the part of a follower to accept the directive of a leader is based on more than a rational calculus of the advantages to be gained from that acceptance. Loyalty to a state, for instance, usually has an emotional component, reinforced by more or less elaborate systems of symbols and rituals. Though there has been much analysis of these non-rational aspects of politics insofar as they affect the individual political participant, there has been little systematic consideration of the dynamic interaction between emotional attachment and material outputs within the leader-follower relationship.

∘ ∘ ∘

The difficulties of the leadership position derive not merely from the fact that the leader must be active in both the instrumental and affective group tasks, but from the fact that these two tasks are closely related. The way in which the group functions in one area will influence functioning in the other. If group members have a satisfactory affective relationship with the leader, they will be more likely to accept his instrumental directives. On the other

hand, if the level of member satisfaction with group leadership is low, members may withdraw from the group, reject the group leader, or reject the group leader's instrumental directives. All these activities lower the instrumental effectiveness of the group. Conversely, the success or failure of the instrumental activity of the group will influence the affective rewards to the members. Group members may derive satisfaction directly from the successful completion of the instrumental task of the group or from certain other rewards that are the by-product of that task completion. Insofar as the group cannot achieve its instrumental goal, satisfactions will be lowered. Maintaining a balance between the satisfactions of the group members and the task achievement of the group may well be the most important task of the group leader.

Equilibrium Problem: Maintaining the balance between affective satisfactions and instrumental performance is, however, a difficult and delicate task. Several studies of group process have suggested that attempts to direct the group toward the accomplishment of its instrumental task may be greeted by negative affective reactions on the part of group members. The theoretical and experimental work of Kurt Lewin and his associates first pinpointed the problem within small groups. In Lewin's theoretical formulation, attempts to direct the group toward the group goal disturb the equilibrium of the group by restricting the freedom of the members. This in turn causes a negative reaction that can take two forms: it may take the form of a rejection of the instrumental directive, in which case equilibrium is restored by negating the directive's effect; or the reaction may be an acceptance of the directive accompanied by increased hostility toward the leader. In the latter

This reading is reprinted from Sidney Verba, Small Groups and Political Behavior: A Study of Leadership *(Princeton: Princeton University Press, 1961), pp. 142, 145–150, 159–165, 168, 172–174, and 176–179. Omission of footnotes.* © *1961 by Princeton University Press.* © *1989 renewed by Princeton University Press. Reprinted with permission of Princeton University Press.*

Sidney Verbs is a political scientist at Harvard University.

case, equilibrium is restored but at a higher level of tension between leader and follower.

Examples of this process of negative reaction to directive leadership can be found in the classic experimental work of Lippitt and White carried out under Lewin's direction. In these experiments with democratic and authoritarian group climates, it was noted that directives from an authoritarian leader, though followed, were accompanied by negative affective reactions on the part of the group members, expressed in hostility toward the leader, a scapegoat, or other groups. Furthermore, the acceptance of the leader's directives in the authoritarian situation was external rather than internal. When the leader left the room and the external pressure was removed, the group members ceased complying with the instrumental directive. Experimental work in field situations produced similar results; attempts to direct change in a group led to negative affective reactions on the part of the group members that in turn limited the effectiveness of the instrumental directive. Coch and French, for instance, found that an attempt by management to direct certain changes in the work process ". . . had the effect for the members of setting Lip management as a hostile power field. They rejected the forces induced by this hostile power field, and group standards to restrict production developed within the group in opposition to management." The problem of leadership is clearly presented by these examples. The achievement of the group's instrumental goal must proceed along with the continuing satisfaction of the individual needs of the group members, but frequently the attempts themselves to achieve the instrumental goal lower the level of affective satisfaction of the group members. This lowering will in turn feed back upon the instrumental achievement and hamper it. Thus the several tasks of the leader may not all be consistent with one another.

The treatment of the problem of control and instrumental achievement in the work of Lewin and his associates bears a significant resemblance to the treatment of the problem in the work of Robert F. Bales and his associates at the Harvard Laboratory of Social Relations. In the small experimental groups used by Bales in the formulation of his theoretical system, the formation of the group takes place around the instrumental task presented to the group by the experimenter. The initial differentiation among the group members evolves in response to the demands of this task. Certain members tend to become more active in directing the group toward the completion of its instrumental task. But attempts to control the group in relation to the instrumental task disturb the equilibrium of the group and cause tensions in the expressive-integrative area of the group's activities. These negative reactions to control attempts may, like the negative reactions found in the work of Lewin and his associates, be directed at the leader or at a group scapegoat.

Evidence for the negative reaction received by the group member who attempts to lead the group in the direction of instrumental task achievement is derived from six measures taken by Bales during the group experiments. Two measures are based on interaction counts using the Bales scheme; these are simply measures of the amount of interactions initiated and the amount received. After each group session the members are asked to rate all members on a sociometric test using three criteria: the member who contributed the best ideas to the group, the member who contributed the best guidance, and the member who was best liked. And after all four group sessions the members are asked to select the one who contributed the best leadership. The percentage of times the same group member occupies the highest position by more than one measure is calculated. Thus on one batch of experimental groups, Slater calculated the percentage of times that the individual selected as the best leader was highest by another criterion. The results follow:

The "best leader" was also ranked highest on guidance 80 per cent of the time; on receiving, 65 per cent; on ideas, 59 per cent; on talking, 55 per cent; and on liking, 25 per cent. Clearly, the member who is best liked is rarely associated in the minds of the group members with the individual who is the best leader. Furthermore, Slater found that "liking" was not associated with any of the other measurements of leadership. The individual chosen highest by the socio-emotional criterion of best-liked was three times as likely to hold the highest position by that measure alone than were those who were most highly chosen by any other measure. Thus, those group members who are active in directing the group, or who are selected by the group members as having contributed to the instrumental task of the group, are not likely to receive choices on a sociometric test using an expressive criterion. The results clearly indicate that the individual who attempts to control the instrumental activities of the group lowers his chances to be highly thought of by the group according to an affective criterion.

External Relations of the Leader: The conflict between directing the group and maintaining one's acceptance by the group would seem to be the unique problem of the group leader. This conflict is heightened in the groups discussed above by the fact that the task toward which the instrumental leader directs the group is set for the group externally by the experimenter. Insofar as the task is set for the group externally rather than chosen by the group, attempts at instrumental control are more likely to engender negative reactions. This proposition is supported in an experimental study by Katz *et al.* of a number of four-man groups. After the performance of one task, the groups were asked to select a leader for a second task. In some cases, the task was one that the group had chosen; in others, it was imposed by the experimenter. The results support the proposition that when the task is imposed upon the group externally, the negative reaction against the leader who attempts to direct the task activity will be greater. In those cases where the group performed a second task that it had selected for itself, all those who had been chosen as leaders after the first task were again so chosen at the end of the second. On the other hand, when the group was assigned a task that it had not selected, only one-third of those who bad been chosen as leaders after the first task retained that position after the second.

. . .

A stable leadership structure is important if the group is to accomplish its instrumental task. But such stability is difficult to achieve because of the conflicting demands for task accomplishment and affective satisfactions. Insofar as the group can achieve some satisfactory balance between the instrumental and the affective aspects of its interaction and a stable leadership structure is developed, the group will be effective and contribute to the satisfaction of its members. Insofar as such a balance cannot be reached and such a structure is not developed, groups will either fall apart or continue operating at high levels of tension. This problem, we can assume, is faced not only by small groups, but by larger organizations and political systems as well. Unless the unlikely prospect of a state totally run by coercion is to be considered, some minimum of acceptance of the system by the participants must be maintained at the same time that the organization or political system carries on instrumental activities that inhibit freedom and, presumably, lower the satisfactions of the members. The importance of affective relations in political systems and of the acceptance by the followers of the leader's directives has long been recognized in political science. As Merriam has written: "No power could stand if it relied upon violence alone, for force is not strong enough to maintain itself against the accidents of rivalry and discontent. The might that makes right must be a different might from that of the right arm. It must be a right deep-rooted in emotion, embedded in feelings and aspirations. . . ." The question must then be asked: how do social systems—whether small experimental groups, on-going groups, organizations or political systems—maintain a satisfactory level of affective integration at the same time that they carry on instrumental activities whose tendency may be to lower the degree of affective satisfaction of the participants?

The Two Leaders. To shed some light upon the way in which the conflict between instrumental and affective leadership is resolved, we turn first to the small group experimental literature. The resolution of the conflict in these small groups will then be compared with the resolution in larger, on-going social systems. In the small groups studied by Bales and his associates, the conflict between instrumental and affective leadership is resolved by a differentiation within the leadership role. In these groups different individuals tend to specialize in the instrumental leadership role and in the socio-emotional leadership role. The evidence for this role differentiation is found in the material cited above: those members highly selected by the group by an affective criterion were not likely to be selected by the group as having contributed to the instrumental task, nor were they likely to be active in giving the

group direction toward the accomplishment of that task. On the other hand, the individual selected by the group as contributing the most to the external task (Best Ideas) was also highly selected as contributing most to the instrumental aspect of the internal group task (Best Guidance). High choice by one criterion was closely correlated with high choice by the other, and the individual rated lowest by one was likely to be lowest by the other. The findings by Bales and his associates that the leadership role tends to be split between a task-oriented instrumental leader and a "sociometric star" is supported by small group studies of other authors.

. . .

Activities of the Two Leaders: The fact that group leadership tends to be split between two individuals is reflected not only in the fact that group members choose different individuals by socio-emotional and instrumental criteria, but also in the fact that the behavior patterns of the individuals thus selected differ. When one looks at the interaction rates of the group members most highly selected on the basis of the socio-emotional and the instrumental (Best Ideas) criteria, one finds significant differences. The socio-emotional leader tends to initiate and receive more interactions in the socio-emotional categories of interaction than does the task specialist. He gives and receives more solidarity and tension-release interactions. The task specialist, on the other hand, is more active in giving opinions and suggestions, and he receives larger amounts of agreement, questions, and negative reactions. The difference between the behavior of the two leaders is best described by Slater: "The most salient general difference between the rates of interaction of the two types of leaders is the tendency for the Idea man to initiate interactions more heavily in Area B (Problem Solving Attempts) and the Best-liked man in Area A (Positive Reactions). . . . On the Receiving end, the situation is largely reversed, with the Idea man receiving more agreement, questions and negative reactions, while the Best-liked man receives more problem solving attempts, and more solidarity and tension release. The general picture is thus one of specialization and complementarity, with the Idea man concentrating on the task and playing a more aggressive role, while the Best-liked man concentrates more on social emotional problems, giving rewards, and playing a more passive role." The qualitative ratings given the two leaders by the group members are thus reflected in their quantitative interaction rates.

The difference between the two specialists extends to the attitudes of these two group members. Not only do they specialize in certain areas of the group activity, but they receive their satisfactions from those areas. The instrumental leader, it has already been suggested, is relatively less motivated to receive positive affective responses from the group. His personal satisfactions derive not from the affective responses of the group members, but from the instrumental task directly. For the "sociometric star," on the other hand, ". . . *primary* satisfaction derives from his success in his role as promoter of solidarity and provider of opportunities for tension release. . . ." The socio-emotional leader also tends to be more accepting of the other group members, while the task specialist differentiates among the other members in the degree to which he accepts them. On the sociometric question in which the group members were asked to rate the other members on the degree to which they liked them, 42 per cent of the socio-emotional leaders did not differentiate among the members (they said, in effect, "I like everybody") while only 20 per cent of the task leaders did not so differentiate.

Relations Between the Two Leaders: The balance between affective tone and instrumental accomplishment is maintained in these groups, then, by the development of two leaders. The disturbance in the expressive area caused by the instrumental directives of the task leader is countered by positive affective reactions from the socio-emotional leader. In understanding this process, it is important to note the relations between the two leaders. Bales and Slater found that the two had close relations, one with the other. The task and socio-emotional leaders tended to interact more frequently with each other than did any other pair of members; and, what is equally significant, tended to agree more frequently with each other. In this way, it may be suggested, the task leader receives indirectly through the socio-emotional leader the expressive support that he could not directly obtain because of his instrumental role. That such a coalition between the two group leaders is important for the effective functioning of the group is suggested by a comparison made by Bales and Slater between High Status Consensus groups and Low Status Consensus groups. In the former type of group—in which, as was pointed out earlier, task accomplishment and member satisfaction are both higher—the relationships between the two leaders are statistically significant. In the Low Consensus groups, though there is a tendency for the two leaders to interact with each other, the pattern is neither as consistent nor as strong.

CONFLICTING EXPECTATIONS:
THEIR RESOLUTION IN ON-GOING SYSTEMS

The conflict in expectations placed upon leaders has now been spelled out. In small experimental groups we have found that this conflict is resolved by the development of two leaders—an affective and a task leader—accompanied by an implicit coalition between the two men. On-going social systems, including political systems, must also deal with instrumental and affective relationships. Political systems, as well as small groups, depend upon inputs from their members of both instrumental activities (contributions of resources, services, etc.) and affect (loyalty, respect, etc.). And these systems maintain the adherence of their members by outputs in both these areas: specific services as well as affective rewards for participation in the

system. The model suggested by the studies of experimental groups suggests that the conflict between the affective and the instrumental aspects might best be resolved by a bifurcation of the leadership function. Faced with this conflict, does the on-going social system develop such a differentiated leadership structure, or are other mechanisms available to it to resolve this conflict?

⚬ ⚬ ⚬

Experimental groups with no previous experience together differ in a systematic way from [on-going groups with a history of interaction]. Insofar as members are similar in age, insofar as they are similar in status in the external culture of the group, and insofar as the experimenter supplies no sanction for any particular leadership structure, any directive attempt by a group member will be looked upon as a challenge to the other members. With no status consensus among the group members at the beginning of interaction and no status guides, would-be leaders in the new experimental groups are placed in a clear power struggle. The increased vigor necessary to control the group increases the negative reaction to the leader and heightens the conflict between acceptance and instrumental control.

⚬ ⚬ ⚬

Role of Norms in Follower Compliance: One of the most effective ways in which the instrumental directives of a group leader acquire legitimacy and avoid being received as personal, arbitrary challenges to the group members is for the leader to be perceived as acting not as an individual but as the agent of some impersonal force, such as the "demands of the situation" or the group traditions and norms. The invocation of some external authority by the group leader relieves the follower of the burden of accepting the control of another individual. Thibault and Kelley, in a study of power relations in the dyad, conclude that group norms have the effect of reducing the tension between the more powerful and the less powerful member of the group. The impersonalization of expectations of behavior through the adoption of norms makes the influence relationship between the more and the less powerful group member more stable and palatable for both of them. For the less powerful member, the use of controls without a normative base would make those controls arbitrary and unpredictable, and lead to resistance on his part. For the more powerful member of a dyad, the use of purely personal power would also be unpleasant. He must either reduce his attempted control (and thereby perhaps endanger the accomplishment of the group goal) or risk the negative reactions of the other member. Thus the exercise of control in the name of a set of norms that legitimizes the control is to the advantage of both leader and follower. Alvin Gouldner makes a similar point in relation to bureaucratic organizations. The advantage of impersonal rules in a bureaucratic situation is not that these rules completely replace interpersonal influence, but that they make that influence less visible. In a society that stresses equalitarian norms, this reduction in the visibility of control increases legitimacy and reduces tensions.

Impersonalization of control has been noted to be an effective means of social control in a number of contexts. Mannheim maintains that a key transition point in the development of human societies occurs when regulation of conduct ceases to be carried on in the name of an individual and begins to be exercised in the name of the needs of the group. Primitive groups, he points out, develop social functions that must be performed if the group is to survive. "Provision for such necessary functions is the external source and motivation of regulation in contrast to mere person-to-person relationships. The collective responsibility calls for recurrent and lasting functions, including that of leadership. The leader may give orders to the subordinate members of his team and on occasion use physical or psychological pressures. In so doing, he links his personal, physical and mental strength to an objective function. . . . In this situation a strange metamorphosis occurs: the 'archaic' experience of purely personal power is linked to and, so to speak, transfused into the social function. . . . The metamorphosis is also significant because it demarcates the beginning of the process that substitutes the control of man by institutions and organizations for that of man by man. . . ."

°   °   °

The Process of Legitimation: The development of the type of leadership found in experimental groups (leadership perceived by followers to be arbitrary and personal) into the type found in most on-going systems (leadership perceived to be impersonal and proper)—i.e., the process of legitimation of leadership—is probably one of the most important processes in political affairs. How does leadership that is seized by an individual with no sanction from the group become leadership that is accepted and expected by the group? Laboratory studies of groups with no expectations of leadership might be an excellent place to study this question. Do the laboratory studies thus far shed light upon this process of the legitimization of leadership? Unfortunately, at this time the answer is probably no.

The development of a legitimate leadership structure out of the leaderless group structure found at the beginning of the experimental studies would have to move through three stages. In the first place, certain members of the group must, in response to the group task, begin to differentiate their activities from those of the other group members. Secondly, the other group members must perceive the difference in the behavior of the group member or members who devote themselves more directly to the group task. And, lastly, the group members must come to regard this differentiated activity as right and proper. The first stage is reached in almost all experimental groups studied. Behavior counts show that significant differences in the behavior of the various members can be found in the first meetings of the new groups. The second stage, the recognition of the differing activity patterns, is also

reached in many small group studies. But it is difficult to say if the third and crucial stage is reached—the stage at which the group members come to consider the differentiated activity of the group leader or leaders right and proper. The problem is that the small groups cited above do not deal with expectations of leadership. This can be seen in the conception of role used in these studies. Role as defined by Slater is ". . . a more or less coherent and unified system of items of interpersonal behavior." A group role is thus defined by the particular behaviors (as measured by interaction counts) in which a member engages. This definition does not take into account the expectations others may hold about the role performer. The existence of expectations as to the leader's behavior is not observed directly in these studies, but is ". . . inferred from consistencies in overt behavior, consensus on ratings, and congruence between behavior and received ratings." This inference is not necessarily valid. That a group member behaves in a certain consistent way and that the other group members agree that he is so behaving do not necessarily imply that the other group members sanction this behavior. The assumption that they do not sanction the leader's behavior is supported by the evidence that he receives negative affect for his instrumental control. In view of the absence of direct measures of expectation, we must agree with the cautious comment of Bales and Slater that "The degree to which differentiated roles in the fully structural sense appear in these small decision-making groups is perhaps a moot point."

Since expectations of behavior are so significant for on-going groups, it is to be hoped that small group researchers will begin to deal with them directly. One problem is that even those studies that do deal with legitimacy deal with it as an independent variable—i.e., legitimacy is introduced by the experimenter to see how it affects some dependent variable such as productivity or acceptance. But if we wish to study the development of legitimate leadership, we must hope for studies of legitimacy as a dependent variable. What group structures, for instance, are conducive to the development of leadership that is accepted by the group? What sort of behavior on the part of an emergent leader indicates to group members that they ought to accord legitimacy to this individual? What type of task encourages the growth of legitimate leadership? These are some of the questions the answers to which would greatly increase our knowledge of political behavior. The small leaderless experimental groups may differ from on-going groups in that they have no pattern of expectations of differentiated leadership behavior. In some ways this limits the usefulness of these small groups for analysis of on-going social systems. But it also presents the possibility of studying in these small groups the process by which such expectations develop.

BIBLIOGRAPHY

Bales, Robert Freed. *Interaction Process Analysis.* Cambridge, Mass.: Harvard University Press, 1950.

Bales, Robert Freed, and Slater, Philip E. "Notes on 'Role Differentiation in Small Decision-Making Groups'; Reply to Dr. Wheeler." *Sociometry,* 20: 152–55.

Coch, Lester, and French, John R. P., Jr. "Overcoming Resistance to Change." In *Basic Studies in Social Psychology,* eds. Harold Proshansky and Bernard Seidenberg. New York: Holt, Rinehart, and Winston, 1965.

Gouldner, Alvin W. *Studies in Leadership: Leadership and Democratic Action.* New York: Harper, 1950.

Katz, Elihu et al. "Leadership Stability and Social Change: An Experiment with Small Groups." *Sociometry,* 20: 36–50.

Lewin, Kurt. *Field Theory in the Social Sciences.* New York: Harper, 1951.

Lippitt, Ronald, and White, Ralph K. "An Experimental Study of Leadership and Group Life." In *Basic Studies in Social Psychology,* eds. Harold Proshansky and Bernard Seidenberg. New York: Holt, Rinehart, and Winston, 1965.

Mannheim, Karl. *Freedom, Power, and Democratic Planning.* London: Routledge and Kegan Paul, 1951.

Merriam, Charles E. *Political Power.* New York: McGraw-Hill, 1934.

Parsons, Talcott, and Bales, Robert Freed. *Family, Socialization, and Interaction Process Analysis.* New York: The Free Press, 1955.

Slater, Philip E. "Role Differentiation in Small Groups." *American Sociological Review,* 20: 300–310.

Thibault, John W., and Kelley, Harold H. *The Social Psychology of Groups.* New York: John Wiley & Sons, 1959.

Leadership

James MacGregor Burns

We search eagerly for leadership yet seek to cage and tame it. We recoil from power yet we are bewitched or titillated by it. We devour books on power—power in the office, power in the bedroom, power in the corridors. Connoisseurs of power purport to teach about it—what it is, how to get it, how to use it, how to "gain total control" over "everything around you." We think up new terms for power: clout, wallop, muscle. We measure the power of the aides of Great Men by the number of yards between their offices and that of Number One. If authority made the powerful "giddy, proud, and vain" as Samuel Butler wrote, today it enhances both the seekers of power and the powerless.

Why this preoccupation, this near-obsession, with power? In part because we in this century cannot escape the horror of it. Stalin controlled an apparatus that, year after year and in prison after prison, quietly put to death millions of persons, some of them old comrades and leading Bolsheviks, with hardly a ripple of protest from others. Between teatime and dinner Adolf Hitler could decide whether to release a holocaust of terror and death in an easterly or westerly direction, with stupendous impact on the fate of a continent and a world. On smaller planes of horror, American soldiers have slaughtered women and children cowering in ditches; village tyrants hold serfs and slaves in thrall; revolutionary leaders disperse whole populations into the countryside, where they dig or die; the

daughter of Nehru jails her political adversaries—and is jailed in turn.

* * *

To define power not as a property or entity or possession but as a *relationship* in which two or more persons tap motivational bases in one another and bring varying resources to bear in the process is to perceive power as drawing a vast range of human behavior into its orbit. The arena of power is no longer the exclusive preserve of a power elite or an establishment or persons clothed with legitimacy. Power is ubiquitous; it permeates human relationships. It exists whether or not it is quested for. It is the glory and the burden of most of humanity. A common, highly asymmetric, and sometimes cruel power relation can exist, for example, when one person is in love with another but the other does not reciprocate. The wants and needs and expectations of the person in love are aroused and engaged by a partner whose resources of attractiveness or desirability are high and whose own cluster of motives is less vulnerable. The person possessed by love can maneuver and struggle but still is a slave to the one loved, as the plight of

Excerpts from LEADERSHIP *by James McGregor Burns. Copyright © 1978 by James McGregor Burns. Reprinted by permission of Harper & Row, Publishers, Inc., pp. 9, 15–16, 18–20, 422–27, 454–56, and 460–62.*
    Burns is a political scientist at Williams College and former president of the American Political Science Association.

Philip in Somerset Maugham's marvelously titled *Of Human Bondage* illustrates.

Because power can take such multifarious, ubiquitous, and subtle forms, it is reflected in an infinite number of combinations and particularities in specific contexts. Even so, observers in those contexts may perceive their particular "power mix" as the basic and universal type, and they will base elaborate descriptions and theories of power on one model—their own. Even Machiavelli's celebrated portrait of the uses and abuses of power, while relevant to a few other cultures and eras, is essentially culturebound and irrelevant to a host of other power situations and systems. Thus popular tracts on power—how to win power and influence people—typically are useful only for particular situations and may disable the student of power coping with quite different power constellations.

∗   ∗   ∗

Leadership and Followership

Leadership is an aspect of power, but it is also a separate and vital process in itself.

Power over other persons, we have noted, is exercised when potential power wielders, motivated to achieve certain goals of their own, marshal in their power base resources (economic, military, institutional, or skill) that enable them to influence the behavior of respondents by activating motives of respondents relevant to those resources and to those goals. This is done in order to realize the purposes of the *power wielders, whether or not these are also the goals of the respondents.* Power wielders also exercise influence by mobilizing their own power base in such a way as to establish direct physical control over others' behavior, as in a war of conquest or through measures of harsh deprivation, but these are highly restricted exercises of power, dependent on certain times, cultures, and personalities, and they are often self-destructive and transitory.

Leadership over human beings is exercised when persons with certain motives and purposes mobilize, in competition or conflict with others, institutional, political, psychological, and other resources so as to arouse, engage, and satisfy the motives of followers. This is done in order to realize goals mutually held by *both* leaders and followers, as in Lenin's calls for peace, bread, and land. In brief, leaders with motive and power bases tap followers' motives in order to realize the purposes of both leaders and followers. Not only must motivation be relevant, as in power generally, but its purposes must be realized and satisfied. Leadership is exercised in a condition of *conflict* or *competition* in which leaders contend in appealing to the motive bases of potential followers. Naked power, on the other hand, admits of no competition or conflict—there is no engagement.

Leaders are a particular kind of power holder. Like power, leadership is relational, collective, and purposeful.

Leadership shares with power the central function of achieving purpose. But the reach and domain of leadership are, in the short range at least, more limited than those of power. Leaders do not obliterate followers' motives though they may arouse certain motives and ignore others. They lead other creatures, not things (and lead animals only to the degree that they recognize animal motives—i.e., leading cattle to shelter rather than to slaughter). To control *things*—tools, mineral resources, money, energy—is an act of power, not leadership, for things have no motives. Power wielders may treat people as things. Leaders may not.

All leaders are actual or potential power holders, but not all power holders are leaders.

These definitions of power and of leadership differ from those that others have offered. Lasswell and Kaplan hold that power must be relevant to people's valued things; I hold that it must be relevant to the *power wielder's* valued things and may be relevant to the *recipient's* needs or values only as necessary to exploit them. Kenneth Janda defines power as "the ability to cause other persons to adjust their behavior in conformance with communicated behavior patterns." I agree, assuming that those behavior patterns aid the purpose of the power wielder. According to Andrew McFarland, "If the leader causes changes that he intended, he has exercised power; if the leader causes changes that he did not intend or want, he has exercised influence, but not power. . . ." I dispense with the concept of influence as unnecessary and unparsimonious. For me the leader is a very special, very circumscribed, but potentially the most effective of power holders, judged by the degree of intended "real change" finally achieved. Roderick Bell et al. contend that power is a relationship rather than an entity—an entity being something that "could be smelled and touched, or stored in a keg"; while I agree that power is a relationship, I contend that the relationship is one in which some entity—part of the "power base"—plays an indispensable part, whether that keg is a keg of beer, of dynamite, or of ink.

The crucial variable, again, is *purpose.* Some define leadership as leaders making followers do what *followers* would not otherwise do, or as leaders making followers do what the *leaders* want them to do; I define leadership as leaders inducing followers to act for certain goals that represent the values and the motivations—the wants and needs, the aspirations and expectations—*of both leaders and followers.* And the genius of leadership lies in the manner in which leaders see and act on their own and their followers' values and motivations.

Leadership, unlike naked power-wielding, is thus inseparable from followers' needs and goals. The essence of the leader-follower relation is the interaction of persons with different levels of motivations and of power potential, including skill, in pursuit of a common or at least joint purpose. That interaction, however, takes two fundamentally different forms. The first I will call *transactional* leadership (the nature of which will be developed in Part III). Such leadership occurs when one person takes the initiative in making contact with others for the purpose of an exchange of valued things. The exchange could be economic or political or psychological in nature: a swap of goods or of one good for money; a trading of votes between candidate and citizen or between legislators; hospitality to another person in exchange for willingness to listen to one's troubles. Each party to the bargain is conscious of the power resources and attitudes of the other. Each person recognizes the other as a *person*. Their purposes are related, at least to the extent that the purposes stand within the bargaining process and can be advanced by maintaining that process. But beyond this the relationship does not go. The bargainers have no enduring purpose that holds them together; hence they may go their separate ways. A leadership act took place, but it was not one that binds leader and follower together in a mutual and continuing pursuit of a higher purpose.

Contrast this with *transforming* leadership. Such leadership occurs when one or more persons *engage* with others in such a way that leaders and followers raise one another to higher levels of motivation and morality. (The nature of this motivation and this morality will be developed in Part II.) Their purposes, which might have started out as separate but related, as in the case of transactional leadership, become fused. Power bases are linked not as counterweights but as mutual support for common purpose. Various names are used for such leadership, some of them derisory: elevating, mobilizing, inspiring, exalting, uplifting, preaching, exhorting, evangelizing. The relationship can be moralistic, of course. But transforming leadership ultimately becomes *moral* in that it raises the level of human conduct and ethical aspiration of both leader and led, and thus it has a transforming effect on both. Perhaps the best modern example is Gandhi, who aroused and elevated the hopes and demands of millions of Indians and whose life and personality were enhanced in the process. Transcending leadership is dynamic leadership in the sense that the leaders throw themselves into a relationship with followers who will feel "elevated" by it and often become more active themselves, thereby creating new cadres of leaders. Transcending leadership is leadership *engagé*. Naked power-wielding can be neither transactional nor transforming; only leadership can be.

Leaders and followers may be inseparable in function, but they are not the same. The leader takes the initiative in making the leader-led connection; it is the leader who creates the links that allow communication and exchange to take place. An office seeker does this in accosting a voter on the street, but if the voter espies and accosts the politician, the voter is assuming a leadership function, at least for that brief moment. The leader is more skillful in evaluating followers' motives, anticipating their responses to an initiative, and estimating their power bases, than the reverse. Leaders continue to take the major part in maintaining and effectuating the relationship with followers and

will have the major role in ultimately carrying out the combined purpose of leaders and followers. Finally, and most important by far, leaders address themselves to followers' wants, needs, and other motivations, as well as to their own, and thus they serve as an *independent force in changing the makeup of the followers' motive base through gratifying their motives.*

* * *

Late in the winter of 1968, in response to my request that I interview President Johnson about his memories of Franklin Roosevelt, I received an invitation from the President and Mrs. Johnson to an informal family dinner. Making my way across Lafayette Park toward the White House a few days later, I was struck by the appearance of the imposing old building. The place now seemed dark, cold, diminished. Was it my imagination that it appeared to be under siege?

After close inspection of my credentials by guards at the gate, I was escorted into the mansion, taken in the little elevator to the second floor, and ushered into the family living room. In addition to the President and First Lady only a staff member and an ex-governor of Texas and their wives were present. The conversation was guarded and subdued, with everyone avoiding the subject that lay over the White House like a shroud, until one of the President's daughters flounced into the room in a housecoat, sat in her father's lap, then beside him on the floor, and suddenly started talking about Vietnam. Most of her friends and those of her husband were military men, she said, but she understood the feelings of young people who hated the war. She then presented those feelings, as simply and eloquently as I could remember having heard. The President listened, saying nothing.

During a lull I turned to my host and inquired about a meeting between Johnson and Franklin Roosevelt during the war years. The President dealt briefly and uninterestedly with the query, then began to reminisce about his boyhood years in Texas. He talked until dinner—about his parents, his mother's expectations of him, his father's discipline, his brothers and sisters. He talked during dinner, hardly bothering to eat, about his life and troubles growing up. He talked on and on after dinner, while his wife and friends listened with apparent interest to stories they must have heard many times. Finally, exhausted by the flow of words and overcome with a feeling of guilt over the presidential time I was monopolizing, I managed to rise to my feet and murmur my apologies. The President accompanied me halfway to the elevator, then announced and conducted a tour of the family living quarters, including a look at the presidential bedside piled with memoranda and reports.

Next day I happened to be standing outside the office of a presidential aide when the tall figure loomed again. The President led me to a tiny room off the oval office, where he produced a bound collection of the messages exchanged between Washington and Moscow during the

Arab–Israeli hostilities of 1967. A large finger pointed to an ominous message from the Kremlin that virtually threatened war, then pointed proudly to the President's de-escalating response. Once again I made my escape. I left with no illusions as to the role I was expected to serve. Deserted by large portions of the constituencies that had given him his landslide victory of 1964, the President was seeking a final victory before the bar of history. Even this academic might have a vote to cast in the ultimate verdict. Every juror would count.

I reflected on the vagaries of power and leadership. Here was a President who had his hand on all the alleged levers of influence. The party he headed enjoyed majorities in both houses of Congress. After five years in the White House he had the constitutional right to run for four more. He had billions to budget and spend. He commanded a huge staff, talent, presidential attention, television screens, planes, cars. Only his finger could pull the nuclear trigger. Yet the man was almost impotent. He could not run again, for reasons of both bodily and political health. His congressional majorities were no longer dependable. He could not win in Southeast Asia with conventional war tactics and dared not employ nuclear strategy. Looking at him, especially from afar, people saw a man of vast power; looking out at the people, he felt lonely and powerless.

At night, I learned later, Johnson dreamed a recurring dream of impotence. He dreamed that he was lying in bed in the Red Room of the White House, paralyzed from the neck down, listening to his aides in the next room quarreling over the division of power. He could hear them but could not speak to them. Waking from his sleep after such a dream, the President would make his way through the empty corridors of the White House to the place where Woodrow Wilson's portrait hung. It soothed him to touch Wilson's portrait, for Wilson had been paralyzed and now was dead but Johnson was still alive and active. In the morning the fears would return—of paralysis of the body, paralysis of his presidency. And soon he would quit.

He would do so with a wretching sense of damaged self-esteem. He felt that he had been, above all, a leader—of the poor, the blacks, the sick, the alienated. Perhaps he did not comprehend that the people he had led—as a result in part of the impact of his leadership—had created their own fresh leadership, which was now in some ways outrunning his. In sensing black wants, recognizing black needs, arousing black aspirations, legitimating black expectations, meeting black demands, Johnson had not only helped focus the effort and reinvigorate the organization of the old Negro groups like the NAACP. He had mobilized in the South and in the ghettos a new breed of militant black who was brassy, noisy, assertive, and moving far beyond the reach of that long presidential arm. Leadership had begat leadership and hardly recognized its offspring. Vietnam was more than perplexing to him, it was sickening. He had followed the responsible, the moderate strategy of Truman, Eisenhower, and Kennedy; he had learned from

earlier wars that if you clung to your course and persevered, victory would come. But victory would not come in Vietnam; and now young men were resisting the draft, religious leaders were demonstrating at the White House gates, college students were so hostile that there was hardly a campus he could visit. And a brash young rival, Bobby Kennedy, and others waited offstage. Political leadership had simply passed out of the President's hands, and with it had gone political power. Followers had become leaders.

On the face of it, there was nothing unusual about Johnson's loss of power. Winston Churchill, Chiang Kai-shek, Nikita Khrushchev, Sukarno, and later Richard Nixon, de Gaulle, Indira Gandhi all suddenly slid—or were pushed—down the "greasy pole." But Johnson's plight was especially poignant and significant. On the one hand, in meeting to some degree the economic needs of blacks and others he had unwittingly aroused higher needs and values that he could neither comprehend fully nor gratify. On the other hand, in not meeting the demands of the anti-Vietnam militants he had generated new dimensions and intensities of conflict, thereby producing a whirlwind he could not control. His "abdication" a few weeks after I visited him was simply recognition of that fact.

If leaders who seemed to wield power often lacked it, followers who seemed impotent might unexpectedly exert influence. The Maoist demand that leaders struggle against self-advancement and privilege has been traced to the Taoist insistence that the sage must make himself lower than the people in order not to offend them. Few would seem more powerless and passive than slaves, but in the American antebellum South slaves were not mere recipients of power; the masters' paternalism aroused expectations other than those intended. "By developing a sense of moral worth and by asserting rights," Eugene Genovese concluded, "the slaves transformed their acquiescence in paternalism into a rejection of slavery itself."

We need not look so far back to glimpse the interlocking of leadership and followership, of power-wielding and power-receiving. The programs of private television are mainly financed by advertisers who make a massive effort to gauge the wants and needs of buyers, whose buying habits in turn are closely influenced by the messages on the tube. Politicians organizing revolutionary movements or planning to run for office take soundings in the villages or through opinion polls to see what the people want—but what the people want is mightily affected by the promises and preachings of politicians. Next to me as I write hangs a cartoon published in London in 1830 showing a frock-coated John Bull reading *The Times,* with a chain running from the *Times* masthead to his nose. The cartoon is captioned, "The man wot is easily led by the nose." But the editors of the newspaper, ever needful of readers, faced the threat of competing papers.

So again the paradox: Who are the leaders and who the led? Who is leading whom to where? For what purposes? With what results?

LEADERSHIP AND COLLECTIVE PURPOSE

To answer such questions we must proceed to the formidable task of seeing the role of leadership, as we have defined it, in historical causation. Let us take stock of the definition. Leadership is the reciprocal process of mobilizing, by persons with certain motives and values, various economic, political, and other resources, in a context of competition and conflict, in order to realize goals independently or mutually held by both leaders and followers. The nature of those goals is crucial. They could be separate but related; that is, two persons may exchange goods or services or other things in order to realize independent objectives. Thus Dutchmen (colonists in America) give beads to Indians in exchange for real estate, and French legislators trade votes in the Assembly on unrelated pieces of legislation. This is *transactional leadership*. The objective in these cases is not a joint effort for persons with common aims acting for the collective interests of followers but a bargain to aid the individual interests of persons or groups going their separate ways.

Leaders can also shape and alter and elevate the motives and values and goals of followers through the vital *teaching* role of leadership. This is *transforming* leadership. The premise of this leadership is that, whatever the separate interests persons might hold, they are presently or potentially united in the pursuit of "higher" goals, the realization of which is tested by the achievement of significant change that represents the collective or pooled interests of leaders and followers.

Both forms of leadership can contribute to human purpose. If the *transactions* between leaders and followers result in realizing the individual goals of each, followers may satisfy certain wants, such as food or drink, in order to realize goals higher in the hierarchy of values, such as aesthetic needs. The chief monitors of transactional leadership are *modal values*, that is, values of means—honesty, responsibility, fairness, the honoring of commitments—without which transactional leadership could not work. Transformational leadership is more concerned with *end-values*, such as liberty, justice, equality. Transforming leaders "raise" their followers up through levels of morality, though insufficient attention to means can corrupt the ends.

Thus both kinds of leadership have moral implications. How can we define that morality? Summoned before the "bar of history," Adolf Hitler would argue that he spoke the true values of the German people, summoned them to a higher destiny, evoked the noblest sacrifice from them. The most crass, favor-swapping politician can point to the followers he helps or satisfies. Three criteria must be used to evaluate these claims. Both Hitler and the politician would have to be tested by modal values of honor and integrity—by the extent to which they advanced or thwarted fundamental standards of good conduct in humankind. They would have to be judged by the end-values of equal-ity and justice. Finally, in a context of free communication and open criticism and evaluation, they would be judged in the balance sheet of history by their impact on the well-being of the persons whose lives they touched.

Because our emphasis is on collective purpose and change we stress the factors that unite leaders and followers as well as those that differentiate them. This distinction may be elusive to an observer who sees leaders leading followers but does not understand that leaders may modify their leadership in recognition of followers' preferences, or in order to anticipate followers' responses, or in order to harmonize the actions of both leader and follower with their common motives, values, and goals. Leaders and followers are engaged in a common enterprise; they are dependent on each other, their fortunes rise and fall together, they share the results of planned change together.

So defined, leadership—especially transforming leadership—is far more pervasive, widespread—indeed, common—than we generally recognize; it is also much more bounded, limited, and uncommon. *Common*, because acts of leadership occur not simply in presidential mansions and parliamentary assemblies but far more widely and powerfully in the day-to-day pursuit of collective goals through the mutual tapping of leaders' and followers' motive bases and in the achievement of intended change. It is an affair of parents, teachers, and peers as well as of preachers and politicians. *Uncommon*, because many acts heralded or bemoaned as instances of leadership—acts of oratory, manipulation, sheer self-advancement, brute coercion—are not such. Much of what commonly passes as leadership—conspicuous position-taking without followers or follow-through, posturing on various public stages, manipulation without general purpose, authoritarianism—is no more leadership than the behavior of small boys marching in front of a parade, who continue to strut along Main Street after the procession has turned down a side street toward the fairgrounds. Also, many apparent leaders will be only partial leaders. They may tap followers' motives or power bases; or they may take value-laden positions; or they may sharpen conflict; or they may operate at the final policy-making or implementation stages; or they may do some or all of these. The test of their leadership function is their contribution to change, measured by purpose drawn from collective motives and values.

Even if we exclude acts of nonleadership from our analysis, we must include an enormous variety. and range of actions that in themselves constitute complete leadership acts—that is, the process and achievement of intended change—or that consciously make up significant links in the total process of achieving intended change. Not only the building of a new political party aimed at mobilizing tribal groups for the sake of social change, or a campaign against illiteracy, or a community development program, but a mother consciously acting in such a way that her small son's sensitivity to others will be improved, a taxi driver deliberately setting an example of considerate driving, a Red Guard leader making sure that food and drink are equally shared on a work project in the country—all these are parts of the totality of the leadership proem. Leadership begins earlier, operates more widely, takes more forms, pervades more sectors of society, and lasts longer in the lives of most persons than has been generally recognized.

* * *

The most lasting tangible act of leadership is the creation of an institution—a nation, a social movement, a political party, a bureaucracy—that continues to exert moral leadership and foster needed social change long after the creative leaders are gone. An institution, it is said, is but the lengthened shadow of a man, but it takes many men and women to establish lasting institutions. The establishment of a new system of government embracing a structure of divided and fragmented powers by the framers of 1787—and by their supporters and adversaries in the various states and by the political theorists who inspired them—was perhaps the most creative and durable act of political planning in modern history. It was ironic that such brilliant leadership would found a system that so hobbled leadership; yet it was a system that could meet, albeit partially and with all deliberate slowness, the moral challenge of slavery in the 1860s and that of black rights a century later.

The most lasting and pervasive leadership of all is intangible and noninstitutional. It is the leadership of influence fostered by ideas embodied in social or religious or artistic movements, in books, in great seminal documents, in the memory of great lives greatly lived.

Leadership is morally purposeful. All leadership is goal-oriented. The failure to set goals is a sign of faltering leadership. Successful leadership points in a direction; it is also the vehicle of continuing and achieving purpose. Where leadership is necessary, Philip Selznick writes, "the problem is always *to choose key values and to create a social structure that embodies them.*" Purpose may be singular, such as the protection and enhancement of individual liberty, or it may be multiple, in which case it will be expressed in a set of priorities. Both leaders and followers are drawn into the shaping of purpose. "Our dilemma, then, is not an absence of leaders" Benjamin Barber observes, "but a paucity of values that might sustain leaders; not a failure of leadership but a failure of followership, a failure of popular will from which leadership might draw strength. . . ." But the transforming leader taps the needs and raises the aspirations and helps shape the values—and hence mobilizes the potential—of followers.

Transforming leadership is elevating. It is moral but not moralistic. Leaders engage with followers, but from higher levels of morality; in the enmeshing of goals and values both leaders and followers are raised to more principled levels of judgment. Leaders most effectively "connect with" followers from a level of morality only one stage higher than that of the followers, but moral leaders who act at much higher levels—Gandhi, for example—relate to followers at all levels either heroically or through the found-

ing of mass movements that provide linkages between persons at various levels of morality and sharply increase the moral impact of the transforming leader. Much of this kind of elevating leadership asks sacrifices *from* followers rather than merely promising them goods.

The most dramatic test in modern democracies of the power of leaders to elevate followers and of followers to sustain leaders was the civil rights struggle in the United States. Myrdal recognized presciently that this was a moral struggle, a struggle for the soul of America. There were those who pandered to the base instincts of persons—the very negation of leadership—but many more who appealed to the spirit of a "moral commitment of the American nation to high ideals," Myrdal said years later. "In spite of all the conspicuous and systematic gross failures of compliance, America of all countries I knew had come to have the most explicitly formulated system of general ideals in reference to human interrelations, shared, on one level of valuations, by all its citizens." Shared by all its citizens—that was the crux of the struggle. The battle was won at lunch counters, on highways, in classrooms, in front of courthouses by followers who had become leaders. On the other side of the globe, the pacific and egalitarian values taught by Mohandas Gandhi were proving to be an elevating force in an even harsher struggle for social justice.

* * *

How, then, do we exert influence as a leader? First, by clarifying within ourselves our own personal goal. If that goal is *only* to secure a livelihood or advance a career, our tactic need only be calculatedly self-serving and manipulative—at least until our career or prominence is assured. We will at least know who has been led where. Alternatively, we may link our career with a cause that rises above considerations of personal success and may provide some social good. In practice leaders so intertwine their motives that they are hard to separate, as leaders variously support causes that in turn support them. But what happens at the fateful moment when career diverges from cause? Students over the years have told their teachers that they first would "make their million" and then go into politics or the public service. A few, like Jeb Magruder, manage the transition, though not always with happy results; most fail to amass their million or do amass it and then concentrate on keeping it or amassing another. *Decide on whether we are really trying to lead anyone but ourselves, and what part of ourselves, and where, and for what purposes.*

The second question is *whom* are we seeking to lead? This is not a matter of defining merely the voters or coalitions we wish to mobilize, but of the motives, aspirations, values, and goals that are to be mobilized within the followers, within their groups. Authentic leadership is a collective process, I contend, and it emerges from the clash and congruence of motives and goals of leaders and followers. It requires neither that leaders slavishly adapt their own motives and goals to those of followers nor vice versa. It means that, in the reaching out by leaders to potential followers, broader and higher ranges of motivation come into play and that both goals and means of achieving them are informed by the force of higher end-values and modal values. Leaders' goals at the start may be only bread and circuses, but as those goals are reached or blocked, their purpose may be converted to the realization of higher needs like esteem, recognition, and fulfillment for both leaders and led. *Define our potential followers, not in the manipulative sense of how to persuade them to our own ends, such as they are, but in terms of mutuality and of future motives that may be stimulated as present motives are variously realized or blocked.*

Third, were are we seeking to go? The answer usually seems obvious: the goal consists of immediate, short-run, easily definable, step-by-step objectives. But often these calculations of tangible objectives fail to allow for the likelihood that goals will be changed as intermediate steps are taken; that targets will be transformed and perhaps elevated as more followers become involved; that conflict will develop and alter outcomes. Above all, the absorption with short-run, specifiable goals may dilute attention to the likely final outcome of a long and complex process of leadership–followership interaction. Attention may continue to center in the predictable, visible matters of technique and process and personality rather than in the prospects and nature of fundamental, substantive alterations in people's lives and welfare and opportunities—of "real change." Political leadership, however, can be defined only in terms of, and to the extent of the realization of, purposeful, substantive change in the conditions of people's lives. *The ultimate test of practical leadership is the realization of intended, real change that meets people's enduring needs.*

Fourth, how do we overcome obstacles to realizing our goals? Only two generalizations can we apply to the hundreds of specific situations a political leader may face. One is to recognize the motivations of potential followers in all their fullness and complexity (and enough has been said above about that). The other is never to assess at face value, or by reputation, or by easy quantification, the power bases of a rival or possible obstructionist (or of pos-

sible supporters). Those power bases—which may look so impressive in the form of the presidency of an institution or the possession of money or the command of armies or the availability of weapons or the support of millions of persons—*must always be assessed in terms of the motivations of those leaders and followers,* as those motivations relate to the disposition of power resources. The question is always one of convertibility, and political power, unlike electric power, is not easily convertible. *Watch out for the towering giant with feet of clay, especially if we are the giant.*

These "rules" for practical influence may seem impractical in some instances, perhaps even utopian. But what is proposed is not all that different from what we do daily and automatically as we make approaches to people and anticipate their reactions—and perhaps anticipate our own reactions to their reactions. The function of leadership is to *engage* followers, not merely to activate them, to commingle needs and aspirations and goals in a common enterprise, and in the process to make better citizens of both leaders and followers. To move from manipulation to power-wielding is to move from the arithmetic of everyday contacts and collisions to the geometry of the structure and dynamics of interaction. It is to move from checkers to chess, for in the "game of kings" we estimate the powers of our chessmen and the intentions and calculations and indeed the motives of our adversary. But democratic leadership moves far beyond chess because, as we play the game, the chessmen come alive, the bishops and knights and pawns take part on their own terms and with their own motivations, values, and goals, and the game moves ahead with new momentum, direction, and possibilities. In real life the most practical advice for leaders is not to treat pawns like pawns, nor princes like princes, but all persons like *persons.*

Woodrow Wilson called for leaders who, by boldly interpreting the nation's conscience, could lift a people out of their everyday selves. That people can be lifted into their better selves is the secret of transforming leadership and the moral and practical theme of this work.

Typically, a group emerges in SIMSOC that is radically discontented with the existing situation in the society. Such groups have many analogues in a real society, and they experience the same dilemmas that protest groups face in the real world. Should they work within the system, pursuing moderate strategies that do not alienate those whom they wish to influence? Should they pursue more dramatic and militant strategies in the spirit of confrontation politics? Should they express their frustration and anger even if this does not necessarily bring about the changes they desire? Can they trust their own leaders not to become a new oppressor in different garb?

The readings in this section examine the issue of protest primarily from the standpoint of groups seeking social change. Societies that are marked by great differences in power and privilege have potential instability, but rebellion by the have-nots is not inevitable. One must ask how people become mobilized for collective action. The well-known community organizer Saul Alinsky offers one possible answer in the selection reprinted here. Even the apparently powerless, he argues, have available to them many tactics for creating power. Gamson, Fireman, and Rytina focus on some of the obstacles to rebellion and the specific organizing acts that challengers can use to overcome them in furthering the process of rebelling against what they consider an unjust authority.

For the leaders of a protest group, discontent is an opportunity—it makes it possible to mobilize people on behalf of desired social changes. But, for those who are attempting to gain sufficient legitimacy to govern, discontent presents a problem in social control. They may tell themselves, "Here I am knocking myself out for the good of the society, and all I get is a lot of attacks and criticism instead of appreciation and cooperation." From their standpoint, the problem is how to win compliance with their policies—a problem of social control. The threat of force or its actual employment has limited utility. It is just not possible to govern effectively for any length of time if one has to constantly enforce decisions by punishing noncompliance. The short selection by Dahl puts the issue very succinctly. When legitimacy is low, leaders must use other political resources to secure compliance, but in democracies they are not permitted to acquire sufficient resources to enforce their policies through naked power. Legitimacy is a necessity of effective governance.

The Process of Power

Saul D. Alinsky

From the moment the organizer enters a community, he lives, dreams, eats, breathes, sleeps only one thing and that is to build the mass power base of what he calls the army. Until he has developed that mass power base, he confronts no major issues. He has nothing with which to confront anything. Until he has those means and power instruments, his "tactics" are very different from power tactics. Therefore, every move revolves around one central point: how many recruits will this bring into the organization, whether by means of local organizations, churches, services groups, labor unions, corner gangs, or as individu-

This reading is condensed by permission of Random House, Inc., from RULES FOR RADICALS, *by Saul D. Alinsky. Pp. 113–20, 126–27, 136, and 140. Copyright © 1971 by Saul D. Alinsky.*

The late Saul D. Alinsky was a long-time community organizer who wrote and lectured extensively on the process of building power among the poor.

als. The only issue is, how will this increase the strength of the organization? If by losing in a certain action he can get more members than by winning, then victory lies in losing and he will lose.

Change comes from power, and power comes from organization. In order to act, people must get together.

Power is the reason for being of organizations. When people agree on certain religious ideas and want the power to propagate their faith, they organize and call it a church. When people agree on certain ideas and want the power to put them into practice, they organize and call it a political party. The same reason holds across the board. Power and organization are one and the same.

The organizer knows, for example, that his biggest job is to give the people the feeling that they can do something, that while they may accept the idea that organization means power, they have to experience this idea in action. The organizer's job is to begin to build confidence and hope in the idea of organization and thus in the people themselves: to win limited victories, each of which will build confidence and the feeling that "if we can do so much with what we have now just think what we will be able to do when we get big and strong." It is almost like taking a prize-fighter up the road to the championship—you have to very carefully and selectively pick his opponents, knowing full well that certain defeats would be demoralizing and end his career. Sometimes the organizer may find such despair among the people that he has to put on a cinch fight.

。 。 。

The organizer simultaneously carries on many functions as he analyzes, attacks, and disrupts the prevailing power pattern. The ghetto or slum in which he is organizing is *not* a disorganized community. There is no such animal as a disorganized community. It is a contradiction in terms to use the two words "disorganization" and "community" together: the word community itself means an organized, communal life; people living in an organized fashion. The people in the community may have experienced successive frustrations to the point that their will to participate has seemed to atrophy. They may be living in anonymity and may be starved for personal recognition. They may be suffering from various forms of deprivation and discrimination. They may have accepted anonymity and resigned in apathy. They may despair that their children will inherit a somewhat better world. From your point of view they may have a very negative form of existence, but the fact is that they are organized in that way of life. Call it organized apathy or organized nonparticipation, but that is their community pattern. They are living under a certain set of arrangements, standards, way of life. They may in short have surrendered—but life goes on in an organized form, with a definite power structure; even if it is as Thoreau called most lives, "quiet desperation."

Therefore, if your function is to attack apathy and get people to participate it is necessary to attack the prevailing patterns of organized living in the community. *The first step in community organization is community disorganization.* The disruption of the present organization is the first step toward community organization. Present arrangements must be disorganized if they are to be displaced by new patterns that provide the opportunities and means for citizen participation. *All change means disorganization of the old and organization of the new.*

This is why the organizer is immediately confronted with conflict. The organizer dedicated to changing the life of a particular community must first rub raw the resentments of the people of the community; fan the latent hostilities of many of the people to the point of overt expression. He must search out controversy and issues, rather than avoid them, for unless there is a controversy people are not concerned enough to act. The use of the adjective "controversial" to qualify the word "issue" is a meaningless redundancy. There can be no such thing as a "non-controversial" issue. When there is agreement there is no issue; issues only arise when there is disagreement or controversy. An organizer must stir up dissatisfaction and discontent; provide a channel into which the people can angrily pour their frustrations. He must create a mechanism that can drain off the underlying guilt for having accepted the previous situation for so long a time. Out of this mechanism, a new community organization arises. But more on this point later.

The job then is getting the people to move, to act, to participate; in short, to develop and harness the necessary power to effectively conflict with the prevailing patterns and change them. When those prominent in the status quo turn and label you an "agitator" they are completely correct, for that is, in one word, your function—to agitate to the point of conflict.

A sound analogy is to be found in the organization of trade unions. A competent union organizer approaches his objective, let's say the organization of a particular industrial plant where the workers are underpaid, suffering from discriminatory practices, and without job security. The workers accept these conditions as inevitable, and they express their demoralization by saying, "what's the use." In private they resent these circumstances, complain, talk about the futility of "bucking the big shots" and generally succumb to frustration—*all because of the lack of opportunity for effective action.*

Enter the labor organizer or the agitator. He begins his "trouble making" by stirring up these angers, frustrations, and resentments, and highlighting specific issues or grievances that heighten controversy. He dramatizes the injustices by describing conditions at other industrial plants engaged in the same kind of work where the workers are far better off economically and have better working conditions, job security, health benefits, and pensions as well as other advantages that had not even been thought of by the workers he is trying to organize. Just as important, he points out that the workers in the other places had also been exploited in the past and had existed under similar circumstances until they used their intelligence and energies to organize into a power instrument known as a trade union, with the result that they achieved all of these other benefits. Generally this approach results in the formation of a new trade union.

Let us examine what this labor organizer has done. He has taken a group of apathetic workers; he has fanned their resentments and hostilities by a number of means, including challenging contrasts of better conditions of other workers in similar industries. Most important, he has demonstrated that something can be done, and that there is a concrete way of doing it that has already proven its effectiveness and success: that by organizing together as a trade union they will have the power and the instrument with which to make these changes. He now has the workers participating in a trade union and supporting its program. We must never forget that so long as there is no opportunity or method to make changes, it is senseless to get people agitated or angry, leaving them no course of action except to blow their tops.

And so the labor organizer simultaneously breeds conflict and builds a power structure. The war between the trade union and management is resolved either through a strike or a negotiation. Either method involves the use of power; the economic power of the strike or the threat of it, which results in successful negotiations. *No one can negotiate without the power to compel negotiation.*

This is the function of a community organizer. Anything otherwise is wishful non-thinking. To attempt to operate on a good-will rather than a power basis would be to attempt something that the world has not yet experienced.

In the beginning the organizer's first job is to create the issues or problems. It sounds mad to say that a community such as a low-income ghetto or even a middle-class community has no issues per se. The reader may feel that this statement borders on lunacy, particularly with reference to low-income communities. The simple fact is that in any community, regardless of how poor, people may have serious problems—but they do not have issues, they have a bad scene. An issue is something you can do something about, but as long as you feel powerless and unable to do anything about it, all you have is a bad scene. The people resign themselves to a rationalization: it's the kind of world, it's a crumby world, we didn't ask to come into it but we are stuck with it and all we can do is hope that something happens somewhere, somehow, sometime. This is what is usually taken as apathy, what we discussed earlier—that policy follows power. Through action, persuasion, and communication the organizer makes it clear that organization will give them the power, the ability, the strength, the force to be able to do something about these particular problems. It is then that a bad scene begins to break up into specific issues, because now the people can do something about it. What the organizer does is convert the plight into a problem. The question is whether they do it this way or that way or whether they do all of it or part of it. But now you have issues.

TACTICS

Tactics means doing what you can with what you have. Tactics are those consciously deliberate acts by which human beings live with each other and deal with the world around them. In the world of give and take, tactics is the art of how to take and how to give. Here our concern is with the tactic of taking; how the Have-Nots can take power away from the Haves.

For an elementary illustration of tactics, take parts of your face as the point of reference; your eyes, your ears, and your nose. First the eyes; if you have organized a vast, mass-based people's organization, you can parade it visibly before the enemy and openly show your power. Second the ears; if your organization is small in numbers, then do what Gideon did: conceal the members in the dark but raise a din and clamor that will make the listener believe that your organization numbers many more than it does. Third, the nose; if your organization is too tiny even for noise, stink up the place.

Always remember the first rule of power tactics:

Power is not only what you have but what the enemy thinks you have.

The second rule is: *Never go outside the experience of your people.* When an action or tactic is outside the experience of the people, the result is confusion, fear, and retreat. It also means a collapse of communication, as we have noted.

The third rule is: *Wherever possible go outside of the experience of the enemy.* Here you want to cause confusion, fear, and retreat.

※ ※ ※

The scene is Rochester, New York, the home of Eastman Kodak—or rather Eastman Kodak, the home of Rochester, New York. Rochester is literally dominated by this industrial giant. For anyone to fight or publicly challenge Kodak is in itself completely outside of Rochester's experience. Even to this day this company does not have a labor union. Its attitudes toward the general public make paternalistic feudalism look like participatory democracy.

Rochester prides itself on being one of America's cultural crown jewels; it has its libraries, school system, university, museums, and its well-known symphony. As previously mentioned we were coming in on the invitation of the black ghetto to organize them (they literally organized to invite us in). The city was in a state of hysteria and fear at the very mention of my name. Whatever I did was news. Even my old friend and tutor, John L. Lewis, called me and affectionately growled, "I resent the fact that you are more hated in Rochester than I was." This was the setting.

※ ※ ※

I have emphasized and re-emphasized that tactics means you do what you can with what you've got, and that power in the main has always gravitated towards those who have money and those whom people follow. The resources of the Have-Nots are (1) no money and (2) lots of people.

All right, let's start from there. People can show their power by voting. What else? Well, they have physical bodies. How can they use them? Now a melange of ideas begins to appear. Use the power of the law by making the establishment obey its own rules. Go outside the experience of the enemy, stay inside the experience of your people. Emphasize tactics that your people will enjoy. The threat is usually more terrifying than the tactic itself. Once all these rules and principles are festering in your imagination they grow into a synthesis.

I suggested that we might buy one hundred seats for one of Rochester's symphony concerts. We would select a concert in which the music was relatively quiet. The hundred blacks who would be given the tickets would first be treated to a three-hour pre-concert dinner in the community, in which they would be fed nothing but baked beans, and lots of them; then the people would go to the symphony hall—with obvious consequences. Imagine the scene when the action began! The concert would be over before the first movement! (If this be a Freudian slip—so be it!)

Let's examine this tactic in terms of the concepts mentioned above.

First, the disturbance would be utterly outside the experience of the establishment, which was expecting the usual stuff of mass meetings, street demonstrations, confrontations and parades. Not in their wildest fears would they expect an attack on their prize cultural jewel, their famed symphony orchestra. Second, all of the action would ridicule and make a farce of the law for there is no law, and there probably never will be, banning natural physical functions. Here you would have a combination not only of noise but also of odor, what you might call natural stink bombs. Regular stink bombs are illegal and cause for immediate arrest, but there would be absolutely nothing here that the Police Department or the ushers or any other servants of the establishment could do about it. The law would be completely paralyzed.

People would recount what had happened in the symphony hall and the reaction of the listener would be to crack up in laughter. It would make the Rochester Symphony and the establishment look utterly ridiculous. There would be no way for the authorities to cope with any future attacks of a similar character. What could they do? Demand that people not eat baked beans before coming to a concert? Ban anyone from succumbing to natural urges during the concert? Announce to the world that concerts must not be interrupted by farting? Such talk would destroy the future of the symphony season. Imagine the tension at the opening of any concert! Imagine the feeling of the conductor as he raised his baton!

With this would come certain fall-outs. On the following morning, the matrons, to whom the symphony season is one of the major social functions, would confront their husbands (both executives and junior executives) at the breakfast table and say "John, we are not going to have our symphony season ruined by *those people!* I don't know what they want but whatever it is, something has got to be done and this kind of thing has to be stopped!"

　　　°　°　°

As Finley Peter Dunne's Mr. Dooley put it:

> Don't ask f'r rights. Take thim. An' don't let anny wan give thim to ye. A right that is handed to ye fer nawthin has somethin the mather with it. It's more thin likely it's only a wrong turned inside out.

The Theory and Practice of Rebellion

William A. Gamson, Bruce Fireman, and Steven Rytina

We have focused much more on *how* people rebel than on *why*. Indeed, we have taken the why for granted. Abuse of authority is the primary theme of the twentieth century, reaching full fruition in Nazi Germany; the Holocaust is its ultimate symbol. Given the myriad abuses of authority that we have all witnessed in our lifetimes, perhaps the more appropriate question is: Why do people not rebel?

The answer is that it is easier said than done. It requires active enterprise, frequently fraught with great risk, to rebel. The enterprise can falter at many points and for many reasons. In attempting to explain *how* groups forge a successful rebellion career, we are implicitly addressing the question of *why* people don't rebel. They falter on one of the many obstacles that can stifle or abort rebellious collective action.

Our explanation has two parts to it. On the one hand, every encounter has a certain context and assets that the participants have brought to it. These are a fixed starting point in any given encounter, but they are of major importance in understanding the problems and opportunities that potential challengers face under different circumstances.

This reading is excerpted from William A. Gamson, Bruce Fireman, and Steven Rytina, ENCOUNTERS WITH UNJUST AUTHORITY *(Homewood, Ill.: The Dorsey Press, 1982), pp. 147–50, 152–55.*

The second part of our explanation is more dynamic. If we analyze the enterprise directly, focusing on a set of identifiable mobilizing acts, we see that each of these acts increases the overall capacity of the group for rebellious collective action in the encounter. We can unpack the overall process of mobilization into three simultaneous sub-processes, to show how the specific mobilizing acts further one or another of these. Progress in each realm facilitates progress in others, allowing them to interact in fostering a successful rebellion career. Under different circumstances, one or another of these processes may be especially problematic, but progress in each of them is necessary. Together they are sufficient for a successful rebellion career—in the absence of active countermeasures by authorities. This is the logic of our explanation.

° ° °

Context and assets exist at the beginning of an encounter, but they do not determine its course. Much of what happens is in the hands of the participants, and they can affect its outcome by what they do in the course of the interaction. Our argument focuses on what potential challengers can do in furthering three processes that underline mobilization: working together, breaking out of the bonds of authority, and adopting an injustice frame. Each process is advanced by different types of mobilizing acts: organizing, divesting, and reframing acts, respectively.

An *organizing act* is one that increases the capacity of the potential challengers to act as a unit. More specifically, these acts serve to build solidarity and loyalty to a challenging organization, create some procedure or apparatus for managing logistical problems, or manage internal conflicts so that they don't disrupt collective action.

A *divesting act* is one that weakens the bonds of authority. More specifically, these acts void obligations to authority, handle fears about making a scene, or personalize responsibility. Potential challengers are free of the bonds of authority when they no longer feel any obligations to comply, they are no longer concerned about disrupting the smooth flow of interaction, and they do not regard the authority system which lays its claim on them as beyond human agency. Considerations of self-interest may still be important, but they are psychologically free for participation in rebellious collective action.

A *reframing act* furthers the collective adoption of the injustice frame at the expense of the legitimating frame. It is accomplished through public acts that call attention to something wrong in what the authorities are doing (attention calling) and that link what is happening with an explicit injustice frame (context setting).

THE PRACTICE OF REBELLION

Sooner or later, many of us will confront a situation in which we are part of a group faced with one or more dilemmas of compliance. Our theory has practical implications for such encounters. It tells us what to do if we want to suc-

ceed in fomenting rebellious collective action. It suggests a how-to manual for rebellion.

One begins by assessing the special vulnerabilities and opportunities that stem from context. With respect to climate, ask how generally supportive it is for potential challengers. If the climate is favorable, you are fortunate and need not worry about it. If it is not favorable, this means that divesting and reframing will require extra attention. The legitimating frame may be expected to seem especially natural and taken-for-granted and the bonds of authority to be especially strong.

° ° °

Assets also require a careful assessment. For resources, it is a matter of determining whether or not what you need is present. In many cases, resource needs are minimal and can be ignored, but the absence of any that might be needed is a constraint. The form of action that you pursue needs to reflect this constraint. If you have read this book, you should now have the necessary repertoire; you can help the group to rebel, as well as polish your skills, by applying this knowledge.

The basic practice of rebellion is to make sure that the various mobilizing acts are performed. When an agent of authority acts in a manner that is questionable, make sure that someone calls attention to it. Even if others probably noticed it, calling attention not only makes sure of this, but, more importantly, it makes everyone aware that it is common knowledge.

Perhaps the problematic behavior will be remedied, in which case no injustice frame is appropriate. Then there is no particular need for mobilizing rebellious collective action. Our advice is intended for a situation in which the agent continues to operate in a way that is likely to produce an injustice. The injustice frame makes sense of the agent's behavior by showing that it is consistent with some objective that the authority system is actively seeking.

A full-fledged injustice frame may not be immediately clear. You may not understand the full context of the authority's behavior without discussion and probing. Consider the development of an injustice frame to be a collective problem, not merely your personal one, and enlist the help of other potential challengers in analyzing the context. Press the agents of authority for the information that would help to make the context clearer. Your objective is to facilitate the *shared* definition of the situation as one in which the unimpeded operation of the authority system will result in an injustice.

° ° °

Authorities frequently have sanctions available to back up their efforts at gaining voluntary compliance. Premature acts of protest may isolate challengers and make them vulnerable to such sanctions. Overt acts of protest are appropriate when the process of breaking out is close to completion, but they can easily backfire if the bonds of authority are still intact.

The first step in breaking out is rim talk, in which the terms and conditions of compliance are actively negotiated, not merely accepted as the natural prerogative of authority. This step weakens several different bonds simultaneously. First, it preserves the fact of the particular agent of authority, allowing divesting to proceed without disrupting the smooth flow of interaction any more than necessary. Second, it either forces into the open or undercuts reification. If the rules are a subject of negotiation and can be altered, then they are not independent of human agency. While such rim talk involves making a contract explicit and negotiating its terms, it does not directly void obligation. But it is likely to provide the basis for later voiding it, by providing a basis for the claim that authorities are operating in violation of its terms. Finally, rim talk is less likely than more overt acts of protest to provide a justification for sanctions—although some authorities might treat it as a sufficient provocation in itself. It does not eliminate risk, but it reduces it.

If authorities refuse to negotiate or if the negotiations break down, it is easier to move then to more advanced acts of protest that void the obligation of potential challengers to comply. An individual act of resistance indicates that a particular person does not feel obliged to comply, but making the claim explicit and public declares it void for other potential challengers as well. If the reframing process has properly advanced, an injustice frame may itself serve as the justification for voiding any obligation to comply.

If potential challengers have some prior history of working together, this existing organizational structure may be useful in enabling them to find a unified course of action. In many encounters, however, the potential challengers have little prior experience in working together,

and this process will require active effort. Part of your job as an organizer in this situation would be to foster a sense of collective identity. If there is an explicit challenging organization involved, then act in the name of it so that potential challengers will recognize it as a carrier of their interests and values.

Be alert to the logistics of collective action. Procedural suggestions at various points will enable challengers to carry out the collective action routines that they consider. Finally, give explicit attention to the handling of disagreements in a way that allows a group to proceed. If one can't find a common course of action on which participants can agree, there are other procedures besides consensus. A straw vote or a show of hands may convince a minority faction to support a course of action that has clear majority support. Voting is a widely recognized and legitimated mechanism for resolving conflicts, and can serve even in ad hoc groups that have no life beyond a single encounter.

CONCLUSION

Perhaps the most hopeful message in our account is the frequency with which ordinary people, with no prior experience of working together, were able to join together in actively resisting an unjust authority. . . . Although earlier studies have suggested that people are overly compliant, our message is a complementary one: people sometimes resist unjust authority when they should, and we can all learn from their efforts in doing so.

Legitimacy and Authority

Robert A. Dahl

How do leaders win compliance for their policies? A leader has certain resources at his disposal—money, police, privileges, weapons, status, and so on. He can use these resources to obtain compliance for his policies. Suppose a leader wished to enforce a policy requiring all peasants to give up their land-holdings and enter collective farms. He could use his resources to increase the rewards for those who comply or to increase the disadvantages to those who failed to comply. Thus he could act in one or more of four ways:

To encourage compliance, he could

1. Increase rewards for complying.
2. Decrease disadvantages of complying.

To discourage non-compliance, he could

3. Decrease rewards from other alternatives.
4. Increase disadvantages of other alternatives.

This reading is reprinted from Robert A. Dahl, MODERN POLITICAL ANALYSIS *(Englewood Cliffs, N.J.: Prentice-Hall, Inc., 1963), pp. 31–32. © 1963 by Prentice-Hall, Inc. Reprinted by permission.*
Robert A. Dahl is a political scientist at Yale University.

Now during any brief period, the more of his resources he uses to secure compliance for one policy, the less he has available for securing compliance with other policies. In general, then, leaders have some interest in economizing on their political resources. Resources are not, in any case, limitless.

Individuals have internal sources of rewards and deprivations as well as external sources. Examples of internalized rewards are the feeling that one has done a good job, followed the dictates of conscience, done what is right, performed one's duty, and so forth; conversely, internalized penalties include the feeling that one has done a bad job, violated one's conscience, committed an evil act, and so on. Now from a leader's point of view, the more that citizens comply with policies because of internal rewards and deprivations, the less resources he needs to allocate to create external rewards and deprivations. If a leader could win compliance for his policies simply by transmitting information as to what he wanted citizens to do, with no external rewards or deprivations whatsoever, securing compliance would be all but costless.

When a political system is widely accepted by its members as legitimate, and when the policies of its officials and other leaders are regarded as morally binding by citizens, then the costs of compliance are low. Conversely, when legitimacy and authority are low, leaders must use more of their money, police, privileges, weapons, status, and other political resources to secure compliance.

Popular governments—democracies—necessarily require more legitimacy and authority than dictatorships. Political leaders cannot impose a democracy on a people if a majority (or even, in practice, a very large minority) reject democracy as an illegitimate system. Policies that lack authority, like Prohibition in the United States, generally cannot be enforced by naked power. A chief executive would have needed such a great array of coercive power to enforce Prohibition as to constitute a threat to the system itself. In general, then, in democracies political leaders need authority because they are not permitted to acquire sufficient resources to enforce their policies through naked power.

PART 4 / SOCIAL CONFLICT: ITS NATURE, FUNCTIONS, AND RESOLUTION

Real societies can be torn apart by destructive conflicts and some SIMSOCs have collapsed because of the inability of the participants to deal with the struggles that arose. But we must not conclude from this that conflict is bad for a society. Most social scientists would accept the argument in the selection by Coser that conflict can and frequently does have positive functions. When we talk about healthy conflicts, we have in mind a conflict that is carried on within certain definite limits—moderate conflict. Too little conflict and a society may stagnate; too much conflict and it may fall apart.

Perhaps the most influential theory of how conflicts are kept within acceptable limits is the theory of pluralist democracy. Once again we turn to Dahl for a succinct summary. The factors that lead to moderate rather than severe conflict in Dahl's paradigm are, essentially, the defining conditions of social and political pluralism.

Although one may be able to predict from prior conditions whether severe conflicts will arise, once they begin they frequently have a dynamic of their own. The selection by Fisher and Ury suggests one major method for breaking through intractable conflicts by finding options from which all the conflicting parties may gain. A successful mechanism of conflict-resolution is one which extracts the positive value of social conflict, while keeping the human costs and destructive consequences to a minimum. The development of creative mechanisms for handling conflict is a major challenge for any society.

The Functions of Conflict

Lewis Coser

Conflict within a group . . . may help to establish unity or to re-establish unity and cohesion where it has been threatened by hostile and antagonistic feelings among the members. Yet, not *every* type of conflict is likely to benefit group structure, nor can that conflict subserve such functions for *all* groups. Whether social conflict is beneficial to internal adaptation or not depends on the type of issues over which it is fought as well as on the type of social structure within which it occurs. However, types of conflict and types of social structure are not independent variables.

Internal social conflicts which concern goals, values or interests that do not contradict the basic assumptions upon which the relationship is founded tend to be positively functional for the social structure. Such conflicts tend to make possible the readjustment of norms and power relations within groups in accordance with the felt needs of its individual members or subgroups.

Internal conflicts in which the contending parties no longer share the basic values upon which the legitimacy of the social system rests threaten to disrupt the structure.

One safeguard against conflict disrupting the consensual basis of the relationship, however, is contained in the social structure itself: it is provided by the institutionalization and tolerance of conflict. Whether internal conflict promises to be a means of equilibration of social relations or readjustment of rival claims, or whether it threatens to "tear apart," depends to a large extent on the social structure within which it occurs.

In every type of social structure there are occasions for conflict, since individuals and subgroups are likely to make from time to time rival claims to scarce resources, prestige or power positions. But social structures differ in the way in which they allow expression to antagonistic claims. Some show more tolerance of conflict than others.

Closely knit groups in which there exists a high fre-

This reading is reprinted with permission of The Macmillan Co. and Routledge & Kegan Paul Ltd., from Lewis Coser, THE FUNCTIONS OF SOCIAL CONFLICT, pp. 151–157. © by The Free Press, a Corporation, 1956.
Lewis Coser is a sociologist at Boston College.

quency of interaction and high personality involvement of the members have a tendency to suppress conflict. While they provide frequent occasions for hostility (since both sentiments of love and hatred are intensified through frequency of interaction), the acting out of such feelings is sensed as a danger to such intimate relationships, and hence there is a tendency to suppress rather than to allow expression of hostile feelings. In close-knit groups, feelings of hostility tend, therefore, to accumulate and hence to intensify. If conflict breaks out in a group that has consistently tried to prevent expression of hostile feelings, it will be particularly intense for two reasons: First, because the conflict does not merely aim at resolving the immediate issue which led to its outbreak; all accumulated grievances which were denied expression previously are apt to emerge at this occasion. Second, because the total personality involvement of the group members makes for mobilization of all sentiments in the conduct of the struggle.

Hence, the closer the group, the more intense the conflict. Where members participate with their total personality and conflicts are suppressed, the conflict, if it breaks out nevertheless, is likely to threaten the very root of the relationship.

In groups comprising individuals who participate only segmentally, conflict is less likely to be disruptive. Such groups are likely to experience a multiplicity of conflicts. This in itself tends to constitute a check against the breakdown of consensus: the energies of group members are mobilized in many directions and hence will not concentrate on *one* conflict cutting through the group. Moreover, where occasions for hostility are not permitted to accumulate and conflict is allowed to occur wherever a resolution of tension seems to be indicated, such a conflict is likely to remain focused primarily on the condition which led to its outbreak and not to revive blocked hostility; in this way, the conflict is limited to "the facts of the case." One may venture to say that multiplicity of conflicts stands in inverse relation to their intensity.

So far we have been dealing with internal social conflict only. At this point we must turn to a consideration of external conflict, for the structure of the group is itself affected by conflicts with other groups in which it engages or which it prepares for. Groups which are engaged in continued struggle tend to lay claim on the total personality involvement of their members so that internal conflict would tend to mobilize all energies and affects of the members. Hence such groups are unlikely to tolerate more than limited departures from the group unity. In such groups there is a tendency to suppress conflict; where it occurs, it leads the group to break up through splits or through forced withdrawal of dissenters.

Groups which are not involved in continued struggle with the outside are less prone to make claims on total personality involvement of the membership and are more likely to exhibit flexibility of structure. The multiple internal conflicts which they tolerate may in turn have an equilibrating and stabilizing impact on the structure.

In flexible social structures, multiple conflicts crisscross each other and thereby prevent basic cleavages along one axis. The multiple group affiliations of individuals makes them participate in various group conflicts so that their total personalities are not involved in any single one of them. Thus segmental participation in a multiplicity of conflicts constitutes a balancing mechanism within the structure.

In loosely structured groups and open societies, conflict, which aims at a resolution of tension between antagonists, is likely to have stabilizing and integrative functions for the relationship. By permitting immediate and direct expression of rival claims, such social systems are able to readjust their structures by eliminating the sources of dissatisfaction. The multiple conflicts which they experience may serve to eliminate the causes for dissociation and to reestablish unity. These systems avail themselves, through the toleration and institutionalization of conflict, of an important stabilizing mechanism.

In addition, conflict within a group frequently helps to revitalize existent norms; or it contributes to the emergence of new norms. In this sense, social conflict is a mechanism for adjustment of norms adequate to new conditions. A flexible society benefits from conflict because such behavior, by helping to create and modify norms, assures it continuance under changed conditions. Such mechanism for readjustment of norms is hardly available to rigid systems: by suppressing conflict, the latter smother a useful warning signal, thereby maximizing the danger of catastrophic breakdown.

Internal conflict can also serve as a means for ascertaining the relative strength of antagonistic interests within the structure, and in this way constitute a mechanism for the maintenance or continual readjustment of the balance of power. Since the outbreak of the conflict indicates a rejection of a previous accommodation between parties, once the respective power of the contenders has been ascertained through conflict, a new equilibrium can be established and the relationship can proceed on this new basis. Consequently, a social structure in which there is room for conflict disposes of an important means for avoiding or redressing conditions of disequilibrium by modifying the terms of power relations.

Conflicts with some produce associations or coalitions with others. Conflicts through such associations or coalitions, by providing a bond between the members, help to reduce social isolation or to unite individuals and groups otherwise unrelated or antagonistic to each other. A social structure in which there can exist a multiplicity of conflicts contains a mechanism for bringing together otherwise isolated, apathetic or mutually hostile parties and for taking them into the field of public social activities. Moreover, such a structure fosters a multiplicity of associations and coalitions whose diverse purposes crisscross each other, we recall, thereby preventing alliances along one major line of cleavage.

Once groups and associations have been formed

through conflict with other groups, such conflict may further serve to maintain boundary lines between them and the surrounding social environment. In this way, social conflict helps to structure the larger social environment by assigning position to the various subgroups within the system and by helping to define the power relations between them.

Not all social systems in which individuals participate segmentally allow the free expression of antagonistic claims. Social systems tolerate or institutionalize conflict to different degrees. There is no society in which any and every antagonistic claim is allowed immediate expression. Societies dispose of mechanisms to channel discontent and hostility while keeping intact the relationship within which antagonism arises. Such mechanisms frequently operate through "safety-valve" institutions which provide substitute objects upon which to displace hostile sentiments as well as means of abreaction of aggressive tendencies.

Safety-valve institutions may serve to maintain both the social structure and the individual's security system, but they are incompletely functional for both of them. They prevent modification of relationships to meet changing conditions and hence the satisfaction they afford the individual can be only partially or momentarily adjustive. The hypothesis has been suggested that the need for safety-valve institutions increases with the rigidity of the social structure, i.e., with the degree to which it disallows direct expression of antagonistic claims.

Safety-valve institutions lead to a displacement of goal in the actor: he need no longer aim at reaching a solution of the unsatisfactory situation, but merely at releasing the tension which arose from it. Where safety-valve institutions provide substitute objects for the displacement of hostility, the conflict itself is channeled away from the original unsatisfactory relationship into one in which the actor's goal is no longer the attainment of specific results, but the release of tension.

This affords us a criterion for distinguishing between realistic and non-realistic conflict.

Social conflicts that arise from frustrations of specific demands within a relationship and from estimates of gains of the participants, and that are directed at the presumed frustrating object, can be called realistic conflicts. Insofar as they are means toward specific results, they can be replaced by alternative modes of interaction with the contending party if such alternatives seem to be more adequate for realizing the end in view.

Nonrealistic conflicts, on the other hand, are not occasioned by the rival ends of the antagonists, but by the need for tension release of one or both of them. In this case the conflict is not oriented toward the attainment of specific results. Insofar as unrealistic conflict is an end in itself, insofar as it affords only tension release, the chosen antagonist can be substituted for by any other "suitable" target.

In realistic conflict, there exist functional alternatives with regard to the means of carrying out the conflict, as well as with regard to accomplishing desired results short of conflict; in nonrealistic conflict, on the other hand, there exist only functional alternatives in the choice of antagonists.

Our hypothesis, that the need for safety-valve institutions increases with the rigidity of the social system, may be extended to suggest that unrealistic conflict may be expected to occur as a consequence of rigidity present in the social structure.

Our discussion of the distinction between types of conflict, and between types of social structures, leads us to conclude that conflict tends to be dysfunctional for a social structure in which there is no or insufficient toleration and institutionalization of conflict. The intensity of a conflict which threatens to "tear apart," which attacks the consensual basis of a social system, is related to the rigidity of the structure. What threatens the equilibrium of such a structure is not conflict as such, but the rigidity itself which permits hostilities to accumulate and to be channeled along one major line of cleavage once they break out in conflict.

Conflict: A Paradigm

Robert A. Dahl

The intensity or severity of a political conflict in a republic is indicated by the extent to which people on each side see the other as an enemy to be destroyed; evidence that political disagreements are becoming severe is an increase in threats or actual use of violence, suppression of opponents, civil war, secession, disloyalty, or a marked increase in demoralization, apathy, indifference, or alienation.

The intensity or severity of a political conflict depends on at least four sets of factors:

1. The way in which politically relevant attitudes are distributed among the citizens and leaders.

This reading is reprinted from Robert A. Dahl, PLURALISTIC DEMOCRACY IN THE UNITED STATES: CONFLICT AND CONSENT *(Chicago: Rand-McNally and Company, 1967), pp. 279–81. © 1967 by Rand-McNally and Company.*

a. The greater the number of citizens who hold extreme (and opposing) views the more severe a conflict is likely to be. Conversely, the greater the number who hold moderate views, the less severe a conflict is likely to be.

b. The more extreme the views of political leaders and activists in comparison with the views of ordinary citizens, the more severe the conflict; conversely, the more moderate the views of leaders and activists in comparison with other citizens, the less severe the conflict is likely to be.

2. The patterns of cleavage.
The more conflicts accumulate along the same lines of cleavage, the more severe they are likely to be; conversely, the more conflicts intersect along different lines of cleavage, the less severe they are.

3. How much is at stake.
a. The more at stake, the more severe a conflict is likely to be.

b. A conflict in which no contestant can possibly make himself better off except by making other contestants worse off is likely to be more severe than a conflict in which there is a possibility that no contes-

tant need be worse off than before, and some may be better off.

c. Conflicts involving incompatible "ways of life" are bound to be particularly severe.

4. The political institutions.
a. Political institutions and processes are likely to intensify conflicts if they require the groups involved to negotiate but do not provide any acceptable way by which leaders can terminate negotiations and arrive at a decision.

b. Political institutions and processes are likely to intensify conflicts if they make it possible for leaders to make decisions without engaging in negotiations to obtain the consent of the persons, groups, or parties involved.

c. Political institutions and processes are most likely to reduce the intensity of conflicts if they embody widespread agreement on procedures, *both* for negotiating in order to gain consent and for terminating the negotiations and arriving at a decision.

These propositions are summarized in the accompanying table.

A Paradigm: Some Factors That Moderate or Intensify Political Conflicts

	Conflict Is More Likely to Be	
	Moderate If:	Severe If:
1. The distribution of attitudes is	convergent	divergent
a. Attitudes of citizens are	convergent	divergent
b. Attitudes of political leaders and activists are	convergent	divergent
2. Lines of cleavage are	overlapping (cross-cutting)	non-overlapping (cumulative)
3. Threats to ways of life are	absent	present
a. Privileged groups feel	secure	seriously threatened
b. Aspiring groups feel	successful	frustrated
4. Political institutions provide		
a. Negotiations for consent but not decisions.	No	Yes
b. Decisions without consent.	No	Yes
c. Agreed processes for negotiating consent and arriving at decisions.	Yes	No

Inventing Options for Mutual Gain

Roger Fisher and William Ury

The case of Israel and Egypt negotiating over who should keep how much of the Sinai Peninsula illustrates both a major problem in negotiation and a key opportunity.

The problem is a common one. There seems to be no way to split the pie that leaves both parties satisfied. Often you are negotiating along a single dimension, such as the amount of territory, the price of a car, the length of a lease on an apartment, or the size of a commission on a sale. At other times you face what appears to be an either/or choice that is either markedly favorable to you or to the other side. In a divorce settlement, who gets the house? Who gets custody of the children? You may see the choice as one between winning and losing—and neither side will agree to lose. Even if you do win and get the car for $12,000, the lease for five years, or the house and kids, you have a sinking feeling that they will not let you forget it. Whatever the situation, your choices seemed limited.

The Sinai example also makes clear the opportunity. A creative option like a demilitarized Sinai can often make the difference between deadlock and agreement. One lawyer we know attributes his success directly to his ability to invent solutions advantageous to both his client and the other side. He expands the pie before dividing it. Skill at inventing options is one of the most useful assets a negotiator can have.

Yet all too often negotiators end up like the proverbial children who quarreled over an orange. After they finally agreed to divide the orange in half, the first child took one half, ate the fruit, and threw away the peel, while the other threw away the fruit and used the peel from the second half in baking a cake. All too often negotiators "leave money on the table"—they fail to reach agreement when they might have, or the agreement they do reach could have been better for each side. Too many negotiations end up with half an orange for each side instead of the whole fruit for one and the whole peel for the other. Why?

DIAGNOSIS

As valuable as it is to have many options, people involved in a negotiation rarely sense a need for them. In a dispute, people usually believe that they know the right answer—their view should prevail. In a contract negotiation they are equally likely to believe that their offer is reasonable and should be adopted, perhaps with some adjustment in the price. All available answers appear to lie along a straight line between their position and yours. Often the only creative thinking shown is to suggest splitting the difference.

In most negotiations there are four major obstacles that inhibit the inventing of an abundance of options: (1) premature judgment; (2) searching for the single answer; (3) the assumption of a fixed pie; and (4) thinking that "solving their problem is their problem." In order to overcome these constraints, you need to understand them.

Premature Judgment

Inventing options does not come naturally. Not inventing is the normal state of affairs, even when you are outside a stressful negotiation. If you were asked to name the one person in the world most deserving of the Nobel Peace Prize, any answer you might start to propose would immediately encounter your reservations and doubts. How could you be sure that that person was the *most* deserving? Your mind might well go blank, or you might throw out a few answers that would reflect conventional thinking: "Well, maybe the Pope, or the President."

Nothing is so harmful to inventing as a critical sense waiting to pounce on the drawbacks of any new idea. Judgment hinders imagination.

Under the pressure of a forthcoming negotiation, your critical sense is likely to be sharper. Practical negotiation appears to call for practical thinking, not wild ideas.

Your creativity may be even more stifled by the presence of those on the other side. Suppose you are negotiating with your boss over your salary for the coming year. You have asked for a $4,000 raise; your boss has offered you $1,500, a figure that you have indicated is unsatisfactory. In a tense situation like this you are not likely to start inventing imaginative solutions. You may fear that if you suggest some bright half-baked idea like taking half the increase in a raise and half in additional benefits, you might look foolish. Your boss might say, "Be serious. You know better than that. It would upset company policy. I am surprised that you even suggested it." If on the spur of the moment you invent a possible option of spreading out the raise over time, he may take it as an offer: "I'm prepared to start negotiating on that basis." Since he may take whatever you say as a commitment, you will think twice before saying anything.

You may also fear that by inventing options you will disclose some piece of information that will jeopardize your bargaining position. If you should suggest, for example, that the company help finance the house you are about to buy, your boss may conclude that you intend to stay and that you will in the end accept any raise in salary he is prepared to offer.

This selection is from Roger Fisher and William Ury, GETTING TO YES, *2nd Edition, pp. 56–80 and is reprinted with permission.*

Roger Fisher is a Professor at the Harvard Law School and with William Ury heads the Harvard Negotiation Project.

Searching for the Single Answer

In most people's minds, inventing simply is not part of the negotiating process. People see their job as narrowing the gap between positions, not broadening the options available. They tend to think, "We're having a hard enough time agreeing as it is. The last thing we need is a bunch of different ideas." Since the end product of negotiation is a single decision, they fear that free-floating discussion will only delay and confuse the process.

If the first impediment to creating thinking is premature criticism, the second is premature closure. By looking from the outset for the single best answer, you are likely to short-circuit a wiser decision-making process in which you select from a large number of possible answers.

The Assumption of a Fixed Pie

A third explanation for why there may be so few good options on the table is that each side sees the situation as essentially either/or—either I get what is in dispute or you do. A negotiation often appears to be a "fixed-sum" game; $100 more for you on the price of a car means $100 less for me. Why bother to invent if all the options are obvious and I can satisfy you only at my own expense?

Thinking that "Solving Their Problem Is Their Problem"

A final obstacle to inventing realistic options lies in each side's concern with only its own immediate interests. For a negotiator to reach an agreement that meets his own self-interest he needs to develop a solution which appeals to the self-interest of the other. Yet emotional involvement on one side of an issue makes it difficult to achieve the detachment necessary to think up wise ways of meeting the interests of both sides: "We've got enough problems of our own; they can look after theirs." There also frequently exists a psychological reluctance to accord any legitimacy to the views of the other side; it seems disloyal to think up ways to satisfy them. Shortsighted self-concern thus leads a negotiator to develop only partisan positions, partisan arguments, and one-sided solutions.

PRESCRIPTION

To invent creative options, then, you will need (1) to separate the act of inventing options from the act of judging them; (2) to broaden the options on the table rather than look for a single answer; (3) to search for mutual gains; and (4) to invent ways of making their decisions easy. Each of these steps is discussed below.

Separate Inventing from Deciding

Since judgment hinders imagination, separate the creative act from the critical one; separate the process of thinking up possible decisions from the process of selecting among them. Invent first, decide later.

As a negotiator, you will of necessity do much inventing by yourself. It is not easy. By definition, inventing new ideas requires you to think about things that are not already in your mind. You should therefore consider the desirability of arranging an inventing or brainstorming session with a few colleagues or friends. Such a session can effectively separate inventing from deciding.

A brainstorming session is designed to produce as many ideas as possible to solve the problem at hand. The key ground rule is to postpone all criticism and evaluation of ideas. The group simply invents ideas without pausing to consider whether they are good or bad, realistic or unrealistic. With those inhibitions removed, one idea should stimulate another, like firecrackers setting off one another.

In a brainstorming session, people need not fear looking foolish since wild ideas are explicitly encouraged. And in the absence of the other side, negotiators need not worry about disclosing confidential information or having an idea taken as a serious commitment.

There is no right way to run a brainstorming session. Rather, you should tailor it to your needs and resources. In doing so, you may find it useful to consider the following guidelines.

Before Brainstorming:

1. *Define your purpose.* Think of what you would like to walk out of the meeting with.

2. *Choose a few participants.* The group should normally be large enough to provide a stimulating interchange, yet small enough to encourage both individual participation and free-wheeling inventing—usually between five and eight people.

3. *Change the environment.* Select a time and place distinguishing the session as much as possible from regular discussions. The more different a brainstorming session seems from a normal meeting, the easier it is for participants to suspend judgment.

4. *Design an informal atmosphere.* What does it take for you and others to relax? It may be talking over a drink, or meeting at a vacation lodge in some picturesque spot, or simply taking off your tie and jacket during the meeting and calling each other by your first names.

5. *Choose a facilitator.* Someone at the meeting needs to facilitate—to keep the meeting on track, to make sure everyone gets a chance to speak, to enforce any ground rules, and to stimulate discussion by asking questions.

During Brainstorming:

1. *Seat the participants side by side facing the problem.* The physical reinforces the psychological. Physically sitting side by side can reinforce the mental attitude of tackling a common problem together. People facing each other tend to respond personally and engage in dialogue or

argument; people sitting side by side in a semicircle of chairs facing a blackboard tend to respond to the problem depicted there.

2. *Clarify the ground rules, including the no-criticism rule.* If the participants do not all know each other, the meeting begins with introductions all around, followed by clarification of the ground rules. Outlaw negative criticism of any kind.

Joint inventing produces new ideas because each of us invents only within the limits set by our working assumptions. If ideas are shot down unless they appeal to all participants, the implicit goal becomes to advance an idea that no one will shoot down. If, on the other hand, wild ideas are encouraged, even those that in fact lie well outside the realm of the possible, the group may generate from these ideas other options that *are* possible and that no one would previously have considered.

Other ground rules you may want to adopt are to make the entire session off the record and to refrain from attributing ideas to any participant.

3. *Brainstorm.* Once the purpose of the meeting is clear, let your imaginations go. Try to come up with a long list of ideas, approaching the question from every conceivable angle.

4. *Record the ideas in full view.* Recording ideas either on a blackboard or, better, on large sheets of newsprint gives the group a tangible sense of collective achievement; it reinforces the no-criticism rule; it reduces the tendency to repeat; and it helps stimulate other ideas.

After Brainstorming:

1. *Star the most promising ideas.* After brainstorming, relax the no-criticism rule in order to winnow out the most promising ideas. You are still not at the stage of deciding; you are merely nominating ideas worth developing further. Mark those ideas that members of the group think are best.

2. *Invent improvements for promising ideas.* Take one promising idea and invent ways to make it better and more realistic, as well as ways to carry it out. The task at this stage is to make the idea as attractive as you can. Preface constructive criticism with: "What I like best about that idea is. . . . Might it be better if . . . ?"

3. *Set up a time to evaluate ideas and decide.* Before you break up, draw up a selective and improved list of ideas from the session and set up a time for deciding which of these ideas to advance in your negotiation and how.

Consider Brainstorming with the Other Side.

Although more difficult than brainstorming with your own side, brainstorming with people from the other side can also prove extremely valuable. It is more difficult because of the increased risk that you will say something that prejudices your interests despite the rules established for a brainstorming session. You may disclose confidential infor-

mation inadvertently or lead the other side to mistake an option you devise for an offer. Nevertheless, joint brainstorming sessions have the great advantages of producing ideas which take into account the interests of all those involved, of creating a climate of joint problem-solving, and of educating each side about the concerns of the other.

To protect yourself when brainstorming with the other side, distinguish the brainstorming session explicitly from a negotiating session where people state official views and speak on the record. People are so accustomed to meeting for the purpose of reaching agreement that any other purpose needs to be clearly stated.

To reduce the risk of appearing committed to any given idea, you can make a habit of advancing at least two alternatives at the same time. You can also put on the table options with which you obviously disagree. "I could give you the house for nothing, or you could pay me a million dollars in cash for it, or . . ." Since you are plainly not proposing either of these ideas, the ones which follow are labeled as mere possibilities, not proposals.

To get the flavor of a joint brainstorming session, let us suppose the leaders of a local union are meeting with the management of a coal mine to brainstorm on ways to reduce unauthorized one- or two-day strikes. Ten people—five from each side—are present, sitting around a table facing a blackboard. A neutral facilitator asks the participants for their ideas and writes them down on the blackboard.

Facilitator: OK, now let's see what ideas you have for dealing with this problem of unauthorized work stoppages. Let's try to get ten ideas on the blackboard in five minutes. OK, let's start. Tom?

Tom (Union): Foremen ought to be able to settle a union member's grievance on the spot.

Facilitator: Good, I've got it down. Jim, you've got your hand up.

Jim (Management): A union member ought to talk to his foreman about a problem before taking any action that—

Tom (Union): They do, but the foremen don't listen.

Facilitator: Tom, please, no criticizing yet. We agreed to postpone that until later, OK? How about you, Jerry? You look like you've got an idea.

Jerry (Union): When a strike issue comes up, the union members should be allowed to meet in the bathhouse immediately.

Roger (Management): Management could agree to let the bathhouse be used for union meetings and could assure the employees' privacy by shutting the doors and keeping the foremen out.

Carol (Management): How about adopting the rule that there will be no strike without giving the union leaders and management a chance to work it out on the spot?

Jerry (Union): How about speeding up the grievance procedure and having a meeting within twenty-four hours if the foreman and union member don't settle it between themselves?

Karen (Union): Yeah. And how about organizing some joint training for the union members and the foremen on how to handle their problems together?

Phil (Union): If a person does a good job, let him know it.

John (Management): Establish friendly relations between union people and management people.

Facilitator: That sounds promising, John, but could you be more specific?

John (Management): Well, how about organizing a union-management softball team?

Tom (Union): And a bowling team too.

Roger (Management): How about an annual picnic get-together for all the families?

And on it goes, as the participants brainstorm lots of ideas. Many of the ideas might never have come up except in such a brainstorming session, and some of them may prove effective in reducing unauthorized strikes. Time spent brainstorming together is surely among the best-spent time in negotiation.

But whether you brainstorm together or not, separating the act of developing options from the act of deciding on them is extremely useful in any negotiation. Discussing options differs radically from taking positions. Whereas one side's position will conflict with another's, options invite other options. The very language you use differs. It consists of questions, not assertions; it is open, not closed: "One option is. . . . What other options have you thought of?" "What if we agreed to this?" "How about doing it this way?" "How would this work?" "What would be wrong with that?" Invent before you decide.

Broaden Your Options

Even with the best of intentions, participants in a brainstorming session are likely to operate on the assumption that they are really looking for the *one* best answer, trying to find a needle in a haystack by picking up every blade of hay.

At this stage in a negotiation, however, you should not be looking for the right path. You are developing room within which to negotiate. Room can be made only by having a substantial number of markedly different ideas—ideas on which you and the other side can build later in the negotiation, and among which you can then jointly choose.

A vintner making a fine wine chooses his grapes from a number of varieties. A baseball team looking for star players will send talent scouts to scour the local leagues and college teams all over the nation. The same principle applies to negotiation. The key to wise decision-making, whether in wine-making, baseball, or negotiation, lies in selecting from a great number and variety of options.

If you were asked who should receive the Nobel Peace Prize this year, you would do well to answer, "Well, let's think about it" and generate a list of about a hundred names from diplomacy, business, journalism, religion, law, agriculture, politics, academia, medicine, and other fields, making sure to dream up a lot of wild ideas. You would almost certainly end up with a better decision this way than if you tried to decide right from the start.

A brainstorming session frees people to think creatively. Once freed, they need ways to think about their problems and go generate constructive solutions.

Multiply options by shuttling between the specific and the general: The Circle Chart. The task of inventing options involves four types of thinking. One is thinking about a particular problem—the factual situation you dislike, for example, a smelly, polluted river that runs by your land. The second type of thinking is descriptive analysis—you diagnose an existing situation in general terms. You sort problems into categories and tentatively suggest causes. The river water may have a high content of various chemicals, or too little oxygen. You may suspect various upstream industrial plants. The third type of thinking, again in general terms, is to consider what ought, perhaps, to be done. Given the diagnoses you have made, you look for prescriptions that theory may suggest, such as reducing chemical effluent, reducing diversions of water, or bringing fresh water from some other river. The fourth and final type of thinking is to come up with some specific and feasible suggestions for action. Who might do what tomorrow to put one of these general approaches into practice? For instance, the state environmental agency might order an upstream industry to limit the quantity of chemical discharge.

The Circle Chart on the next page illustrates these four types of thinking and suggests them as steps to be taken in sequence. If all goes well, the specific action invented in this way will, if adopted, deal with your original problem.

The Circle Chart provides an easy way of using one good idea to generate others. With one useful action idea before you, you (or a group of you who are brainstorming) can go back and try to identify the general approach of which the action idea is merely one application. You can then think up other action ideas that would apply the same general approach to the real world. Similarly, you can go back one step further and ask, "If this theoretical approach appears useful, what is the diagnosis behind it?" Having articulated a diagnosis, you can generate other approaches for dealing with a problem analyzed in that way, and then look for actions putting these new approaches into practice. One good option on the table thus opens the door to asking about the theory that makes this option good and then using that theory to invent more options.

An example may illustrate the process. In dealing with the conflict over Northern Ireland, one idea might be to have Catholic and Protestant teachers prepare a common workbook on the history of Northern Ireland for use in the primary grades of both school systems. The book would present Northern Irish history as seen from different points of view and give the children exercises that involve role-playing and putting themselves in other people's shoes. To generate more ideas, you might start with this ac-

CIRCLE CHART
The Four Basic Steps in Inventing Options

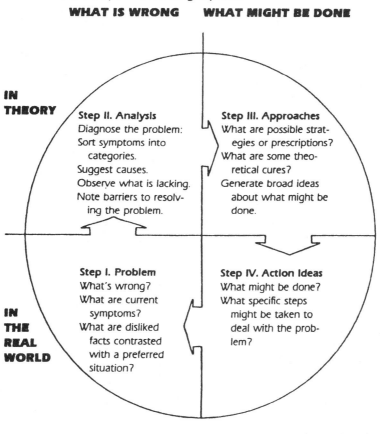

tion suggestion and then search out the theoretical approach that underlies it. You might find such general propositions as:

"There should be some common educational content in the two school systems."

"Catholics and Protestants should work together on small, manageable projects."

"Understanding should be promoted in young children before it is too late."

"History should be taught in ways that illuminate partisan perceptions."

Working with such theory you may be able to invent additional action suggestions, such as a joint Catholic and Protestant film project that presents the history of Northern Ireland as seen through different eyes. Other action ideas might be teacher exchange programs or some common classes for primary-age children in the two systems.

Look through the eyes of different experts. Another way to generate multiple options is to examine your problem from the perspective of different professions and disciplines.

In thinking up possible solutions to a dispute over custody of a child, for example, look at the problem as it might be seen by an educator, a banker, a psychiatrist, a civil rights lawyer, a minister, a nutritionist, a doctor, a feminist, a football coach, or one with some other special point of view. If you are negotiating a business contract, invent options that might occur to a banker, an inventor, a labor leader, a speculator in real estate, a stockbroker, an economist, a tax expert, or a socialist.

You can also combine the use of the Circle Chart with this idea of looking at a problem through the eyes of different experts. Consider in turn how each expert would diagnose the situation, what kinds of approaches each might suggest, and what practical suggestions would follow from those approaches.

Invent agreements of different strengths. You can multiply the number of possible agreements on the table by thinking of "weaker" versions you might want to have on hand in case a sought-for agreement proves beyond reach. If you cannot agree on substance, perhaps you can agree on procedure. If a shoe factory cannot agree with a wholesaler on who should pay for a shipment of damaged shoes, perhaps they can agree to submit the issue to an arbitrator. Similarly, where a permanent agreement is not possible, perhaps a provisional agreement is. At the very least, if you and the other side cannot reach first-order agreement, you can usually reach second-order agreement—that is, agree on where you disagree, so that you both know the issues in dispute, which are not always obvious. The pairs of adjectives below suggest potential agreements of different "strengths":

Stronger	Weaker
Substantive	Procedural
Permanent	Provisional
Comprehensive	Partial
Final	In principle
Unconditional	Contingent
Binding	Nonbinding
First-order	Second-order

Change the scope of a proposed agreement. Consider the possibility of varying not only the strength of the agreement but also its scope. You could, for instance, "fractionate" your problem into smaller and perhaps more manageable units. To a prospective editor for your book, you might suggest: "How about editing the first chapter for $300, and we'll see how it goes?" Agreements may be partial, involve fewer parties, cover only selected subject matters, apply only to a certain geographical area, or remain in effect for only a limited period of time.

It is also provocative to ask how the subject matter might be enlarged so as to "sweeten the pot" and make agreement more attractive. The dispute between India and Pakistan over the waters of the Indus River became more amenable to settlement when the World Bank entered the discussions; the parties were challenged to invent new irrigation projects, new storage dams, and other engineering works for the benefit of both nations, all to be funded with the assistance of the Bank.

Look for Mutual Gain

The third major block to creative problem-solving lies in the assumption of a fixed pie: the less for you, the more for me. Rarely if ever is the assumption true. First of all, both sides can always be worse off than they are now. Chess looks like a zero-sum game; if one loses, the other wins—until a dog trots by and knocks over the table, spills the beer, and leaves you both worse off than before.

Even apart from a shared interest in averting joint loss, there almost always exists the possibility of joint gain. This may take the form of developing a mutually advantageous relationship, or of satisfying the interests of each side with a creative solution.

Identify shared interests. In theory it is obvious that shared interests help produce agreement. By definition, inventing an idea which meets shared interests is good for you and good for them. In practice, however, the picture seems less clear. In the middle of a negotiation over price, shared interests may not appear obvious or relevant. How then can looking for shared interests help?

Let's take an example. Suppose you are the manager of an oil refinery. Call it Townsend Oil. The mayor of Pageville, the city where the refinery is located, has told you he wants to raise the taxes Townsend Oil pays to Pageville from one million dollars a year to two million. You have told him that you think one million a year is quite sufficient. The negotiation stands there: he wants more, you want to pay what you have been paying. In this negotiation, a typical one in many ways, where do shared interests come into play?

Let's take a closer look at what the mayor wants. He wants money—money undoubtedly to pay for city services, a new civic center, perhaps, and to relieve the ordinary taxpayers. But the city cannot obtain all the money it needs for now and for the future just from Townsend Oil. They will look for money from the petrochemical plant across the street, for example, and, for the future, from new businesses and from the expansion of existing businesses. The mayor, a businessman himself, would also like to encourage industrial expansion and attract new businesses that will provide new jobs and strengthen Pageville's economy.

What are your company's interests? Given the rapid changes in the technology of refining oil, and the antiquated condition of your refinery, you are presently considering a major refurbishment and expansion of the plant. You are concerned that the city may later increase its assessment of the value of the expanded refinery, thus making taxes even higher. Consider also that you have been encouraging a plastics plant to locate itself nearby to make convenient use of your product. Naturally, you worry that the plastics plant will have second thoughts once they see the city increasing taxes.

The shared interests between the mayor and you now become more apparent. You both agree on the goals of fostering industrial expansion and encouraging new industries. If you did some inventing to meet these shared goals, you might come up with several ideas: a tax holiday of seven years for new industries, a joint publicity campaign with the Chamber of Commerce to attract new companies, a reduction in taxes for existing industries that choose to expand. Such ideas might save you money while filling the city's coffers. If on the other hand the negotiation soured the relationship between company and town, both would lose. You might cut back on your corporate contributions to city charities and school athletics. The city might become unreasonably tough on enforcing the building code and other ordinances. Your personal relationship with the city's political and business leaders might grow unpleasant. The relationship between the sides, often taken for granted and overlooked, frequently outweighs in importance the outcome of any particular issue.

As a negotiator, you will almost always want to look for solutions that will leave the other side satisfied as well. If the customer feels cheated in a purchase, the store owner has also failed; he may lose a customer and his reputation may suffer. An outcome in which the other side gets absolutely nothing is worse for you than one which leaves them mollified. In almost every case, your satisfaction depends to a degree on making the other side sufficiently content with an agreement to want to live up to it.

Three points about shared interests are worth remembering. First, shared interests lie latent in every negotiation. They may not be immediately obvious. Ask yourself: Do we have a shared interest in preserving our relationship? What opportunities lie ahead for cooperation and mutual benefit? What costs would we bear if negotiations broke off? Are there common principles, like a fair price, that we both can respect?

Second, shared interests are opportunities, not godsends. To be of use, you need to make something out of them. It helps to make a shared interest explicit and to formulate it as a shared *goal*. In other words, make it concrete and future-oriented. As manager of Townsend Oil, for example, you could set a joint goal with the mayor of bringing five new industries into Pageville within three years. The tax holiday for new industries would then represent not a concession by the mayor to you but an action in pursuit of your shared goal.

Third, stressing your shared interests can make the negotiation smoother and more amicable. Passengers in a lifeboat afloat in the middle of the ocean with limited rations will subordinate their differences over food in pursuit of their shared interest in getting to shore.

Dovetail differing interests. Consider once again the two children quarreling over an orange. Each child wanted the orange, so they split it, failing to realize that one wanted only the fruit to eat and the other only the peel for baking. In this case as in many others, a satisfactory agreement is made possible because each side wants *different* things. This is genuinely startling if you think about it. People generally assume that differences between two parties create the problem. Yet differences can also lead to a solution.

Agreement is often based on disagreement. It is as absurd to think, for example, that you should always begin by reaching agreement on the facts as it is for a buyer of stock to try to convince the seller that the stock is likely to go up. If they did agree that the stock would go up, the seller would probably not sell. What makes a deal likely is that the buyer believes the price will go up and the seller believes it will go down. The difference in belief provides the basis for a deal.

Many creative agreements reflect this principle of reaching agreement through differences. Differences in interests and belief make it possible for an item to be high benefit to you, yet low cost to the other side. Consider the nursery rhyme:

> Jack Sprat could eat no fat
> His wife could eat no lean,
> And so betwixt them both
> They licked the platter clean.

The kinds of differences that best lend themselves to

dovetailing are differences in interests, in beliefs, in the value placed on time, in forecasts, and in aversion to risk.

Any difference in interests? The following brief checklist suggests common variations in interests to look for:

One party cares more about:	The other party cares more about:
Form	Substance
Economic considerations	Political considerations
Internal considerations	External considerations
Symbolic considerations	Practical considerations
Immediate future	More distant future
Ad hoc results	The relationship
Hardware	Ideology
Progress	Respect for tradition
Precedent	This case
Prestige, reputation	Results
Political points	Group welfare

Different beliefs? If I believe I'm right, and you believe you're right, we can take advantage of this difference in beliefs. We may both agree to have an impartial arbitrator settle the issue, each confident of victory. If two factions of the union leadership cannot agree on a certain wage proposal, they can agree to submit the issue to a membership vote.

Different values placed on time? You may care more about the present while the other side cares more about the future. In the language of business, you discount future value at different rates. An installment plan works on this principle. The buyer is willing to pay a higher price for the car if he can pay later; the seller is willing to accept payment later if he gets a higher price.

Different forecasts? In a salary negotiation between an aging baseball star and a major league baseball team, the player may expect to win a lot of games while the team owner has the opposite expectation. Taking advantage of these different expectations, they can both agree on a base salary of $750,000 plus $500,000 if the player pitches so well that on average he permits less than three earned runs per game.

Differences in aversion to risk? One last kind of difference which you may capitalize on is aversion to risk. Take, for example, the issue of deep-seabed mining in the Law of the Sea negotiations. How much should the mining companies pay the international community for the privilege of mining? The mining companies care more about avoiding big losses than they do about making big gains. For them deep-seabed mining is a major investment. They want to reduce the risk. The international community, on the other hand, is concerned with revenue. If some company is going to make a lot of money out of "the common heritage of mankind," the rest of the world wants a generous share.

In this difference lies the potential for a bargain advantageous to both sides. Risk can be traded for revenue. Exploiting this difference in aversion to risk, the proposed treaty provides for charging the companies low rates until they recover their investment—in other words, while their risk is high—and much higher rates thereafter, when their risk is low.

Ask for their preferences. One way to dovetail interests is to invent several options all equally acceptable to you and ask the other side which one they prefer. You want to know what is preferable, not necessarily what is acceptable. You can then take that option, work with it some more, and again present two or more variants, asking which one they prefer. In this way, without anyone's making a decision, you can improve a plan until you can find no more joint gains. For example, the agent for the baseball star might ask the team owner: "What meets your interests better, a salary of $875,000 a year for four years, or $1,000,000 a year for three years? The latter? OK, how about between that and $900,000 a year for three years with a $500,000 bonus in each year if Fernando pitches better than a 3.00 ERA?"

If dovetailing had to be summed up in one sentence, it would be: Look for items that are of low cost to you and high benefit to them, and vice versa. Differences in interests, priorities, beliefs, forecasts, and attitudes toward risk all make dovetailing possible. A negotiator's motto could be *"Vive la différence!"*

Make Their Decision Easy

Since success for you in a negotiation depends upon the other side's making a decision you want, you should do what you can to make that decision an easy one. Rather than make things difficult for the other side, you want to confront them with a choice that is as painless as possible. Impressed with the merits of their own case, people usually pay too little attention to ways of advancing their case by taking care of interests on the other side. To overcome the shortsightedness that results from looking too narrowly at one's immediate self-interest, you will want to put yourself in their shoes. Without some option that appeals to them, there is likely to be no agreement at all.

Whose shoes? Are you trying to influence a single negotiator, an absent boss, or some committee or other collective decision-making body? You cannot negotiate successfully with an abstraction like "Houston" or "the University of California." Instead of trying to persuade "the insurance company" to make a decision, it is wiser to focus your efforts on getting one claims agent to make a recommendation. However complex the other side's decisional process may seem, you will understand it better if you pick one person—probably the person with whom you are dealing—and see how the problem looks from his or her point of view.

By focusing on one person you are not ignoring complexities. Rather, you are handling them by understanding how they impinge on the person with whom you are negotiating. You may come to appreciate your negotiating role in a new light, and see your job, for example, as strength-ening that person's hand or giving her arguments that she will need to persuade others to go along. One British ambassador described his job as "helping my opposite number get new instructions." If you place yourself firmly in the shoes of your opposite number, you will understand his problem and what kind of options might solve it.

What decision? In Chapter 2 we discussed how one can understand the other side's interests by analyzing their currently perceived choice. Now you are trying to generate options that will so change their choice that they might then decide in a way satisfactory to you. Your task is to give them not a problem but an answer, to give them not a tough decision but an easy one. It is crucial in that process to focus your attention on the content of the decision itself. That decision is often impeded by uncertainty.

Frequently you want as much as you can get, but you yourself do not know how much that is. You are likely to say, in effect, "Come up with something, and I will tell you if it is enough." That may seem reasonable to you, but when you look at it from the other's point of view, you will understand the need to invent a more appealing request. For whatever they do or say, you are likely to consider that merely a floor—and ask for more. Requesting the other side to be "more forthcoming" will probably not produce a decision you want.

Many negotiators are uncertain whether they are asking for words or for performance. Yet the distinction is critical. If it is performance you want, do not add something for "negotiating room." If you want a horse to jump a fence, don't raise the fence. If you want to sell a soft drink from a vending machine for seventy-five cents, don't mark the price at a dollar to give yourself room to negotiate.

Most of the time you will want a promise—an agreement. Take a pencil and paper in hand and try drafting a few possible agreements. It is never too early in a negotiation to start drafting as an aid to clear thinking. Prepare multiple versions, starting with the simplest possible. What are some terms that the other party could sign, terms that would be attractive to them as well as to you? Can you reduce the number of people whose approval would be required? Can you formulate an agreement that will be easy for them to implement? The other side will take into account difficulties in carrying out an agreement; you should too.

It is usually easier, for example, to refrain from doing something not being done than to stop action already underway. And it is easier to cease doing something than to undertake an entirely new course of action. If workers want music on the job, it will be easier for the company to agree not to interfere for a few weeks with an experimental employee-run program of playing tapes than for the company to agree to run such a program.

Because most people are strongly influenced by their notions of legitimacy, one effective way to develop solutions easy for the other side to accept is to shape them so that they will appear legitimate. The other side is more likely to accept a solution if it seems the right thing to do—right in terms of being fair, legal, honorable, and so forth.

Few things facilitate a decision as much as precedent. Search for it. Look for a decision or statement that the other side may have made in a similar situation, and try to base a proposed agreement on it. This provides an objective standard for your request and makes it easier for them to go along. Recognizing their probable desire to be consistent, and thinking about what they have done or said, will help you generate options acceptable to you that also take their point of view into account.

Making threats is not enough. In addition to the content of the decision you would like them to make, you will want to consider from their point of view the consequences of following that decision. If you were they, what results would you most fear? What would you hope for?

We often try to influence others by threats and warnings of what will happen if they do not decide as we would like. Offers are usually more effective. Concentrate both on making them aware of the consequences they can expect if they do decide as you wish and on improving those consequences from their point of view. How can you make your offers more credible? What are some specific things that they might like? Would they like to be given credit for having made the final proposal? Would they like to make the announcement? What can you invent that might be attractive to them but low in cost to yourself?

To evaluate an option from the other side's point of view, consider how they might be criticized if they adopted it. Write out a sentence or two illustrating what the other side's most powerful critic might say about the decision you are thinking of asking for. Then write out a couple of sentences with which the other side might reply in defense. Such an exercise will help you appreciate the restraints within which the other side is negotiating. It should help you generate options that will adequately meet their interests so that they can make a decision that meets yours.

A final test of an option is to write it out in the form of a "yesable proposition." Try to draft a proposal to which their responding with the single word "yes" would be sufficient, realistic, and operational. When you can do so, you have reduced the risk that your immediate self-interest has blinded you to the necessity of meeting concerns of the other side.

In a complex situation, creative inventing is an absolute necessity. In any negotiation it may open doors and produce a range of potential agreements satisfactory to each side. Therefore, generate many options before selecting among them. Invent first; decide later. Look for shared interests and differing interests to dovetail. And seek to make their decision easy.

Members of SIMSOC confront problems of scarcity, social protest, power struggles, and the like. They have an unusual opportunity to create a different kind of society. Yet most societies that actually emerge in the course of the game are beset with many of the same problems that characterize existing societies. The creation of a new and better society is no simple task, especially when participants begin with a situation as fraught with difficulty as the one SIMSOC provides.

The readings in this section give some perspective on the difficulties of the task involved. Handy suggests that one important step is a change in the way we think about public corporations. He urges us to think of corporations not as property but as a community created by common purpose. The core members of communities are citizens rather than employees or "human resources." The selection by Slater focuses on some of the dilemmas of American society and culture. He examines the challenge which the "counterculture," with its communal values, presents to the dominant culture, with its emphasis on individual success. He is strongly critical of the old culture and sympathetic to the new. But his sympathy does not prevent him from recognizing and anticipating many of the emerging problems and tensions which the new culture has yet to confront successfully.

The selection by Putnam introduces the idea of *social capital*—aspects of social organization such as networks, norms, and social trust that facilitate coordination and cooperation for mutual benefit. Putnam reviews evidence suggesting that social capital has declined in America during the past 25 years. The final selection by Lemann builds on the idea of social capital. He raises questions about whether it has in fact declined and argues for the continuing role of government in helping to stimulate its creation and to supply the necessary support where it is lacking.

The Citizen Corporation

by Charles Handy

"Language is the dress of thought," said Samuel Johnson 200 years ago. The way we talk colors the way we think, and the way we think shapes the way we act. We are the unconscious prisoners of our language. While most of the time this constraint matters little, at times of momentous change in culture or society, our use of old words to describe new things can hide the emerging future from our eyes.

The old language of property and ownership no longer serves us in modern society because it no longer describes what a company really is. The old language suggests the wrong priorities, leads to inappropriate policies, and screens out new possibilities. The idea of a corporation as the property of the current holders of its shares is confusing because it does not make clear where power lies. As

such, the notion is an affront to natural justice because it gives inadequate recognition to the people who work in the corporation and who are, increasingly, its principal assets. To talk of owning other people, as shareholders implicitly do, might even be considered immoral. Moreover, the language of property and ownership is an insult to democracy. One of the great paradoxes of our time is that it is totalitarian, centrally planned organizations, owned by outsiders, that are providing the material wherewithal of the great democracies. Free people do not relish being the instruments of others. The best of them will, increasingly, either

This selection by Charles Handy is reprinted with permission from the HARVARD BUSINESS REVIEW 75 (Sept.–Oct., 1997).

Charles Handy is a former oil company executive turned writer and social commentator.

refuse to join such institutions or demand a high price for the sacrifice of their rights.

We need a new language to release our thinking, and I suggest that it be the language of polity. A public corporation should now be regarded not as a piece of property but as a community—although a community created by common purpose rather than by common place. No one owns a community. Communities, as democracies know them, have constitutions that recognize the rights of their different constituencies and that lay down the methods of governance. The core members of communities are more properly regarded as citizens rather than as employees or "human resources"—citizens with responsibilities as well as rights. Even where organizational entities such as the Internet have already taken on new forms—which may be models for the future—we lack the language to describe them. No one "owns" the Internet. It is indeed a community of common purpose, which serves its constituencies and is supported by them.

The corporation is changing, but it is still spoken of as if it were a licensed, self-appointed oligopoly, dominated, in the Anglo-Saxon world, by the pressures of the stock market. Yet the research on long-lasting and successful organizations (see "The Living Company," by Arie de Geus, HBR March-April 1997) suggest that what enables a corporation to succeed in the longer term is a wish for immortality, or at least a long life; a consistent set of values based on an awareness of the organization's own identity; a willingness to change; and a passionate concern for developing the capacity and self-confidence of its core inhabitants,

whom the company values more than its physical assets. I suggest that those conditions are best met when organizations live up to the literal meaning of the word company—"the sharing of bread"—and regard themselves as communities, not property.

What difference would it make if we were to regard corporations as communities, as sovereign states within states? The key difference is that a community is something to which one belongs, while it, in turn, belongs to no one. This inversion of the property concept has implications for the way in which the community is governed. It requires a clearer definition of the bond between individual and organization—something that could be called the citizen contract—as well as of the relationships with the other stakeholders, particularly the providers of capital, who must receive their due rewards. Last, the culture and the purpose of the community have to pervade the organization.

In time, a new theory of the corporation will develop. Profits are the lifeblood of any business, but life consists of more than keeping the blood flowing; otherwise, it would not be worth living. As more corporations realize this truth, they will become increasingly interested in enriching the lives of the people who work in them. In time, the laws governing corporations will change to reflect the new reality. First, however, we need a language to explain this new theory—a language of community and citizenship, not of property. As Ludwig Wittgenstein said, "Words enable deeds."

The Pursuit of Loneliness

Philip E. Slater

Societies are more complex than individuals, and have more available outlets for unacceptable impulses. Still, the pressures remain, and often build up to a pitch of intense distress. Whether today's pressures could lead to a cultural flip-flop or not I cannot say, but I would like to suggest three human desires that are deeply and uniquely frustrated by American culture:

1. The desire for *community*—the wish to live in trust, cooperation, and friendship with those around one.
2. The desire for *engagement*—the wish to come directly to grips with one's social and physical environment.
3. The desire for *dependence*—the wish to share responsibility for the control of one's impulses and the direction of one's life.

When I say that these three desires are frustrated by American culture, I don't want to conjure up romantic images of the individual struggling against society. In each case we participate eagerly in producing the frustration we endure—it isn't merely something done to us. For each of these desires is subordinate to its opposite in the American character. The thesis of this chapter is that Americans have voluntarily created, and voluntarily maintain, a society that increasingly frustrates and aggravates these secondary

This reading is reprinted from Philip E. Slater, THE PURSUIT OF LONELINESS: AMERICAN CULTURE AT THE BREAKING POINT *(Boston: Beacon Press, Revised Edition, 1976), pp. 8–14, 108–110, 112–114, 116–120, 123–120, 157–160, and 164–167. Copyright © 1970, 1976, by Philip E. Slater. Reprinted by permission of Beacon Press.*

Philip E. Slater is a sociologist and free-lance writer.

yearnings to the point where they threaten to become primary. Groups that in any way personify this threat have always been feared in an exaggerated way, and always will be until Americans are able to recognize and accept those needs within themselves.

I. COMMUNITY AND COMPETITION: GETTING TOGETHER

We are so used to living in an individualistic society that we need to be reminded that collectivism has been the more usual lot of humans. Most people in most societies have lived and died in stable communities that took for granted the subordination of the individual to the welfare of the group. The aggrandizement of the individual at the expense of his neighbors was simply a crime.

This is not to say that competition is an American invention—all societies involve some mixture of cooperative and competitive institutions. But our society lies near the competitive extreme, and although it contains cooperative institutions, we suffer from their weakness and peripherality. Studies of business executives reveal a deep hunger for an atmosphere of trust and fraternity with their colleagues. The competitive life is a lonely one and its satisfactions short-lived, for each race leads only to a new one.

In the past our society had many oases in which one could take refuge from the frenzied invidiousness of our economic system—institutions such as the extended family and the stable local neighborhood in which people could take pleasure from something other than winning symbolic victories over their neighbors. But these have disappeared one by one, leaving us more and more in a situation in which we must try to satisfy our vanity and our needs for intimacy in the same place and at the same time. This has made the appeal of cooperative living more seductive, and the need to suppress our longing for it more acute.

The main vehicle for the expression of this longing has been the mass media. Popular songs and film comedies for fifty years have been engaged in a sentimental rejection of our dominant mores, maintaining that the best things in life are free, that love is more important than success, that keeping up with the Joneses is futile, that personal integrity should take precedence over winning, and so on. But these protestations must be understood for what they are: a safety valve. The same man who chuckles and sentimentalizes over a happy-go-lucky hero in a film would view his real-life counterpart as frivolous and irresponsible, and suburbanites who philosophized over the back fence with complete sincerity about their "dog-eat-dog-world," and what-is-it-all-for, and you-can't-take-it-with-you, and success-doesn't-make-you-happy-it-just-gives-you-ulcers-and-a-heart-condition, were enraged in the sixties when their children began to pay serious attention to these ideas. To the young this seemed hypocritical, but if adults didn't feel these things they wouldn't have had to fight them so vigorously. The exaggerated hostility that young people aroused in the "flower child" era argues that the life they led was highly seductive to middle-aged Americans.

When a value is strongly held, as individualism is in America, the illnesses it produces tend to be treated in the same way an alcoholic treats a hangover or a drug addict his withdrawal symptoms. Technological change, mobility, and individualistic ways of thinking all rupture the bonds that tie a man to a family, a community, a kinship network, a geographical location—bonds that give him a comfortable sense of himself. As this sense of himself erodes, he seeks ways of affirming it. Yet his efforts accelerate the very erosion he seeks to halt.

This loss of a sense of oneself, a sense of one's place in the scheme of things, produces a jungle of competing egos, each trying to *create* a place. Huge corporations are fueled on this energy—the stockholders trying to buy place with wealth, executives trying to grasp it through power and prestige, public relations departments and advertisers trying to persuade people that the corporation can confer a sense of place to those who believe in it or buy its products.

Americans love bigness, mostly because they feel so small. They feel small because they're unconnected, without a place. They try to overcome that smallness by associating themselves with bigness—big projects, big organizations, big government, mass markets, mass media, "nationwide," "worldwide." But it's that very same bigness that rips away their sense of connectedness and place and makes them feel small. A vicious circle.

Notice the names of corporations: "Universal," "Continental," "International," "General," "National," "Trans-World"—the spirit of grandiosity and ego-inflation pervades our economic life. Corporations exist not to feed or supply the people, but to appease their own hungry egos. Advertising pays scant attention to price or quality and leans heavily on our needs for acceptance and respect. The economic structure of our society continually frustrates those needs, creating an artificial scarcity that in turn motivates the entire economy. This is why the quality of life in America is so unsatisfying. Since our economy is built on inflated vanity, rather than being grounded in the real material needs of the people, it must eventually collapse, when these illusions can no longer be maintained.

Much of the unpleasantness, abrasiveness, and costliness of American life comes from the fact that we're always dealing with strangers. This is what bureaucracy is: a mechanism for carrying on transactions between strangers. Who would need all those offices, all that paperwork, all those lawyers, contracts, rules and regulations, if all economic transactions took place between lifelong neighbors? A huge and tedious machinery has evolved to cope with the fact that we prefer to carry on our activities among strangers. The preference is justified, as are most of the sicknesses in American society, by the alleged economic benefits of bigness, but like many economic arguments, it's a con.

On the surface, it seems convincing. Any big company can undersell a little one. Corporations keep getting bigger and bigger and fewer and fewer. Doesn't that prove it? Survival of the fittest? Yet for some reason, what should be providing economic benefits to the consumer has in fact produced nothing but chronic inflation. If bigness lowers the cost of production, why does everything cost more and break sooner? Management, of course, blames it on labor, and each industry cites the rising prices of its own suppliers. Isn't it obvious that a few big nationwide companies can produce things cheaper than many local ones?

It all depends on what you leave out of your analysis (which is why a chimp pressing buttons randomly could predict as well as our economic forecasters). The fewer the companies, the less influence supply and demand have on prices. A heavy investment in advertising and public relations is necessary to keep a national reputation alive. And what about the transportation costs involved when all firms are national? Not to mention the air pollution costs, which are also passed on to the consumer. Chronic inflation suggests that someone is leaving something vital out of his analysis. How does one measure in dollars the cost of economic mistrust? It may be subtle, but it's clearly enormous.

The Great Illusion

It's easy to produce examples of the many ways in which Americans try to minimize, circumvent, or deny the interdependence upon which all human societies are based. We seek a private house, a private laundry, self-service stores, and do-it-yourself skills of every kind. An enormous technology seems to have set itself the task of making it unnecessary for one human being ever to ask anything of another in the course of going about his or her daily business. Even within the family Americans are unique in their feeling that each member should have a separate room, and even a separate telephone, television, and car, when economically possible. We seek more and more privacy, and feel more and more alienated and lonely when we get it. And what accidental contacts we do have seem more intrusive, not only because they're unsought, but because they're not connected with any familiar pattern of interdependence.

Most important, our encounters with others tend increasingly to be competitive as we search for more privacy. We less and less often meet our fellow humans to share and exchange, and more and more often encounter them as an impediment or a nuisance: making the highway crowded when we're rushing somewhere, cluttering and littering the beach or park or wood, pushing in front of us at the supermarket, taking the last parking place, polluting our air and water, building a highway through our house, blocking our view, and so on. Because we've cut off so much communication with each other we keep bumping into each other, so that a higher and higher percentage of our interpersonal contacts are abrasive.

We seem unable to foresee that the gratification of a wish might turn out to be a monkey's paw if the wish were shared by many others. We cheer the new road that shaves ten minutes off the drive to our country retreat but ultimately transforms it into a crowded resort and increases both the traffic and the time. We're continually surprised to find, when we want something, that thousands or millions of others want it, too—that other human beings get hot in summer and cold in winter. The worst traffic jams occur when a mass of vacationing tourists start home early to "beat the traffic." We're too enamored of the individualistic fantasy that everyone is, or should be, different—that a man could somehow build his entire life around some single eccentricity without boring himself and everyone else to death. We all have our quirks, which provide surface variety, but aside from this, human beings have little basis for their persistent claim that they are not all members of the same species.

∘ ∘ ∘

The Two Cultures

A culture is largely a symbolic thing—a set of values, ways of behaving, ways of looking at the world, ideas, beliefs, designs. It is not a collection of people. (The word "counterculture," however, was often used to refer to collections of people—students, New Left radicals, communards, flower people, and so on, which is why I put it in quotation marks.) When I talk about two cultures in the United States, then I'm not referring to warring groups of people, but rather to colliding idea systems. Each system is more or less consistent within itself. Each is based on a set of assumptions and has an internal logic that hangs together as long as those assumptions hold. Hence both are valid, although they are diametrically opposite and cannot be combined.

The basic assumption of the old culture is that human gratification is in short supply; the new culture assumes that it is plentiful. Like all basic assumptions, they're both self-validating—that is, whichever one you believe and act on tends to be true.

Based on these assumptions, the old culture tends to choose property rights over personal rights, technological requirements over human needs, competition over cooperation, violence over sexuality, concentration over distribution, producers over consumers, means over ends, secrecy over openness, social forms over personal expression, striving over gratification, Oedipal love over communal love, and so on. The new culture tends to reverse all these priorities.

Now it's important to realize that these differences can't be resolved by some sort of compromise. Every cultural system is a dynamic whole, and change must affect the motivational roots of a society or it isn't change at all. If you introduce some isolated new element into such a system, it will either be redefined and absorbed if the culture is strong, or will have a disorganizing effect if the culture is weak. As Margaret Mead points out, to introduce cloth garments into a grass-clad population without simultaneously introducing closets, soap, sewing, and furniture, merely transforms a neat and attractive tribe into a dirty and slovenly one. Cloth is part of a complex cultural pattern that includes storing, cleaning, mending, and protecting—just as the automobile is part of a system that includes fueling, maintenance, and repair. You can't just graft lungs onto a shark and expect it to survive out of water.

∘ ∘ ∘

Core Beliefs

Thus it's important to know the motivational foundations of the old and the new cultures, for a prolonged head-on collision would nullify both of them, like bright pigments combining into gray. The transition must be as deft as possible if we're to minimize the destructive chaos that accompanies major cultural transformations. There must be room for them to exist side by side while the energy is gradually siphoned from one to the other. The complexity and richness of our society lends itself to this, and it's happening today in a small but significant way.

The core of the old culture is scarcity. Everything in it rests on the assumption that the world does not contain the wherewithal to satisfy the needs of its human inhabitants. From this it follows that people must compete with one another for these scarce resources—lie, swindle, steal, and kill, if necessary. These basic assumptions, however, create the danger of a "war of all against all" and must be qualified by moral commandments that will mute and restrain the intensity of the struggle. Those who can take the largest share of the scarce resources are said to be successful, and if they can do it without violating the moral commandments, they are said to have character and moral fibre.

The key flaw in the old culture is that so much of its scarcity is spurious—that it creates most of the needs it fails to satisfy and often deliberately frustrates others. We suffer from an energy shortage, for example, because we've learned to "need" cars, the presence of which frustrates our more basic needs for community stability, closeness, warmth, and physical contact. Even world hunger is to a considerable extent man-made, by maldistribution of food, overpopulation, and dependence on agriculture, which in turn comes from human anxiety to create food surpluses. Malnutrition and famine are less common in hunter-gatherer societies, for example, than in agricultural ones. During severe droughts agricultural peoples sometimes have to turn to their "poor" neighbors in order to survive. Since they have few wants, many "poor" hunter-gatherers feel rich indeed.

Most scarcity in our own society exists for the purpose of maintaining the system that depends upon it. Americans are often in the position of having killed someone to avoiding sharing a meal which turns out to be too large to eat alone.

The new culture is based on the assumption that important human needs are easily satisfied and that the resources for doing so are plentiful. Competition is unnecessary, and the only danger to humans is human aggression.

There is no reason outside of human perversity for peace not to reign and for life not to be spent in joy and the cultivation of beauty. Those who can do this in the face of the old culture's ubiquity are considered "beautiful."

The flaw in the new culture is the fact that the old culture has succeeded in making real the scarcity it believes in—that a certain amount of work will be needed to release all this bounty from the restraints under which it is now placed. A man may learn that his nearsightedness is "all psychological" and still need his glasses to see. And should our transportation system break down, New York City will starve to death, despite the abundance of food around the nation.

It's important to recognize the internal logic of the old culture, however faulty its premise. If you assume scarcity, then the knowledge that others want what you want leads with some logic to preparations for defense, and ultimately (since the best defense is offense) for attack. The same assumption leads people to place a high value on the ability to postpone gratification (since there's not enough to go around). The expression of feelings is a luxury, since this might alert the scarce gratifications to the fact that a hunter is near.

∘ ∘ ∘

Inequality

Another logical consequence of scarcity is structured inequality. If there isn't enough to go around, then those who have more will find ways to prolong their advantage, and even try to legitimize it. The law itself, although equalitarian in theory, is in large part a social device for maintaining structured inequality—keeping the rich rich and the poor poor. One of the major thrusts of the new culture, on the other hand, is equality: since the good things of life are plentiful, everyone should share them—rich and poor, black and white, female and male.

In the old culture, means habitually become ends, and ends means. Instead of people working to obtain goods in order to be happy, for example, we find that people should be made happy in order to work better in order to obtain more goods. Inequality, originally a result of scarcity, is now a means of *creating* it. And for the old culture, the manufacture of scarcity is paramount, as hostile comments toward new-culture customs ("people won't want to work if they can get things for nothing") reveal. Scarcity, the supposedly unfortunate but unavoidable foundation for the whole system, has now become its most treasured and sacred resource, and in order to maintain this resource in the midst of plenty, it has been necessary to make invidiousness the foremost criterion of worth. Old-culture Americans are peculiarly drawn to anything that seems to be the exclusive possession of some group or other, and they find it difficult to enjoy anything unless they can be sure that there are people to whom this pleasure is denied. For those in power, life itself derives value invidiously. Numbed by their busy lives, many officials gain reassurance of their vitality from their proximity to blowing up the world.

Invidiousness also provides a *raison d'être* for the advertising industry, whose primary function is to manufacture illusions of scarcity. In a society engorged to the point of strangulation with useless and joyless products, advertisements show people calamitously running out of their food or beer, avidly hoarding potato chips, stealing each other's cigarettes, guiltily borrowing each other's deodorants, and so on. In a land of plenty there should be little to fight over, but in the world of advertising, men and women will fight before changing their brand, in a kind of parody of the Vietnam war.

The fact that property takes precedence over human life in the old culture also follows logically from scarcity assumptions. Since possessions are "scarce" relative to people (in the sense that there are always some people who don't own a given form of property), they come to have more value than people. This is especially true of people with few possessions, who come to be considered so worthless as to be sub-human and eligible for extermination. Having many possessions, on the other hand, entitles the owner to a status somewhat more affluent, these priorities begin to change—human life increases in value and property decreases. Yet it's still permissible to kill someone who's stealing your property under certain conditions—especially if that person is without property himself. Thus although the death of a wealthy kleptomaniac, killed while stealing, would probably be thought worthy of a murder trial, that of a poor black looter would not. Noise control provides another example: Police are called to prevent distraction by the joyous noises of laughter and song, but not to stop the harsh and abrasive roar of power saws, air hammers, power mowers, snow blowers, and other baneful machines.

Old Loves New, New Loves Old

It would be easy to show how various aspects of the new culture derive from the premise that life's satisfactions exist in abundance and sufficiency for all, but I would like to look instead at the relationship the new culture bears to the old—the continuities and discontinuities it offers.

To begin with, the new culture takes the position that instead of throwing away your body in order to accumulate possessions, you should throw away the possessions and enjoy your body. This is based on the idea that possessions actually create scarcity. The more emotion you invest in them, the more chances for real gratification are lost—the more committed to them you get, the more deprived you feel, like a thirsty man drinking salt water. To accumulate possessions is to deliver pieces of yourself to dead things. Possessions can absorb emotion, but unlike people, they feel nothing back. Americans have combined love of possessions with the disruption and trivialization of most personal relationships. An alcoholic becomes malnourished because drinking obliterates his hunger; Americans be-

come alienated because amassing possessions obliterates their loneliness. This is why manufacturing in the United States has always seemed to be on an endless upward spiral: every time we buy something we deepen our emotional deprivation, and hence our need to buy something. This is good for business, of course, but those who profit from it are just as trapped as everyone else. The new culture seeks to substitute an adequate emotional diet for this crippling addiction.

Yet the new culture is a product of the old, not just a rejection of it. It picks up themes that are dormant or secondary in the old culture and magnifies them. It's full of nostalgia—nostalgia for the Old West, Amerindian culture, the wilderness, the simple life, the utopian community—all venerable American traditions. But for the old culture they represent a minor aspect of the culture, appropriate for recreational occasions for fantasy—a kind of pastoral relief from everyday striving—whereas for the new culture they're dominant themes. The new culture's passion for memorabilia, paradoxically, causes uneasiness in old-culture adherents, whose striving leads them to sever themselves from the past. Yet for the most part the new culture is simply making the old culture's secondary themes primary, rather than just discarding the old culture's primary theme. Even the notion of "dropping out" is an important American tradition—neither the United States itself nor its populous suburbs would exist were this not so.

Americans have always been deeply ambivalent about social involvement. On the one hand they're suspicious of it, and share romantic dreams of running off to live in the woods. On the other hand they're much given to acting out grandiose fantasies of taking society by storm through the achievement of wealth, power, or fame. This ambivalence has led to many strange institutions—the suburb and the automobile being the most obvious. But note that both fantasies take the viewpoint of an outsider. Americans have a profound tendency to feel like outsiders—they wonder where the action is and wander about in search of it (this puts a great burden on celebrities, who are supposed to know, but in fact feel just as doubtful as everyone else). Americans have created a society in which they are automatic nobodies, since no one has any stable place or enduring connection. The village idiot of earlier times was less a "nobody" in this sense than the mobile junior executive or academic. An American has to "make a place for himself" because he does not have one.

Since our society rests on scarcity assumptions, involvement in it has always meant competition, while oddly enough, the idea of a cooperative, communal life has always been associated with bucolic withdrawal. So consistently have cooperative communities established themselves in the wilderness, we can only infer that society as we know it makes cooperative life impossible.

It's important to remember that the New England colonies grew out of utopian communes, so that the drop-out tradition is not only old but extremely important to our history. Like so many of the more successful nineteenth century communities (Oneida and Amana, for example), the puritans became corrupted by economic success until the communal aspect eroded away—another example of a system being destroyed by what it tries to ignore. The new culture is thus a kind of reform movement, trying to revive a decayed tradition once important to our civilization.

∘ ∘ ∘

SPLITS IN THE NEW CULTURE

1. Inner and Outer

Up to this point we have rather awkwardly discussed the new culture as if it were integrated and monolithic, which it certainly is not. There are many contradictory streams feeding the new culture, and some of these deserve particular attention since they provide the raw material for future conflict.

The most important split in the new culture is that which divides outward, political change from internal, psychological transformation. The first requires confrontation, revolutionary action, and radical commitment to changing the structure of modern industrial society. The second involves a renunciation of that society in favor of the cultivation of inner experience, psychic balance, or enlightenment. Heightening sensory receptivity, committing oneself to the here-and-now, and attuning oneself to the physical environment are also sought, since in the old culture immediate experience is overlooked or grayed out by the preoccupation with utility and mastery.

Since political activism is task-oriented, it partakes of certain old-culture traits: postponement of gratification, preoccupation with power, and so on. To seek political change is to live in the future, to be absorbed in means, in achievement. Psychological change can be sought in the same way, of course—you can make anything into a task—but to do so is to treat yourself as an object to be manipulated. No significant psychological change can occur if the change is sought as a means to some other end. The change must be an end in itself. True psychological change then, whether we call it "sensory awakening," "enlightenment," "mental health," or just "getting your shit together," is a "salvation now" approach. Thus it's more radical, since it's uncontaminated with old-culture values. It's also less realistic, since it ignores the fact that the status quo provides a totally antagonistic milieu in which the psychological changes will be undermined. The "flower children" of the sixties, for example, tried to survive in a state of highly vulnerable parasitic dependence, and were severely victimized by the old culture. They had no social base of their own and evaporated at the first sign of trouble. Yet, on the other hand, an attempt at political change based on old-culture premises is lost before it's begun, for even if its authors are victorious, they will have been corrupted by the process of winning.

The dilemma is a real one wherever radical change is sought. For every society tries to exercise rigid control over the mechanisms by which it can be altered—defining some as legitimate and others as criminal or disloyal. When we look at the characteristics of these mechanisms, however, we find that the "legitimate" ones require a sustained commitment to the core assumptions of the culture. In other words, if a person follows the "legitimate" pathway, there's a very good chance that her initial radical intent will be eroded in the process. If she feels that some fundamental change in the system is required, then she has a choice between following a path that subverts her goal or one that leads to some form of victimization.

This isn't a Machiavellian invention of American capitalism, but simply the way all viable societies protect themselves from instability. When the society is no longer viable, however, this technique must be exposed for the swindle that it is; otherwise the needed radical changes will be rendered ineffectual.

The key to the technique is the powerful human reluctance to admit that an achieved goal was not worth the unpleasant experience required to achieve it. This is the principle on which initiation rituals are based: "If I had to suffer so much pain and humiliation to get into this club, it must be a wonderful group." The evidence of thousands of years is that the mechanism works extremely well. Most professionals are reluctant to admit that their graduate training was boring, trivial, nitpicking, or irrelevant, as so much of it is, and up to some point war leaders can count on high casualties to increase popular commitment to military adventures.

So when a political leader says to a radical, "Why don't you run for political office and try to change the system from within," or the teacher says to the student, "Wait until you have your Ph.D. and then you can criticize our program," they're dealing a stacked deck, in that the protester, if she accepts the condition, will in most cases be converted to her opponent's point of view rather than admit to having worked, struggled, and suffered pointlessly.

The dilemma of the radical, then, is that she is likely to be corrupted if she fights the *status quo* on its own terms, but is not permitted to fight it in any other way. And even if she succeeds in solving this dilemma, after a lifetime spent altering the power structure, won't she become old-culture—utilitarian, invidious, scarcity-oriented, future-centered, and so on? Having made the world safe for the enlightened, can she afford to relinquish it to them?

There is no way to resolve this dilemma and, indeed, it's better left unresolved. Political change requires discipline and unity of purpose, which lead to all kinds of abuses when the goal is won. Discipline and unity become ends in themselves (the usual old-culture pattern) and any victory becomes an empty one. It's important to have someone living out the goals of any political change even before it's achieved, so that the new political condition can be compared to a living reality, however small and insignificant, instead of just to some visionary fantasy.

The new culture is amorphous, and since it no longer

has any significant spokespersons to give it a false air of purpose and unity, almost anything we can say about it is arguable. Millions of Americans are trying to break old-culture habits, but for every one they break a dozen are reinforced. The new culture is very divided about violence, for example: in the sixties nonviolence seemed to be a central tenet, to the point where assertiveness and anger were in danger of being crossed off the list of allowable human traits; but the violence of the establishment finally converted many dedicated pacifists to terrorism.

2. Technology

Technology is another point of division. The new culture tends to be suspicious of technology as a whole, but everyone has his favorite exception when it gets down to cases. Any large-scale assault on technology would produce a host of defenders even from within the attacking armies—each rushing to place some prized possession on the endangered appliance list. Most nature lovers, who dream of living peacefully in the wilderness after all the nasty bulldozers and jets and factories have been magically whisked away, fail to notice that their fantasy includes a stereo or a blender or a Ferrari. Americans are hopelessly enmeshed in equipment and won't escape it in the lifetime of anyone now living. Some people take almost as much equipment camping as they have in their homes; it's just more expensive and lighter weight.

Other new-culture types are more sophisticated and attack only mechanical technology, exempting all that's electronic from their ire. Even though it disrupts the environment just as badly, they argue, it doesn't create bad habits of thought: being circuitry, it reminds people of their interconnectedness and of the importance of feedback. The electronic buffs like to demonstrate how video equipment, for example, can connect people who wouldn't otherwise be connected. So far I'm unmoved by these demonstrations, which always remind me of two kids rigging up toy telephones so they can talk to each other across the room without shouting. They also talk of the marvels of videotape, where one can see oneself and alter one's behavior without the embarrassment of getting feedback directly from other people. But I'm a little suspicious of solipsistic learning. The more you can control your environment, the less you can learn from it. A videotape, like an audiotape, is just a better mirror, and insofar as mirrors are bad for us, videotape is worse. Anything that offers to take risk out of the environment is a bad bargain, since it always costs too much and puts as much risk in it as it takes out.

3. Individualism

But the most important ideological confusion in the new culture has to do with individualism and collectivism. On this question the new culture talks out of both sides of its mouth, one moment pitting ideals of cooperation and community against old-culture competitiveness, the next moment espousing the old culture in its most extreme form with exhortations to "do your own thing." New-culture enterprises often collapse because of a dogmatic unwillingness to subordinate the whim of the individual to the needs of the group. This problem is rarely faced honestly by new-culture people, who seem unaware of the conservatism involved in their attachment to individualistic principles.

This is one reason why the new culture cannot be left entirely in the hands of the young and still prevail. Despite all attempts to reverse direction, our society is still moving away from the instinctive sense of community that villagers had in the past—still moving with dizzying speed toward greater anonymity, impersonality, and disconnectedness. By and large, the younger a person is, the less likely he or she is to have any instinctive communal responses left. Once gone, they're very difficult to re-create. Older people, on the other hand, still retain some vestigial ability to care what happens to a group or community, and this is a valuable resource for those seeking a more communal society.

The loss of communal skills in the young isn't all a result of mobility and transience. Spockian child-rearing, in the anxious form in which it was frequently carried out, often encouraged narcissism and insensitivity in its products, and this was profoundly reinforced by television. For when people created their own amusements, they were very much aware that a good time was something that happened when people *did* something—that your enjoyment was a product of the energy you invested—that it combined with other people's energy and accumulated and produced something new. In other words, when you create your own fun, you realize that you only get pleasure when you commit your whole being to a situation. Television teaches a different viewpoint. Those brought up on it often show an irritating passivity in communal situations. They want the group to amuse them whether they put anything into it or not. Otherwise they continually threaten to withdraw. If the group doesn't please them, they switch the channel instead of redirecting the group with their own energy, of which they often have very little.

Because of this weakness, young people often find it difficult in their personal lives to avoid drifting into the same capitalistic behavior they scorn when they see it on a large scale. This is the weakest point in the new culture, for any social change feeds on youth, and young people are even more unsteady on this issue than their elders. Yet if individualism in the United States isn't sharply diminished, everything in the new culture will be perverted and caricatured into simply another bizarre old-culture product. There must be continuities between the old and the new, but not about something so basic to the whole conflict. Nothing will change in America until individualism is assigned a subordinate place in the American value system—for individualism lies at the core of the old culture, and individualism is not a viable foundation for any society in a nuclear age.

◦   ◦   ◦

CHANGE AND POWER

Americans have always thought that change could occur without pain. This pleasant idea springs from a confusion between change (the alteration of a pattern) and novelty (the rotation of stimuli within a pattern). Americans talk about social change as if it involved nothing more than rearranging the contents of a display window. But real change is difficult and painful, which perhaps explains why Americans have abandoned all responsibility for initiating it to technology and the rotation of generations.

Severe illness sometimes leads to great strengths, madness to inspiration, and decay to new growth. Building on its tortured history, the United States could become the center of the most beautiful and exciting culture the world has ever known. We have always been big, and have done things in big ways. Having lately become in many ways the worst of societies we could just as easily become the best. No society, after all, has ever solved the problems that now confront us. Potentiality has always been our most attractive characteristic, which is one reason we've always been so reluctant to commit ourselves to anything. But perhaps the time has come to make that commitment—to abandon our adolescent dreams of limitlessness and demonstrate that we can create some kind of palatable society. America is like a student who is proud of having survived school without serious work, and likes to imagine that if he really put any effort into it, he could achieve everything, but is unwilling to endanger so lovely a dream by making an actual commitment to a single project. Yet we have a great deal to work with. Our democratic institutions—tattered as they are—are a great resource, although we've been too caught up in individualistic dreams of glory to make much use of it. Despite our lack of community and our chronic flirtations with authoritarianism, no society of comparable size is as responsive to popular sentiment.

The fundamental political goal of the new culture is the diffusion of power, just as its basic economic goal is the diffusion of wealth. Marxists want to transfer concentrated power into the hands of revolutionaries first, in order to secure the diffusion of wealth. In the United States, however, the diffusion of wealth is a more easily attained goal than the diffusion of power, so that it becomes more important to ensure the latter, and to be skeptical of its postponement.

Media

Activists have often achieved some dispersion of power on a local scale merely by unmasking, exposing, or threatening to expose those at the centers of power. The ability to maintain a concentration of power depends upon the ability to maintain and enforce secrecy, and dispersal of power tends to follow automatically upon the breakdown of such secrecy. Old-culture leaders are peculiarly vulnerable on this point because they're not sensitive to the nature of mass media. They think in terms of news management

and press releases and public statements—of *controlling* the media in the old-fashioned propagandistic sense. Traditional Marxists share their views, and devote their energies to worrying about the fact that all news media are controlled by a relatively small number of wealthy and conservative men. New-culture activists, on the other hand, are attuned to the media. They know that *the media are inherently stimulus-hungry,* and must by their very nature seek exposure and drama. They know that a crowd is more interesting than a press conference, a march more interesting than a speech. Successful use of television today requires an improvisational looseness and informality that old-culture leaders lack. Their carefully managed statements become too obviously hollow with repetition, their pomposity too easily punctured by an awkward incident, their lies too recently stated and well-remembered to be ignored. It seems astonishing to us when statesmen and generals constantly put themselves in the position of saying, in effect, "Well, I lied to you before, but this time I'm telling the truth." But prior to television it was quite possible to assume that the mass of the population was substantially without memory.

I'm suggesting that the diffusion of power could occur with little change in the *formal* machinery of government which, after all, lends itself to a wide range of political types. Yet it can't be denied that at present the power of the executive is overwhelming and could in theory easily crush any dissident group. I say "in theory" because if all the other parts of the system are working properly, any such repression will automatically invalidate the presidency and bring it down.

° ° °

Individualism: The Midwife of Fascism

Mostly this has been stimulating to the democratic process, since it creates hope where there was cynicism and despair. Lest it also create complacency, however, I might point out that the temptation to give power away is very strong in Americans because of our individualistic heritage. We're always wanting to give power to leaders so we can do our own thing and not be bothered by the demands of collective commitment. This trend is most exaggerated in universities, where professors are always in a frenzy because some administrator has actually used the power they've abdicated to him. Individualism is so rampant in the university that meetings of any kind are peculiarly unbearable—a group of managers seems in warm and telepathic rapport by comparison. Academics as a group are so alienated from their feelings that they tend to invest them in every trivial procedural question rather than expressing them directly. This makes cooperation virtually impossible, and rather than put up with each other's posing and sermonizing any more than they already have to, they are seldom able to resist putting crucial power into the hands of administrators.

This is a violation of democracy's first rule: never delegate authority upward. It's a rule violated by liberals more than anyone else, since liberals are most uncomfortable with the demands of communal existence. Cooperation is so irksome to individualistic natures that they spend half their political lives giving power to centralized governments and the other half fearing for their personal liberties, without ever considering the contradiction.

I have said that it's important to diffuse power, to detach it from those who hate life and would rather die themselves than see others enjoying it. But this raises an awkward dilemma: in a satisfying society, who else would want power? What but a kind of sickness would drive people to attain such power over others? Wouldn't the sickest people wind up with the most power, even more regularly than they do now? If power is diffused, on the other hand, won't the entire population be corrupted by this sickness?

The answer to this last question is No. Nothing is poisonous if taken in small enough quantities, and the more power is diffused, the more the assumption of power looks like the assumption of responsibility. It's when power is concentrated that the pursuit of it takes on an unhealthy hue. One of the best arguments for participatory democracy is that the alternative to participating in the drudgery of government is being governed by the sick and perverse.

Evil is created by negation—to use the word is to extend its domain. When we reject some human trait, exile it, push it down, wall it up, and scorn it, it becomes malevolent, perverse, vicious. Those who refuse to dirty their hands by exercising power and responsibility for the coordination of community affairs often find themselves murdered in the night by those with dirty hands. Any trait that's harmless when accepted as part of the human condition assumes a poisonous concentration when it isn't. Anger becomes implacable malice, self-respect becomes vanity, the wish for a place becomes individualism, the desire for stability becomes reactionary conservatism, the need for order becomes tyranny, the need for coordination becomes witch-hunting.

One of the oldest and deepest myths in the American psyche is the fantasy of being special—a treat that American society promises, and withholds, more than any society in history. The unstated rider to "do your own thing" is that everybody will watch—that a special superiority will be granted and acknowledged by others. But in a satisfying society this specialness isn't needed, and a satisfying society rests on the recognition that people can and must make demands on one another. Any community worthy of the name—one in which the relationships between people are regulated by the people themselves instead of by machines—would probably seem "totalitarian" to today's youth, not in the sense of having authoritarian leadership, but in the sense of permitting a group intrusion into what most Americans consider private. We have long been accustomed to an illusory freedom based on subtle compulsion by technology and bureaucratic institutions. But there is no way for large numbers of people to co-exist without governing and being governed by one another unless they establish machines to do it, at which point they risk losing sight (and understanding) of their interconnections—a loss well advanced in our society today. There's something wildly comic about cars stopping and starting in response to a traffic light for example, but most Americans have lost the capacity to experience it. It seems right and natural for machines to tell us how to relate to each other.

The goal of many early Americans was to create a utopian community, but they became distracted by dreams of personal aggrandizement and found themselves farther and farther from this goal. When we think today of the kind of social compliance that exists in such communities (as well as in the primitive communities we romanticize so much), we shrink in horror. We tell each other chilling stories of people in imagined societies of the future being forced to give up their dreams for the good of the group, or of not being allowed to stand out. But this, in some degree, is just the price one must pay for a tolerable life in a tolerable community. We need to consider this price, to reflect both on its consequences and on the consequences of not paying it. Is an occasional group viciousness really worse than the unfocused universal snarl that has replaced it in our mechanically regulated society? It's the structured narcissism of the old culture that brings down on our heads the evils we detest, and we will only escape those evils when we have abandoned the narcissistic dreams that sustain them.

Bowling Alone: America's Declining Social Capital

Robert D. Putnam

Many students of the new democracies that have emerged over the past decade and a half have emphasized the importance of a strong and active civil society to the consolidation of democracy. Especially with regard to the postcommunist countries, scholars and democratic activists alike have lamented the absence or obliteration of traditions of independent civic engagement and a widespread tendency toward passive reliance on the state. To those concerned with the weakness of civil societies in the developing or postcommunist world, the advanced Western democracies and above all the United States have typically been taken as models to be emulated. There is striking evidence, however, that the vibrancy of American civil society has notably declined over the past several decades. Ever since the publication of Alexis de Tocqueville's *Democracy in America,* the United States has played a central role in systematic studies of the links between democracy and civil society. Although this is in part because trends in American life are often regarded as harbingers of social modernization, it is also because America has traditionally been considered unusually "civic" (a reputation that, as we shall later see, has not been entirely unjustified).

When Tocqueville visited the United States in the 1830s, it was the Americans' propensity for civic association that most impressed him as the key to their unprecedented ability to make democracy work. "Americans of all ages, all stations in life, and all types of disposition," he observed, "are forever forming associations. There are not only commercial and industrial associations in which all take part, but others of a thousand different types—religious, moral, serious, futile, very general and very limited, immensely large and very minute. . . . Nothing, in my view, deserves more attention than the intellectual and moral associations in America."[1]

Recently, American social scientists of a neo-Tocquevillean bent have unearthed a wide range of empirical evidence that the quality of public life and the performance of social institutions (and not only in America) are indeed powerfully influenced by norms and networks of civic engagement. Researchers in such fields as education, urban poverty, unemployment, the control of crime and drug abuse, and even health have discovered that successful outcomes are more likely in civically engaged communities. Similarly, research on the varying economic attainments of different ethnic groups in the United States has demonstrated the importance of social bonds within each group. These results are consistent with research in a wide range of settings that demonstrates the vital importance of social networks for job placement and many other economic outcomes.

Meanwhile, a seemingly unrelated body of research on the sociology of economic development has also focused attention on the role of social networks. Some of this work is situated in the developing countries, and some of it elucidates the peculiarly successful "network capitalism" of East Asia.[2] Even in less exotic Western economies, however, researchers have discovered highly efficient, highly flexible "industrial districts" based on networks of collaboration among workers and small entrepreneurs. Far from being paleoindustrial anachronisms, these dense interpersonal and interorganizational networks undergird ultramodern industries, from the high tech of Silicon Valley to the high fashion of Benetton.

The norms and networks of civic engagement also powerfully affect the performance of representative government. That, at least, was the central conclusion of my own 20-year, quasi-experimental study of subnational governments in different regions of Italy.[3] Although all these regional governments seemed identical on paper, their levels of effectiveness varied dramatically. Systematic inquiry showed that the quality of governance was determined by longstanding traditions of civic engagement (or its absence). Voter turnout, newspaper readership, membership in choral societies and football clubs—these were the hallmarks of a successful region. In fact, historical analysis suggested that these networks of organized reciprocity and civic solidarity, far from being an epiphenomenon of socioeconomic modernization, were a precondition for it.

No doubt the mechanisms through which civic engagement and social connectedness produce such results—better schools, faster economic development, lower crime, and more effective government—are multiple and complex. While these briefly recounted findings require further confirmation and perhaps qualification, the parallels across hundreds of empirical studies in a dozen disparate disciplines and subfields are striking. Social scientists in several fields have recently suggested a common framework for understanding these phenomena, a framework that rests on the concept of *social capital.*[4] By analogy with notions of physical capital and human capital—tools and training that enhance individual productivity—"social capital" refers to features of social organization such as networks, norms, and social trust that facilitate coordination and cooperation for mutual benefit.

For a variety of reasons, life is easier in a community blessed with a substantial stock of social capital. In the first

The selection by Robert D. Putnam first appeared in the JOURNAL OF DEMOCRACY *Vol. 6: 65–78 (January, 1995) and is reprinted here by permission. Robert D. Putnam is Dillon Professor of International Affairs at Harvard University.*

place, networks of civic engagement foster sturdy norms of generalized reciprocity and encourage the emergence of social trust. Such networks facilitate coordination and communication, amplify reputations, and thus allow dilemmas of collective action to be resolved. When economic and political negotiation is embedded in dense networks of social interaction, incentives for opportunism are reduced. At the same time, networks of civic engagement embody past success at collaboration, which can serve as a cultural template for future collaboration. Finally, dense networks of interaction probably broaden the participants' sense of self, developing the "I" into the "we," or (in the language of rational-choice theorists) enhancing the participants' "taste" for collective benefits.

I do not intend here to survey (much less contribute to) the development of the theory of social capital. Instead, I use the central premise of that rapidly growing body of work—that social connections and civic engagement pervasively influence our public life, as well as our private prospects—as the starting point for an empirical survey of trends in social capital in contemporary America. I concentrate here entirely on the American case, although the developments I portray may in some measure characterize many contemporary societies.

Whatever Happened to Civic Engagement?

We begin with familiar evidence on changing patterns of political participation, not least because it is immediately relevant to issues of democracy in the narrow sense. Consider the well-known decline in turnout in national elections over the last three decades. From a relative high point in the early 1960s, voter turnout had by 1990 declined by nearly a quarter; tens of millions of Americans had forsaken their parents' habitual readiness to engage in the simplest act of citizenship. Broadly similar trends also characterize participation in state and local elections.

It is not just the voting booth that has been increasingly deserted by Americans. A series of identical questions posed by the Roper Organization to national samples ten times each year over the last two decades reveals that since 1973 the number of Americans who report that "in the past year" they have "attended a public meeting on town or school affairs" has fallen by more than a third (from 22 percent in 1973 to 13 percent in 1993). Similar (or even greater) relative declines are evident in responses to questions about attending a political rally or speech, serving on a committee of some local organization, and working for a political party. By almost every measure, Americans' direct engagement in politics and government has fallen steadily and sharply over the last generation, despite the fact that average levels of education—the best individual-level predictor of political participation—have risen sharply throughout this period. Every year over the last decade or two, millions more have withdrawn from the affairs of their communities.

Not coincidentally, Americans have also disengaged psychologically from politics and government over this era. The proportion of Americans who reply that they "trust the government in Washington" only "some of the time" or "almost never" has risen steadily from 30 percent in 1966 to 75 percent in 1992.

These trends are well known, of course, and taken by themselves would seem amenable to a strictly political explanation. Perhaps the long litany of political tragedies and scandals since the 1960s (assassinations, Vietnam, Watergate, Irangate, and so on) has triggered an understandable disgust for politics and government among Americans, and that in turn has motivated their withdrawal. I do not doubt that this common interpretation has some merit, but its limitations become plain when we examine trends in civic engagement of a wider sort.

Our survey of organizational membership among Americans can usefully begin with a glance at the aggregate results of the General Social Survey, a scientifically conducted, national-sample survey that has been repeated 14 times over the last two decades. Church-related groups constitute the most common type of organization joined by Americans; they are especially popular with women. Other types of organizations frequently joined by women include school-service groups (mostly parent-teacher associations), sports groups, professional societies, and literary societies. Among men, sports clubs, labor unions, professional societies, fraternal groups, veterans' groups, and service clubs are all relatively popular.

Religious affiliation is by far the most common associational membership among Americans. Indeed, by many measures America continues to be (even more than in Tocqueville's time) an astonishingly "churched" society. For example, the United States has more houses of worship per capita than any other nation on Earth. Yet religious sentiment in America seems to be becoming somewhat less tied to institutions and more self-defined.

How have these complex crosscurrents played out over the last three or four decades in terms of Americans' engagement with organized religion? The general pattern is clear: the 1960s witnessed a significant drop in reported weekly churchgoing—from roughly 48 percent in the late 1950s to roughly 41 percent in the early 1970s. Since then, it has stagnated or (according to some surveys) declined still further. Meanwhile, data from the General Social Survey show a modest decline in membership in all "church-related groups" over the last 20 years. It would seem, then, that net participation by Americans, both in religious services and in church-related groups, has declined modestly (by perhaps a sixth) since the 1960s.

For many years, labor unions provided one of the most common organizational affiliations among American workers. Yet union membership has been falling for nearly four decades, with the steepest decline occurring between 1975 and 1985. Since the mid-1950s, when union membership peaked, the unionized portion of the nonagricultural work force in America has dropped by more than half, falling from 32.5 percent in 1953 to 15.8 percent in 1992.

By now, virtually all of the explosive growth in union membership that was associated with the New Deal has been erased. The solidarity of union halls is now mostly a fading memory of aging men.[5]

The parent-teacher association (PTA) has been an especially important form of civic engagement in twentieth-century America because parental involvement in the educational process represents a particularly productive form of social capital. It is, therefore, dismaying to discover that participation in parent-teacher organizations has dropped drastically over the last generation, from more than 12 million in 1964 to barely 5 million in 1982 before recovering to approximately 7 million now.

Next, we turn to evidence on membership in (and volunteering for) civic and fraternal organizations. These data show some striking patterns. First, membership in traditional women's groups has declined more or less steadily since the mid-1960s. For example, membership in the national Federation of Women's Clubs is down by more than half (59 percent) since 1964, while membership in the League of Women Voters (LWV) is off 42 percent since 1969.[6]

Similar reductions are apparent in the numbers of volunteers for mainline civic organizations, such as the Boy Scouts (off by 26 percent since 1970) and the Red Cross (off by 61 percent since 1970). But what about the possibility that volunteers have simply switched their loyalties to other organizations? Evidence on "regular" (as opposed to occasional or "drop-by") volunteering is available from the Labor Department's Current Population Surveys of 1974 and 1989. These estimates suggest that serious volunteering declined by roughly one-sixth over these 15 years, from 24 percent of adults in 1974 to 20 percent in 1989. The multitudes of Red Cross aides and Boy Scout troop leaders now missing in action have apparently not been offset by equal numbers of new recruits elsewhere.

Fraternal organizations have also witnessed a substantial drop in membership during the 1980s and 1990s. Membership is down significantly in such groups as the Lions (off 12 percent since 1983), the Elks (off 18 percent since 1979), the Shriners (off 27 percent since 1979), the Jaycees (off 44 percent since 1979), and the Masons (down 39 percent since 1959). In sum, after expanding steadily throughout most of this century, many major civic organizations have experienced a sudden, substantial, and nearly simultaneous decline in membership over the last decade or two. The most whimsical yet discomfiting bit of evidence of social disengagement in contemporary America that I have discovered is this: more Americans are bowling today than ever before, but bowling in organized leagues has plummeted in the last decade or so. Between 1980 and 1993 the total number of bowlers in America increased by 10 percent, while league bowling decreased by 40 percent. (Lest this be thought a wholly trivial example, I should note that nearly 80 million Americans went bowling at least once during 1993, *nearly a third more than voted in the 1994 congressional elections* and roughly the same number

as claim to attend church regularly. Even after the 1980s' plunge in league bowling, nearly 3 percent of American adults regularly bowl in leagues.) The rise of solo bowling threatens the livelihood of bowling-lane proprietors because those who bowl as members of leagues consume three times as much beer and pizza as solo bowlers, and the money in bowling is in the beer and pizza, not the balls and shoes. The broader social significance, however, lies in the social interaction and even occasionally civic conversations over beer and pizza that solo bowlers forgo. Whether or not bowling beats balloting in the eyes of most Americans, bowling teams illustrate yet another vanishing form of social capital.

Countertrends

At this point, however, we must confront a serious counterargument. Perhaps the traditional forms of civic organization whose decay we have been tracing have been replaced by vibrant new organizations. For example, national environmental organizations (like the Sierra Club) and feminist groups (like the National Organization for Women) grew rapidly during the 1970s and 1980s and now count hundreds of thousands of dues-paying members. An even more dramatic example is the American Association of Retired Persons (AARP), which grew exponentially from 400,000 card-carrying members in 1960 to 33 million in 1993, becoming (after the Catholic Church) the largest private organization in the world. The national administrators of these organizations are among the most feared lobbyists in Washington, in large part because of their massive mailing lists of presumably loyal members.

These new mass-membership organizations are plainly of great political importance. From the point of view of social connectedness, however, they are sufficiently different from classic "secondary associations" that we need to invent a new label—perhaps "tertiary associations." For the vast majority of their members, the only act of membership consists in writing a check for dues or perhaps occasionally reading a newsletter. Few ever attend any meetings of such organizations, and most are unlikely ever (knowingly) to encounter any other member. The bond between any two members of the Sierra Club is less like the bond between any two members of a gardening club and more like the bond between any two Red Sox fans (or perhaps any two devoted Honda owners): they root for the same team and they share some of the same interests, but they are unaware of each other's existence. Their ties, in short, are to common symbols, common leaders, and perhaps common ideals, but not to one another. The theory of social capital argues that associational membership should, for example, increase social trust, but this prediction is much less straightforward with regard to membership in tertiary associations. From the point of view of social connectedness, the Environmental Defense Fund and a bowling league are just not in the same category.

If the growth of tertiary organizations represents one

potential (but probably not real) counterexample to my thesis, a second countertrend is represented by the growing prominence of nonprofit organizations, especially nonprofit service agencies. This so-called third sector includes everything from Oxfam and the Metropolitan Museum of Art to the Ford Foundation and the Mayo Clinic. In other words, although most secondary associations are nonprofits, most nonprofit agencies are not secondary associations. To identify trends in the size of the nonprofit sector with trends in social connectedness would be another fundamental conceptual mistake.[7]

A third potential countertrend is much more relevant to an assessment of social capital and civic engagement. Some able researchers have argued that the last few decades have witnessed a rapid expansion in "support groups" of various sorts. Robert Wuthnow reports that fully 40 percent of all Americans claim to be "currently involved in [a] small group that meets regularly and provides support or caring for those who participate in it."[8] Many of these groups are religiously affiliated, but many others are not. For example, nearly 5 percent of Wuthnow's national sample claim to participate regularly in a "self-help" group, such as Alcoholics Anonymous, and nearly as many say they belong to book-discussion groups and hobby clubs.

The groups described by Wuthnow's respondents unquestionably represent an important form of social capital, and they need to be accounted for in any serious reckoning of trends in social connectedness. On the other hand, they do not typically play the same role as traditional civic associations. As Wuthnow emphasizes,

> Small groups may not be fostering community as effectively as many of their proponents would like. Some small groups merely provide occasions for individuals to focus on themselves in the presence of others. The social contract binding members together asserts only the weakest of obligations. Come if you have time. Talk if you feel like it. Respect everyone's opinion. Never criticize. Leave quietly if you become dissatisfied. . . . We can imagine that [these small groups] really substitute for families, neighborhoods, and broader community attachments that may demand lifelong commitments, when, in fact, they do not.[9]

All three of these potential countertrends—tertiary organizations, nonprofit organizations, and support groups—need somehow to be weighed against the erosion of conventional civic organizations. One way of doing so is to consult the General Social Survey.

Within all educational categories, total associational membership declined significantly between 1967 and 1993. Among the college-educated, the average number of group memberships per person fell from 2.8 to 2.0 (a 26-percent decline); among high-school graduates, the number fell from 1.8 to 1.2 (32 percent); and among those with fewer than 12 years of education, the number fell from 1.4 to 1.1 (25 percent). In other words, at *all* educational (and hence social) levels of American society, and counting *all* sorts of group memberships, *the average number of associational memberships has fallen by about a fourth over the last quarter-century.* Without controls for educational levels, the trend is not nearly so clear, but the central point is this: *more Americans than ever before are in social circumstances that foster associational involvement (higher education, middle age, and so on), but nevertheless aggregate associational membership appears to be stagnant or declining.*

Broken down by type of group, the downward trend is most marked for church-related groups, for labor unions, for fraternal and veterans' organizations, and for school-service groups. Conversely, membership in professional associations has risen over these years, although less than might have been predicted, given sharply rising educational and occupational levels. Essentially the same trends are evident for both men and women in the sample. In short, the available survey evidence confirms our earlier conclusion: American social capital in the form of civic associations has significantly eroded over the last generation.

Good Neighborliness and Social Trust

I noted earlier that most readily available quantitative evidence on trends in social connectedness involves formal settings, such as the voting booth, the union hall, or the PTA. One glaring exception is so widely discussed as to require little comment here: the most fundamental form of social capital is the family, and the massive evidence of the loosening of bonds within the family (both extended and nuclear) is well known. This trend, of course, is quite consistent with—and may help to explain—our theme of social decapitalization.

A second aspect of informal social capital on which we happen to have reasonably reliable time-series data involves neighborliness. In each General Social Survey since 1974 respondents have been asked, "How often do you spend a social evening with a neighbor?" The proportion of Americans who socialize with their neighbors more than once a year has slowly but steadily declined over the last two decades, from 72 percent in 1974 to 61 percent in 1993. (On the other hand, socializing with "friends who do not live in your neighborhood" appears to be on the increase, a trend that may reflect the growth of workplace-based social connections.)

Americans are also less trusting. The proportion of Americans saying that most people can be trusted fell by more than a third between 1960, when 58 percent chose that alternative, and 1993, when only 37 percent did. The same trend is apparent in all educational groups; indeed, because social trust is also correlated with education and because educational levels have risen sharply, the overall decrease in social trust is even more apparent if we control for education.

Our discussion of trends in social connectedness and

civic engagement has tacitly assumed that all the forms of social capital that we have discussed are themselves coherently correlated across individuals. This is in fact true. Members of associations are much more likely than nonmembers to participate in politics, to spend time with neighbors, to express social trust, and so on.

The close correlation between social trust and associational membership is true not only across time and across individuals, but also across countries. Evidence from the 1991 World Values Survey demonstrates the following.[10]

(1) Across the 35 countries in this survey, social trust and civic engagement are strongly correlated; the greater the density of associational membership in a society, the more trusting its citizens. Trust and engagement are two facets of the same underlying factor—social capital.

(2) America still ranks relatively high by cross-national standards on both these dimensions of social capital. Even in the 1990s, after several decades' erosion, Americans are more trusting and more engaged than people in most other countries of the world.

(3) The trends of the past quarter-century, however, have apparently moved the United States significantly lower in the international rankings of social capital. The recent deterioration in American social capital has been sufficiently great that (if no other country changed its position in the meantime) another quarter-century of change at the same rate would bring the United States, roughly speaking, to the midpoint among all these countries, roughly equivalent to South Korea, Belgium, or Estonia today. Two generations' decline at the same rate would leave the United States at the level of today's Chile, Portugal, and Slovenia.

Why Is U.S. Social Capital Eroding?

As we have seen, something has happened in America in the last two or three decades to diminish civic engagement and social connectedness. What could that "something" be? Here are several possible explanations, along with some initial evidence on each.

The movement of women into the labor force. Over these same two or three decades, many millions of American women have moved out of the home into paid employment. This is the primary, though not the sole, reason why the weekly working hours of the average American have increased significantly during these years. It seems highly plausible that this social revolution should have reduced the time and energy available for building social capital. For certain organizations, such as the PTA, the League of Women Voters, the Federation of Women's Clubs, and the Red Cross, this is almost certainly an important part of the story. The sharpest decline in women's civic participation seems to have come in the 1970s; membership in such "women's" organizations as these has been virtually halved since the late 1960s. By contrast, most of the decline in

participation in men's organizations occurred about ten years later; the total decline to date has been approximately 25 percent for the typical organization. On the other hand, the survey data imply that the aggregate declines for men are virtually as great as those for women. It is logically possible, of course, that the male declines might represent the knock-on effect of women's liberation, as dishwashing crowded out the lodge, but time-budget studies suggest that most husbands of working wives have assumed only a minor part of the housework. In short, something besides the women's revolution seems to lie behind the erosion of social capital.

Mobility: The "re-potting" hypothesis. Numerous studies of organizational involvement have shown that residential stability and such related phenomena as homeownership are clearly associated with greater civic engagement. Mobility, like frequent re-potting of plants, tends to disrupt root systems, and it takes time for an uprooted individual to put down new roots. It seems plausible that the automobile, suburbanization, and the movement to the Sun Belt have reduced the social rootedness of the average American, but one fundamental difficulty with this hypothesis is apparent: the best evidence shows that residential stability and homeownership in America have risen modestly since 1965, and are surely higher now than during the 1950s, when civic engagement and social connectedness by our measures was definitely higher.

Other demographic transformations. A range of additional changes have transformed the American family since the 1960s—fewer marriages, more divorces, fewer children, lower real wages, and so on. Each of these changes might account for some of the slackening of civic engagement, since married, middle-class parents are generally more socially involved than other people. Moreover, the changes in scale that have swept over the American economy in these years—illustrated by the replacement of the corner grocery by the supermarket and now perhaps of the supermarket by electronic shopping at home, or the replacement of community-based enterprises by outposts of distant multinational firms—may perhaps have undermined the material and even physical basis for civic engagement.

The technological transformation of leisure. There is reason to believe that deep-seated technological trends are radically "privatizing" or "individualizing" our use of leisure time and thus disrupting many opportunities for social-capital formation. The most obvious and probably the most powerful instrument of this revolution is television. Time-budget studies in the 1960s showed that the growth in time spent watching television dwarfed all other changes in the way Americans passed their days and nights. Television has made our communities (or, rather, what we experience as our communities) wider and shallower. In the language of economics, electronic technology enables individual tastes to be satisfied more fully, but at the cost of the positive social externalities associated with more primitive forms of entertainment. The same logic applies to the replacement of vaudeville by the movies and now of movies by the VCR. The new "virtual reality" helmets that we will soon don to be entertained in total isolation are merely the latest extension of this trend. Is technology thus driving a wedge between our individual interests and our collective interests? It is a question that seems worth exploring more systematically.

What Is to Be Done?

The last refuge of a social-scientific scoundrel is to call for more research. Nevertheless, I cannot forbear from suggesting some further lines of inquiry.

- We must sort out the dimensions of social capital, which clearly is not an unidimensional concept, despite language (even in this essay) that implies the contrary. What types of organizations and networks most effectively embody—or generate—social capital, in the sense of mutual reciprocity, the resolution of dilemmas of collective action, and the broadening of social identities? In this essay I have emphasized the density of associational life. In earlier work I stressed the structure of networks, arguing that "horizontal" ties represented more productive social capital than vertical ties.[11]
- Another set of important issues involves macrosociological crosscurrents that might intersect with the trends described here. What will be the impact, for example, of electronic networks on social capital? My hunch is that meeting in an electronic forum is not the equivalent of meeting in a bowling alley—or even in a saloon—but hard empirical research is needed. What about the development of social capital in the workplace? Is it growing in counterpoint to the decline of civic engagement, reflecting some social analogue of the first law of thermodynamics—social capital is neither created nor destroyed, merely redistributed? Or do the trends described in this essay represent a deadweight loss?
- A rounded assessment of changes in American social capital over the last quarter-century needs to count the costs as well as the benefits of community engagement. We must not romanticize small-town, middle-class civic life in the America of the 1950s. In addition to the deleterious trends emphasized in this essay, recent decades have witnessed a substantial decline in intolerance and probably also in overt discrimination, and those beneficent trends may be related in complex ways to the erosion of traditional social capital. Moreover, a balanced accounting of the social-capital books would need to reconcile the insights of this approach with the undoubted insights offered by Mancur Olson and others who stress that closely knit social, economic, and political organizations are prone to inefficient cartelization and to what political economists term "rent seeking" and ordinary men and women call corruption.[12]
- Finally, and perhaps most urgently, we need to explore creatively how public policy impinges on (or might impinge on) social-capital formation. In some well-known instances, public policy has destroyed highly effective social networks and norms. American slum-clearance policy of the 1950s and 1960s, for example, renovated physical capital, but at a very high cost to existing social capital. The consolidation of country post offices and small school districts has promised administrative and financial efficiencies, but full-cost accounting for the effects of these policies on social capital might produce a more negative verdict. On the other hand, such past initiatives as the country agricultural-agent system, community colleges, and tax deductions for charitable contributions illustrate that government can encourage social-capital formation. Even a recent proposal in San Luis Obispo, California, to require that all new houses have front porches illustrates the power of government to influence where and how networks are formed.

The concept of "civil society" has played a central role in the recent global debate about the preconditions for democracy and democratization. In the newer democracies this phrase has properly focused attention on the need to foster a vibrant civic life in soils traditionally inhospitable to self-government. In the established democracies, ironically, growing numbers of citizens are questioning the effectiveness of their public institutions at the very moment when liberal democracy has swept the battlefield, both ideologically and geopolitically. In America, at least, there is reason to suspect that this democratic disarray may be linked to a broad and continuing erosion of civic engagement that began a quarter-century ago. High on our scholarly agenda should be the question of whether a comparable erosion of social capital may be under way in other advanced democracies, perhaps in different institutional and behavioral guises. High on America's agenda should be the question of how to reverse these adverse trends in social connectedness, thus restoring civic engagement and civic trust.

Notes

1. Alexis de Tocqueville, *Democracy in America*, ed. J.P. Maier, trans. George Lawrence (Garden City, N.Y.: Anchor Books, 1969), 513–17.
2. On social networks and economic growth in the developing world, see Milton J. Esman and Norman Uphoff, *Local Organizations: Intermediaries in Rural Development* (Ithaca: Cornell University Press, 1984), esp. 15–42 and 99–180; and Albert O. Hirschman, *Getting Ahead Collectively: Grassroots Experiences in Latin America* (Elmsford, N.Y.: Pergamon Press, 1984), esp. 42–77. On East

Asia, see Gustav Papanek, "The New Asian Capitalism: An Economic Portrait," in Peter L. Berger and Hsin-Huang Michael Hsiao, eds., *In Search of an East Asian Development Model* (New Brunswick, N.J.: Transaction, 1987), 27–80; Peter B. Evans, "The State as Problem and Solution: Predation, Embedded Autonomy and Structural Change," in Stephan Haggard and Robert R. Kaufman, eds., *The Politics of Economic Adjustment* (Princeton: Princeton University Press, 1992), 139–81; and Gary G. Hamilton, William Zeile, and Wan-Jin Kim, "Network Structure of East Asian Economies," in Stewart R. Clegg and S. Gordon Redding, eds., *Capitalism in Contrasting Cultures* (Hawthorne, N.Y.: De Gruyter, 1990), 105–29. See also Gary G. Hamilton and Nicole Woolsey Biggart, "Market, Culture, and Authority: A Comparative Analysis of Management and Organization in the Far East," *American Journal of Sociology* (Supplement) 94 (1988): S52–S94; and Susan Greenhalgh, "Families and Networks in Taiwan's Economic Development," in Edwin Winckler and Susan Greenhalgh, eds., *Contending Approaches to the Political Economy of Taiwan* (Armonk, N.Y.: M.E. Sharpe, 1987), 224–45.

3. Robert D. Putnam, *Making Democracy Work: Civic Traditions in Modern Italy* (Princeton: Princeton University Press, 1993).

4. James S. Coleman deserves primary credit for developing the "social capital" theoretical framework. See his "Social Capital in the Creation of Human Capital," *American Journal of Sociology* (Supplement) 94 (1988): S95–S120, as well as his *The Foundations of Social Theory* (Cambridge: Harvard University Press, 1990), 300–21. See also Mark Granovetter, "Economic Action and Social Structure: The Problem of Embeddedness," *American Journal of Sociology* 91 (1985): 481–510; Glenn C. Loury, "Why Should We Care About Group Inequality?" *Social Philosophy and Policy* 5 (1987): 249–71; and Robert D. Putnam, "The Prosperous Community: Social Capital and Public Life," *American Prospect* 13 (1993): 35–42. To my knowledge, the first scholar to use the term "social capital" in its current sense was Jane Jacobs, in *The Death and Life of Great American Cities* (New York: Random House, 1961), 138.

5. Any simplistically political interpretation of the collapse of American unionism would need to confront the fact that the steepest decline began more than six years before the Reagan administration's attack on PATCO. Data from the General Social Survey show a roughly 40-percent decline in reported union membership between 1975 and 1991.

6. Data for the LWV are available over a longer time span and show an interesting pattern: a sharp slump during the Depression, a strong and sustained rise after World War II that more than tripled membership between 1945 and 1969, and then the post–1969 decline, which has already erased virtually all the postwar gains and continues still. This same historical pattern applies to those men's fraternal organizations for which comparable data are available—steady increases for the first seven decades of the century, interrupted only by the Great Depression, followed by a collapse in the 1970s and 1980s that has already wiped out most of the postwar expansion and continues apace.

7. Cf. Lester M. Salamon, "The Rise of the Nonprofit Sector," *Foreign Affairs* 73 (July–August 1994): 109–22. See also Salamon, "Partners in Public Service: The Scope and Theory of Government-Nonprofit Relations," in Walter W. Powell, ed., *The Nonprofit Sector: A Research Handbook* (New Haven: Yale University Press, 1987), 99–117. Salamon's empirical evidence does not sustain his broad claims about a global "associational revolution" comparable in significance to the rise of the nation-state several centuries ago.

8. Robert Wuthnow, *Sharing the Journey: Support Groups and America's New Quest for Community* (New York: The Free Press, 1994), 45.

9. Ibid., 3–6.

10. I am grateful to Ronald Inglehart, who directs this unique cross-national project, for sharing these highly useful data with me. See his "The Impact of Culture on Economic Development: Theory, Hypotheses, and Some Empirical Tests" (unpublished manuscript, University of Michigan, 1994).

11. See my *Making Democracy Work*, esp. ch. 6.

12. See Mancur Olson, *The Rise and Decline of Nations: Economic Growth, Stagflation, and Social Rigidities* (New Haven: Yale University Press, 1982), 2.

Kicking in Groups

by Nicholas Lemann

In 1958 Edward Banfield published *The Moral Basis of a Backward Society*, a study of underdevelopment in a village at the southern tip of Italy—"the extreme poverty and backwardness of which," he write, "is to be explained largely (but not entirely) by the inability of the villagers to act together for their common good." Banfield called the prevailing ethos of the village "amoral familism": "Maximize the material, short-run advantage of the nuclear family; assume that all others will do likewise." The best way to improve the village's economic condition, he said, would be for "the southern peasant to acquire the ways of the north."

Ten years later, in *The Unheavenly City*, Banfield applied a similar line of argument to American inner-city black ghettos, without benefit of the kind of firsthand research he had done in Italy. This time he identified "present-mindedness" as the quality that caused the communities' problems. Whereas *The Moral Basis of a Backward Society* had been respectfully received. *The Unheavenly City* was so controversial that for years Banfield required police protection when he spoke in public. The lesson seems to be that studying the difference between northern and southern Italy is a safe way of addressing a question still very much on Americans' minds: Why is there such a wide variation in the social and economic health of our neighborhoods and ethnic groups and, for that matter, of different societies all over the world?

Robert Putnam, a professor of government at Harvard, has to decide whether to confront just this issue. In 1993 Putnam published a book called *Making Democracy Work: Civic Traditions in Modern Italy*. Though its main text is only 185 pages long, *Making Democracy Work* is the fruit of immense labor. In 1970 Italy created local governments in its twenty regions and turned over many of the functions of the central government to them. Putnam and a team of colleagues almost immediately embarked on a study of the new governments' performance, covering the entire nation and focusing particularly on a few localities, including a town quite near the one where Banfield researched his book.

The finding that leaped out at Putnam was that the governments in the prosperous north of Italy outperformed the ones in the benighted south. Through a variety of statistical exercises he tried to demonstrate that their success was not simply a case of the rich getting richer. For example, he showed that regional government officials are less well educated in the north than in the south, and that in the northern provinces economic-development levels are not especially predictive of government performance. He found the north's secret to be a quality that Machiavelli called *virtu civile* ("civic virtue")—an ingrained tendency to form small-scale associations that create a fertile ground for political and economic development, even if (especially if, Putnam would probably say) the associations are not

themselves political or economic. "Good government in Italy is a by-product of singing groups and soccer clubs," he wrote. Civic virtue both expresses and builds trust and co-operation in the citizenry, and it is these qualities—which Putnam called "social capital," borrowing a phrase from Jane Jacobs—that make everything else go well.

Putnam was arguing against the conventional wisdom in the social sciences, which holds that civic virtue is an appurtenance of a traditional society—"an atavism destined to disappear" with modernization, which replaces small organizations that operate by custom with big ones that operate by rules. Instead, he said, even the biggest and most modern societies can't function well if the local civic dimension is weak. He hinted here and there that it was actually the large bureaucratic overlay that was going to wind up being obsolete.

What causes some societies to become more civic-minded than others? In Italy, Putnam said, the north-south difference dates from the 1100s, when the Normans established a centralized, autocratic regime in the south, and a series of autonomous republics arose in the north. The southern system stressed what Putnam called "vertical bonds": it was rigidly hierarchical, with those at the bottom dependent on the patronage of landowners and officials rather than on one another. In the north small organizations such as guilds and credit associations generated "horizontal bonds," fostering a sense of mutual trust that doesn't exist in the south. Putnam continually stressed the "astonishing constancy" of the north-south difference: it survived the demise of the independent northern republics in the seventeenth century and the Risorgimento in the nineteenth. "The southern territories once ruled by the Norman kings," he wrote, "constitute exactly the seven least civic regions in the 1970s." We shouldn't expect the situation to change anytime soon, because "where institution building . . . is concerned, time is measured in decades."

Social science has become a statistical art, overwhelmingly concerned with using correlation coefficients to express the effect of one thing on another—or, to use the jargon, to discover and isolate the independent variable that has the greatest influence on the dependent variable. Civic virtue can be understood as Putnam's contribution to an ongoing quest for the magic independent variable that will explain economic development; he belongs to an intellectual tradition that tries to locate it in intrinsic cultural tendencies. In this sense civic virtue is a descendant of Max Weber's Protestant ethic, and is the opposite of Oscar Lewis's culture of poverty and Banfield's amoral familism. The venerability of the tradition and its powerful common-

The reading by Nicholas Lemann, is reprinted with permission from the AT-LANTIC MONTHLY 277: 22–26 (April, 1996).
Nicholas Lemann is a writer and social commentator.

sense appeal shouldn't obscure the fact that all such independent variables are, necessarily, artificial constructs. Civic virtue is measured (to three decimal places!) by cobbling together such indices as newspaper-readership figures, voter turnout, and the abundance of sports clubs, and is not, as Putnam admitted, all-powerful as a predictor. Even in parts of northern Italy "the actual administrative performance of most of the new governments"— the subject under study, after all—"has been problematical."

* * *

Nonetheless, when Putnam tentatively brought his theory home to the United States, it created a sensation— of exactly the opposite kind from the one Banfield created a quarter century ago with *The Unheavenly City.* An article called "Bowling Alone," which Putnam published in the January 1995 issue of the *Journal of Democracy,* had an impact far, far beyond the usual for academic writing. In the wake of "Bowling Alone," Putnam has been invited to Camp David to consult with President Bill Clinton. His terminology has heavily influenced the past two *State of the Union* addresses; *Making Democracy Work,* initially ignored by the general-interest press, was reviewed on the front page of *The New York Times Book Review;* Putnam was prominently mentioned in the musings of Senator Bill Bradley about his disillusionment with politics; and, unlikeliest of all, he was the subject of a profile in *People* magazine.

The thesis of "Bowling Alone" is that "the vibrancy of American civil society"—the magic variable—"has notably declined over the past several decades." Putnam gets his title from the finding that from 1980 to 1993 league bowling declined by 40 percent while the number of individual bowlers rose by 10 percent. The rest of his evidence is less whimsical: voter turnout, church attendance, and union membership are down. The percentage of people who trust the government and who attend community meetings has dropped. The leading indicator for Putnam—membership in voluntary associations—is down. Look at the Boy Scouts, the Lions, the Elks, the Shriners, the Jaycees, the Masons, the Red Cross, the Federation of Women's Clubs, and the League of Women Voters: "Serious volunteering declined by roughly one-sixth" from 1974 to 1989. The logic of *Making Democracy Work* would suggest that the true import of these changes is not that they are inherently unfortunate so much as that they predict a broader decline in our society's economic vitality—since, according to Putnam, that vitality rests on a cultural bedrock of local associational strength.

Putnam is scrupulously careful in "Bowling Alone" not to push his theory too hard. Earlier this year, though, he stated the thesis more firmly, in an article in *The American Prospect* called "The Strange Disappearance of Civic America," and offered an explanation for it: Americans who were born after the Second World War are far less civic-minded than their elders, and the main reason is that they grew up after the introduction of television, which "privatizes our leisure time." Putnam is now working up a book on the subject.

* * *

"Bowling Alone" struck a nerve in part because it provided a coherent theory to explain the dominant emotion in American politics: a feeling that the quality of our society at the everyday level has deteriorated severely. An economic statistic like the "misery index" doesn't match the political mood; Putnam's theory does. It is especially appealing to liberal politicians, who see in it the possibility of a rhetoric they can use to address an issue that has been owned by conservatives. Also, if Putnam is right that as local associations go, so goes the nation, his work suggests the possibility of solving our problems through relatively low-cost association-strengthening local initiatives that don't require higher taxes. This makes a wonderful message for Democrats, who want to offer a positive program that is not vulnerable to anti-tax rhetoric. Foundation executives, who want to believe that the limited grants they make can reap large social benefits, also tend to be Putnam fans. Even people whose interests aren't directly affected have eagerly subscribed to the theory of "Bowling Alone," partly because of its apparent validity and partly for reasons I'll discuss later.

It must be said, however, that the talk about "Bowling Alone," and to a lesser extent the article itself, directly contradict the logic of *Making Democracy Work.* In Putnam's Italian model the kind of overnight deterioration of civic virtue that he proposes regarding America would be inconceivable—once civic virtue is in place it is incredibly durable over the centuries. Putnam heartily endorses a theory from economic history called "path dependence," which he has summarized this way: "Where you can get to depends on where you're coming from, and some destinations you simply cannot get to from here." In "Bowling Alone" he quotes Tocqueville's view that "nothing . . . deserves more attention" than Americans' amazing associational predilections; by the standards of *Making Democracy Work,* these ought to have held us in good stead well into the next century. Putnam plainly believes that we were in pretty good associational shape as recently as 1960. How can a tendency toward civic engagement vanish in a single generation?

Not only was Putnam in *Making Democracy Work* insistent upon the lasting good effects of civic virtue, but he was elaborately pessimistic about the possibility of establishing civic virtue where it doesn't already exist. He predicted disaster in the former Communist dictatorships of Europe, because of their weakness in the local-associational area: "Palermo may represent the future of Moscow." Putnam drew this lesson from a comprehensive survey of Third World development efforts:

> Unhappily from the point of view of social engineering . . . local organizations 'implanted' from the outside have a high failure rate. The most successful local organizations represent indigenous, participa-

tory initiatives in relatively cohesive local communities.

If Putnam was right the first time, and civic virtue is deeply rooted, then it's worth wondering whether the United States might actually still have as much of it as ever, or nearly. If that is the case, the dire statistics in "Bowling Alone" reflect merely a mutation rather than a disappearance of civic virtue, because civic virtue has found new expressions in response to economic and social changes. From bowling leagues on up, many of the declining associations Putnam mentioned are like episodes of *The Honeymooners* seen today—out of date.

I spent a couple of days phoning around in search of examples of new associations that have sprung up to take their place. Putnam mentions several of these in "Bowling Alone" in order to dismiss them as real replacements for the lost bowling leagues, either because they don't involve regular face-to-face contact (the many associations in cyberspace; the 33-million-member American Association of Retired Persons) or because they don't encourage people to build lasting ties based on mutual strength (Alcoholics Anonymous and other support groups). The most dramatic example I could find—and a nicely apposite one, too—is U.S. Youth Soccer, which has 2.4 million members, up from 1.2 million ten years ago and from 127,000 twenty years ago. As a long-standing coach in this organization, I can attest that it involves incessant meetings, phone calls, and activities of a kind that create links between people which ramify, in the manner described by Putnam, into other areas.

Another intriguing statistic is the number of restaurants in the United States, which has risen dramatically, from 203,000 in 1972 to 368,000 in 1993. True, this probably means that fewer people are eating a family dinner at home. But from Putnam's perspective, that might be good news, because it means that people who are eating out are expanding their civic associations rather than pursuing amoral familism. (If you've ever visited northern Italy, the connection between restaurants and *virtu civile* seems obvious.) The growth in restaurants is not confined to fastfood restaurants, by the way, although it is true that the number of bars and taverns—institutions singled out for praise in "Bowling Alone"—has declined over the past two decades.

The number of small businesses—what the Internal Revenue Service calls "non-farm proprietorships"—has about doubled since 1970. These can be seen as both generators and results of civic virtue, since they involve so much personal contact and mutual trust. A small subset, Community Development Corporations (organizations that are often explicitly Putnamlike schemes to promote association locally in the hope of a later economic payoff), have grown in number from 500 to 2,200 over the past twenty years. Individual contributions to charity, which are still made by more than three quarters of Americans, grew from $16.2 billion in 1970 to $101.8 billion in 1990. Although church attendance is, as Putnam says, down, the Pentecostal denominations are booming: their domestic membership has burgeoned over the past quarter century. Little League membership has increased every year. Membership in the PTA has risen over the past decade or so, though it's still far below its peak, which occurred in 1962–1963. Homeownership is high and steady, and, as Putnam admits in "Bowling Alone," Americans move less frequently now than they did in the 1950s and 1960s.

᳆   ᳆   ᳆

Weighed against all this, the statistics in "Bowling Alone" are still impressive, and no doubt Putnam will nail down his case in his book. Let's say, however, for the sake of argument, that Putnam's thesis that civic virtue is rapidly collapsing in America isn't true. What would account for its being so widely and instantly accepted as gospel?

Bowling leagues, Elks and Lions, and the League of Women Voters are indisputably not what they used to be. Large internal population shifts have taken place since the 1960s: to the Sunbelt and, within metropolitan areas, to the suburbs. Birth rates dropped substantially and then rose again. Most mothers now work. All these changes could have resulted in atrophied forms of association that are culturally connected to older cities and to old-fashioned gender roles (bowling leagues are a good example), while other forms more oriented to open space and to weekends (like youth soccer) have grown.

I have lived in five American cities: New Orleans, Cambridge, Washington, Austin, and Pelham, New York. The two that stand out in my memory as most deficient in the Putnam virtues—the places where people I know tend not to have elaborate hobbies and not to devote their evenings and weekends to neighborhood meetings and activities—are Cambridge and Washington. The reason is that these places are the big time. Work absorbs all the energy. It is what people talk about at social events. Community is defined functionally, not spatially: it's a professional peer group rather than a neighborhood. Hired hands, from nannies to headmasters to therapists, bear more of the civic-virtue load than is typical.

To people living this kind of life, many of whom grew up in a bourgeois provincial environment and migrated to one of the capitals, the "Bowling Alone" theory makes sense, because it seems to describe their own situation too well. It is natural for people to assume that if their own life trajectories have been in the direction of reduced civic virtue, this is the result not of choices they have made but of a vast national trend. I wonder if the pre-presidential Bill Clinton—the man who spent the morning after Election Day in 1992 wandering around Little Rock engaging in front-porch visits with lifelong friends—would have found "Bowling Alone" so strongly resonant.

A second reason for the appeal of "Bowling Alone" is that it avoids the Banfield problem. A true application of the line of thinking in *Making Democracy Work* would require searching the United States for internal differences in civic virtue and then trying to explain those differences.

One inevitable result would be the shining of a harsh spotlight on the ghettos, with their high rates of crime, welfare dependency, and family breakup. In an article that appeared in *The American Prospect* in 1993 Putnam made a point of saying, "It would be a dreadful mistake, of course, to overlook the repositories of social capital within America's minority communities." This doesn't mean that the spotlight wouldn't still fall on the ghettos, because Putnam was clearly referring to minority communities most of whose members are not poor. But with this caveat he demonstrates at least that he is aware of the sensitive areas into which his Italian inquiry could lead in the United States. So far he has resolutely kept his examples of the decline of civic virtue in America in the realm of middle- or even upper-middle-class culture.

In the 1993 *American Prospect* article Putnam wrote,

> Classic liberal social policy is designed to enhance the opportunities of *individuals,* but if social capital is important, this emphasis is partially misplaced, Instead we must focus on community development, allowing space for religious organizations and choral societies and Little Leagues that may seem to have little to do with politics or economics.

With respect to the United States, the opposite of Putnam's theory would be this: There has been relatively little general decline in civic virtue. To the extent that the overall civic health of the nation did deteriorate, the dip was confined mainly to the decade 1965 to 1975—when, for example, crime and divorce rates rose rapidly—and things have been pretty stable since then. The overwhelming social and moral problem in American life is instead the disastrous condition of poor neighborhoods, almost all of which are in cities.

The model of a healthy country and needy ghettos would suggest a program much closer to the "liberal social policy" from which Putnam wants us to depart. Rather than assume, with Putnam, that such essential public goods as safety, decent housing, and good education can be generated only from within a community, we could assume that they might be provided from without—by government. If quite near the ghettos are working-class neighborhoods (and not insuperably distant are suburbs) of varying ethnic character and strong civic virtue, then the individual-opportunity model might be precisely the answer for ghetto residents—opportunity, that is, to move to a place that is part of the healthy American mainstream.

The difficulty with such a program is that it is politically inconvenient. It would involve, by contemporary standards, far too much action on the part of the government, with the benefits far too skewed toward blacks. The model of an entire United States severely distressed in a way that is beyond the power of government to correct is more comforting.

simsoc
simulated society

3 FORMS

Choice Sheet

Form A

Name _____ Date _____

1. Preferred type of group (place a 1 next to your first choice, a 2 next to your second choice, and a 3 next to your third choice):

   industry _____   political party _____   human services organization _____

   employee organization _____   mass media _____   judicial council _____

2. Individual goals (check those you intend to pursue):

   power _____   center of attention _____   style of life _____

   security _____   popularity _____   fun and excitement _____

   other (please specify) _____

   _____

- -

Assignment Sheet

Form B

Name _____ Date _____

(The remainder of this form is to be filled out by the coordinator—please leave it blank.)

1. You are the head of the following basic group: (circle one)

   None   BASIN   RETSIN   POP   SOP   EMPIN   HUMSERVE   MASMED   JUDCO

2. You are head of the following agency: (circle one)

   None   Subsistence   Travel

3. You live in the following region: (circle one)

   Red   Yellow   Blue   Green

4. (Circle one, if appropriate.)

   Minority-Group   Non-Minority-Group
   Member   Member

Moving Sheet

Form C

Session # _____

Please record the fact that _____ is moving

name

from the (circle one)   *Red*   *Yellow*   *Blue*   *Green*   Region to the (circle one)

Red   *Yellow*   *Blue*   *Green*   Region.

Note: A fee of $10 must be paid to the bank.

- -

Private Transportation Certificate

Form D

Session # _____

This is to certify that _____ has

name

purchased a Private Transportation Certificate and henceforth is free to travel at will.

Fee = $25

_____

(signature or initials of coordinator or assistant)

Withdrawal of Assets Form

Form I

Session # _____

Please give me _____ to be charged to the

(specify amount)

assets of: (circle one)   BASIN   RETSIN

_____

(signature of head)

- -

Withdrawal of Assets Form

Form I

Session # _____

Please give me _____ to be charged to the

(specify amount)

assets of: (circle one)   BASIN   RETSIN

_____

(signature of head)

Withdrawal of Assets Form

Form I

Session # _____

Please give me _____ to be charged to the
(specify amount)

assets of: (circle one)   BASIN   RETSIN

_____
(signature of head)

Withdrawal of Assets Form

Form I

Session # _____

Please give me _____ to be charged to the
(specify amount)

assets of: (circle one)   BASIN   RETSIN

_____
(signature of head)

Withdrawal of Assets Form

Form I

Session # _____

Please give me _____ to be charged to the
(specify amount)

assets of: (circle one)   BASIN   RETSIN

_____
(signature of head)

Withdrawal of Assets Form

Form I

Session # _____

Please give me _____ to be charged to the
(specify amount)

assets of: (circle one)   BASIN   RETSIN

_____
(signature of head)

Minority-Group Member Action Sheet

Form K

Session # _____

Please remove the following Minority-Group Members from all positions (including head) they hold with any basic groups, and from all subsistence and travel agencies they may hold:

(list names)

_____   _____

_____   _____

_____   _____

Authorization (must be signed by any two non-Minority-Group Members):

_____   _____

- -

Minority-Group Member Action Sheet

Form K

Session # _____

Please remove the following Minority-Group Members from all positions (including head) they hold with any basic groups, and from all subsistence and travel agencies they may hold:

(list names)

_____   _____

_____   _____

_____   _____

Authorization (must be signed by any two non-Minority-Group Members):

_____   _____

Job Schedule

Name of Group _____ Session # _____

Name of Head _____

1. List the following people as employees (to be filled in during first session):

   _____   _____   _____

   _____   _____   _____

   _____   _____   _____

   _____   _____   _____

2. Changes in employment (to be used in later sessions)

   a) Make the following additions to the list of employees:

   _____   _____   _____

   _____   _____   _____

   b) Remove the following people from the list of employees:

   _____   _____   _____

   _____   _____   _____

3. Change the head of the group as follows:

   Name of Old Head _____

   Name of New Head _____

   Authorization for change (must include either (1) the signature of the old head or (2) the signature of all employees present for the session in which filed):

   _____   _____   _____

   _____   _____   _____

   _____   _____   _____

   _____   _____   _____

4. Resignation.
   Please remove my name from the list of employees.

   _____
   (signature)

Job Schedule

Name of Group _____ Session # _____

Name of Head _____

1. List the following people as employees (to be filled in during first session):

   _____   _____   _____

   _____   _____   _____

   _____   _____   _____

   _____   _____   _____

2. Changes in employment (to be used in later sessions)

   a) Make the following additions to the list of employees:

   _____   _____   _____

   _____   _____   _____

   b) Remove the following people from the list of employees:

   _____   _____   _____

   _____   _____   _____

3. Change the head of the group as follows:

   Name of Old Head _____

   Name of New Head _____

   Authorization for change (must include either (1) the signature of the old head or (2) the signature of all employees present for the session in which filed):

   _____   _____   _____

   _____   _____   _____

   _____   _____   _____

   _____   _____   _____

4. Resignation.
   Please remove my name from the list of employees.

   _____
   (signature)

Job Schedule

Name of Group _____ Session # _____

Name of Head _____

1. List the following people as employees (to be filled in during first session):

    _____ _____ _____

    _____ _____ _____

    _____ _____ _____

    _____ _____ _____

2. Changes in employment (to be used in later sessions)

    a) Make the following additions to the list of employees:

    _____ _____ _____

    _____ _____ _____

    b) Remove the following people from the list of employees:

    _____ _____ _____

    _____ _____ _____

3. Change the head of the group as follows:

    Name of Old Head _____

    Name of New Head _____

    Authorization for change (must include either (1) the signature of the old head or (2) the signature of all employees present for the session in which filed):

    _____ _____ _____

    _____ _____ _____

    _____ _____ _____

    _____ _____ _____

4. Resignation.
   Please remove my name from the list of employees.

    _____
    (signature)

Job Schedule

Form G

Name of Group _____ Session # _____

Name of Head _____

1. List the following people as employees (to be filled in during first session):

_____   _____   _____

_____   _____   _____

_____   _____   _____

_____   _____   _____

2. Changes in employment (to be used in later sessions)

    a) Make the following additions to the list of employees:

_____   _____   _____

_____   _____   _____

    b) Remove the following people from the list of employees:

_____   _____   _____

_____   _____   _____

3. Change the head of the group as follows:

    Name of Old Head _____

    Name of New Head _____

    Authorization for change (must include either (1) the signature of the old head *or* (2) the signature of all employees present for the session in which filed):

_____   _____   _____

_____   _____   _____

_____   _____   _____

_____   _____   _____

4. Resignation.
Please remove my name from the list of employees.

_____
(signature)

Industry Manufacturing Form

Form H

Industry: (circle one)   BASIN   RETSIN   Session # _____

1. For BASIN:

Number of Vowels

Passage #	a's	e's	i's	o's	u's
# _____	_____	_____	_____	_____	_____
# _____	_____	_____	_____	_____	_____
# _____	_____	_____	_____	_____	_____
# _____	_____	_____	_____	_____	_____
# _____	_____	_____	_____	_____	_____

2. For RETSIN:

Anagram   List of possible marketable words

_____   _____

                                 _____

_____   _____

                                 _____

_____   _____

                                 _____

_____   _____

                                 _____

_____   _____

                                 _____

Industry Manufacturing Form

Form H

Industry: (circle one) BASIN RETSIN Session # _____

1. For BASIN:

	Number of Vowels				
Passage #	a's	e's	i's	o's	u's
# _____	_____	_____	_____	_____	_____
# _____	_____	_____	_____	_____	_____
# _____	_____	_____	_____	_____	_____
# _____	_____	_____	_____	_____	_____
# _____	_____	_____	_____	_____	_____

2. For RETSIN:

Anagram	List of possible marketable words
_____	_____
	_____
_____	_____
	_____
_____	_____
	_____
_____	_____
	_____
_____	_____
	_____

Industry Manufacturing Form

Form H

Industry: (circle one)   BASIN   RETSIN   Session # _____

1. For BASIN:

Number of Vowels

Passage #	*a*'s	*e*'s	*i*'s	*o*'s	*u*'s
# _____	_____	_____	_____	_____	_____
# _____	_____	_____	_____	_____	_____
# _____	_____	_____	_____	_____	_____
# _____	_____	_____	_____	_____	_____
# _____	_____	_____	_____	_____	_____

2. For RETSIN:

Anagram   List of possible marketable words

_____   _____

                         _____

_____   _____

                         _____

_____   _____

                         _____

_____   _____

                         _____

_____   _____

Judco Decision Form

Form J

Session # _____

The following question has arisen:

It is the opinion of the JUDCO that:

Concurring in this opinion:

_____

_____

_____

_____

_____

Judco Decision Form

Session # _____

The following question has arisen:

It is the opinion of the JUDCO that:

Concurring in this opinion:

_____

_____

_____

_____

_____

Judco Decision Form

Form J

Session # _____

The following question has arisen:

It is the opinion of the JUDCO that:

Concurring in this opinion:

_____

_____

_____

_____

_____

Simforce Action Form

Session # _____

1. Creating and maintaining a Simforce.

    a. Name of head _____

    b. Authorization rule. List the individual or the combination of individuals who are authorized to issue orders to the coordinator:

    _____   _____   _____

    _____   _____   _____

    Conditions (e.g., any of the above, two or more of the above, majority of the above, etc.):

    _____

	Additions	Session #
c. Initial size _____	_____	_____
	_____	_____

    d. Renewal: Session # _____ ($10 paid to the coordinator)

2. Protected individuals (all of those who can issue orders are automatically protected and need not be listed again; to remove such a person from protection, list his or her name under 2*b.* below):

    _____   _____   _____

    _____   _____   _____

    Changes in protection: *a.* Add: *b.* Remove from protection:

    _____   _____

    _____   _____

3. Arrest the following individuals ($10 per individual required):

    _____   _____   _____

    Changes in arrest:

    a. Add the following: _____

    b. Release from arrest the following: _____

4. Attack.
   Head of Simforce being attacked: _____

5. Change the original authorization rule as follows: _____

    _____

6. Change the Simforce head.

    Name of new head _____

Simforce Action Form

Session # _____

1. Creating and maintaining a Simforce.

    a. Name of head _____

    b. Authorization rule. List the individual or the combination of individuals who are authorized to issue orders to the coordinator:

    _____   _____   _____

    _____   _____   _____

    Conditions (e.g., any of the above, two or more of the above, majority of the above, etc.):

    _____

	Additions	Session #

    c. Initial size _____   _____   _____

    _____   _____

    d. Renewal: Session # _____ ($10 paid to the coordinator)

2. Protected individuals (all of those who can issue orders are automatically protected and need not be listed again; to remove such a person from protection, list his or her name under 2*b.* below):

    _____   _____   _____

    _____   _____   _____

    Changes in protection: *a.* Add: *b.* Remove from protection:

    _____   _____

    _____   _____

3. Arrest the following individuals ($10 per individual required):

    _____   _____   _____

    Changes in arrest:

    a. Add the following: _____

    b. Release from arrest the following: _____

4. Attack.
   Head of Simforce being attacked: _____

5. Change the original authorization rule as follows: _____

   _____

6. Change the Simforce head.

   Name of new head _____

Simforce Action Form

Session # _____

1. Creating and maintaining a Simforce.

   a. Name of head _____

   b. Authorization rule. List the individual or the combination of individuals who are authorized to issue orders to the coordinator:

   _____   _____   _____

   _____   _____   _____

   Conditions (e.g., any of the above, two or more of the above, majority of the above, etc.):

   _____

	Additions	Session #
c. Initial size _____	_____	_____
	_____	_____

   d. Renewal: Session # _____ ($10 paid to the coordinator)

2. Protected individuals (all of those who can issue orders are automatically protected and need not be listed again; to remove such a person from protection, list his or her name under 2*b.* below):

   _____   _____   _____

   _____   _____   _____

   Changes in protection: *a.* Add: *b.* Remove from protection:

   _____   _____

   _____   _____

3. Arrest the following individuals ($10 per individual required):

   _____   _____   _____

   Changes in arrest:

   a. Add the following: _____

   b. Release from arrest the following: _____

4. Attack.
   Head of Simforce being attacked: _____

5. Change the original authorization rule as follows: _____

   _____

6. Change the Simforce head.

   Name of new head _____

Simriot Form

Session # _____

The following people wish to indicate that they will participate in a riot:

_____   _____   _____

_____   _____   _____

_____   _____   _____

_____   _____   _____

_____   _____   _____

_____   _____   _____

Location of riot: (circle one)   Red   Yellow   Blue   Green

Guard Post Form

Session # _____

Post an anti-riot guard in:

Region: (circle one)   RED   YELLOW   BLUE   GREEN

(Fee: $20)

Simriot Form

Session # _____

The following people wish to indicate that they will participate in a riot:

_____   _____   _____

_____   _____   _____

_____   _____   _____

_____   _____   _____

_____   _____   _____

_____   _____   _____

Location of riot: (circle one)   Red   Yellow   Blue   Green

Guard Post Form

Form N

Session # _____

Post an anti-riot guard in:

Region: (circle one)   RED   YELLOW   BLUE   GREEN

(Fee: $20)

Self-Test on SIMSOC Rules

1. What is the consequence of failing to get subsistence? (Check all that apply.)

    (   ) a.   One can't be employed.

    (   ) b.   One can't talk to anyone.

    (   ) c.   One can't travel.

    (   ) d.   One dies if it happens twice in a row.

    (   ) e.   One must surrender one's Simbucks and travel tickets.

    (   ) f.   One can't invest in public programs.

    (   ) g.   One can't start a Simforce or riot.

    (   ) h.   One can't turn in a Party Support Card or MASMED Subscription.

    (   ) i.   One can't turn in an EMPIN Membership Card.

    (   ) j.   One loses one's travel or subsistence agency if one owns one.

2. What is the consequence of unemployment? (Check all that apply.)

    (   ) a.   One can't provide subsistence.

    (   ) b.   One can't travel.

    (   ) c.   One must surrender one's Simbucks and Travel and Subsistence tickets.

    (   ) d.   One can't invest in Public Programs.

    (   ) e.   One can't start a Simforce or riot.

    (   ) f.   One can't turn in a Party Support Card or MASMED Subscription.

    (   ) g.   One can't turn in an EMPIN Membership Card.

    (   ) h.   Some of the National Indicators will be lowered.

3. What happens when the National Indicators go down? (Check all that apply.)

    (   ) a.   Basic group income is lowered.

    (   ) b.   Fewer jobs will be available.

    (   ) c.   Fewer subsistence tickets will be available.

    (   ) d.   The society collapses if any of the National Indicators goes below zero.

Answers: 1. a, d, i; 2. g, h; 3. a, d.

Individual Goal Declaration — Session #10

Name _____

Are you satisfied with how well you are meeting your individual goals? (check one)

_____ Yes, I'm satisfied.

_____ No, I'm not satisfied.

_____ I've changed my individual goals:

from _____ to _____ .

Individual Goal Declaration — Session #7

Name _____

Are you satisfied with how well you are meeting your individual goals? (check one)

_____ Yes, I'm satisfied.

_____ No, I'm not satisfied.

_____ I've changed my individual goals:

from _____ to _____ .

Individual Goal Declaration — Session #4

Name _____

Are you satisfied with how well you are meeting your individual goals? (check one)

_____ Yes, I'm satisfied.

_____ No, I'm not satisfied.

_____ I've changed my individual goals:

from _____ to _____ .

Individual Goal Declaration — Session #1

Name _____

Are you satisfied with how well you are meeting your individual goals? (check one)

_____ Yes, I'm satisfied.

_____ No, I'm not satisfied.

_____ I've changed my individual goals:

from _____ to _____ .

Individual Goal Declaration — Session #11

Name _____

Are you satisfied with how well you are meeting your individual goals? (check one)

_____ Yes, I'm satisfied.

_____ No, I'm not satisfied.

_____ I've changed my individual goals:

from _____ to _____ .

Individual Goal Declaration — Session #8

Name _____

Are you satisfied with how well you are meeting your individual goals? (check one)

_____ Yes, I'm satisfied.

_____ No, I'm not satisfied.

_____ I've changed my individual goals:

from _____ to _____ .

Individual Goal Declaration — Session #5

Name _____

Are you satisfied with how well you are meeting your individual goals? (check one)

_____ Yes, I'm satisfied.

_____ No, I'm not satisfied.

_____ I've changed my individual goals:

from _____ to _____ .

Individual Goal Declaration — Session #2

Name _____

Are you satisfied with how well you are meeting your individual goals? (check one)

_____ Yes, I'm satisfied.

_____ No, I'm not satisfied.

_____ I've changed my individual goals:

from _____ to _____ .

Individual Goal Declaration — Session #12

Name _____

Are you satisfied with how well you are meeting your individual goals? (check one)

_____ Yes, I'm satisfied.

_____ No, I'm not satisfied.

_____ I've changed my individual goals:

from _____ to _____ .

Individual Goal Declaration — Session #9

Name _____

Are you satisfied with how well you are meeting your individual goals? (check one)

_____ Yes, I'm satisfied.

_____ No, I'm not satisfied.

_____ I've changed my individual goals:

from _____ to _____ .

Individual Goal Declaration — Session #6

Name _____

Are you satisfied with how well you are meeting your individual goals? (check one)

_____ Yes, I'm satisfied.

_____ No, I'm not satisfied.

_____ I've changed my individual goals:

from _____ to _____ .

Individual Goal Declaration — Session #3

Name _____

Are you satisfied with how well you are meeting your individual goals? (check one)

_____ Yes, I'm satisfied.

_____ No, I'm not satisfied.

_____ I've changed my individual goals:

from _____ to _____ .

Individual Goal Declaration

Session #1

Name _____

Are you satisfied with how well you are meeting your individual goals? (check one)

_____ Yes, I'm satisfied.

_____ No, I'm not satisfied.

_____ I've changed my individual goals:

from _____ to _____ .

Individual Goal Declaration

Session #2

Name _____

Are you satisfied with how well you are meeting your individual goals? (check one)

_____ Yes, I'm satisfied.

_____ No, I'm not satisfied.

_____ I've changed my individual goals:

from _____ to _____ .

Individual Goal Declaration

Session #3

Name _____

Are you satisfied with how well you are meeting your individual goals? (check one)

_____ Yes, I'm satisfied.

_____ No, I'm not satisfied.

_____ I've changed my individual goals:

from _____ to _____ .

Individual Goal Declaration

Session #4

Name _____

Are you satisfied with how well you are meeting your individual goals? (check one)

_____ Yes, I'm satisfied.

_____ No, I'm not satisfied.

_____ I've changed my individual goals:

from _____ to _____ .

Individual Goal Declaration

Session #5

Name _____

Are you satisfied with how well you are meeting your individual goals? (check one)

_____ Yes, I'm satisfied.

_____ No, I'm not satisfied.

_____ I've changed my individual goals:

from _____ to _____ .

Individual Goal Declaration

Session #6

Name _____

Are you satisfied with how well you are meeting your individual goals? (check one)

_____ Yes, I'm satisfied.

_____ No, I'm not satisfied.

_____ I've changed my individual goals:

from _____ to _____ .

Individual Goal Declaration

Session #7

Name _____

Are you satisfied with how well you are meeting your individual goals? (check one)

_____ Yes, I'm satisfied.

_____ No, I'm not satisfied.

_____ I've changed my individual goals:

from _____ to _____ .

Individual Goal Declaration

Session #8

Name _____

Are you satisfied with how well you are meeting your individual goals? (check one)

_____ Yes, I'm satisfied.

_____ No, I'm not satisfied.

_____ I've changed my individual goals:

from _____ to _____ .

Individual Goal Declaration

Session #9

Name _____

Are you satisfied with how well you are meeting your individual goals? (check one)

_____ Yes, I'm satisfied.

_____ No, I'm not satisfied.

_____ I've changed my individual goals:

from _____ to _____ .

Individual Goal Declaration

Session #10

Name _____

Are you satisfied with how well you are meeting your individual goals? (check one)

_____ Yes, I'm satisfied.

_____ No, I'm not satisfied.

_____ I've changed my individual goals:

from _____ to _____ .

Individual Goal Declaration

Session #11

Name _____

Are you satisfied with how well you are meeting your individual goals? (check one)

_____ Yes, I'm satisfied.

_____ No, I'm not satisfied.

_____ I've changed my individual goals:

from _____ to _____ .

Individual Goal Declaration

Session #12

Name _____

Are you satisfied with how well you are meeting your individual goals? (check one)

_____ Yes, I'm satisfied.

_____ No, I'm not satisfied.

_____ I've changed my individual goals:

from _____ to _____ .